THE
DEFENCE
TEAM

THE DEFENCE TEAM:

Military and Civilian Partnership in the Canadian Armed Forces and the Department of National Defence

EDITED BY:

Irina Goldenberg, Angela R. Febbraro,
and Waylon H. Dean

CANADIAN DEFENCE ACADEMY PRESS

Canadian Defence Academy Press
PO Box 17000 Stn Forces
Kingston, Ontario   K7K 7B4

Produced for the Canadian Defence Academy Press
by 17 Wing Winnipeg Publishing Office.
WPO31076

Library and Archives Canada Cataloguing in Publication

The Defence Team : military and civilian partnership in the Canadian Armed Forces and Department of National Defence / edited by Irina Goldenberg, Angela R. Febbraro, and Waylon H. Dean.

Produced for the Canadian Defence Academy Press by 17 Wing Winnipeg Publishing Office.
Issued by: Canadian Defence Academy Press.
Available also on the Internet.
Includes bibliographical references and index.
ISBN 978-1-100-25356-5 (pbk.).
ISBN 978-1-100-25357-2 (bound)
Cat. no.: D2-352/1-2015E (pbk.)
Cat. no.: D2-352/2-2015E (bound)

1. Civil-military relations--Canada. 2. Canada--Armed Forces--Organization. 3. Canada. Canadian Armed Forces. 4. Canada. Department of National Defence. 5. Canada--Military policy. I. Febbraro, Angela R. (Angela Rosa), 1963- II. Goldenberg, Irina, 1974- III. Dean, Waylon IV. Canadian Defence Academy V. Canada. Canadian Armed Forces. Wing, 17 VI. Title: Military and civilian partnership in the Canadian Armed Forces and Department of National Defence.

JF195 D44 2014   322'.5   C2014-980055-X

TABLE OF CONTENTS

TABLE OF CONTENTS

FOREWORD

The partnership between civilian public servants in the Department of National Defence (DND) and military members in the Canadian Armed Forces (CAF) is unique – one of only a few such relationships in the world, existing largely in other defence and security organizations. Our Defence Team allows us to draw on the specialized expertise of military and civilian personnel to perform the critical work needed to achieve operational effectiveness, and it is their diverse and complementary skills that have made the Defence Team so successful. Indeed, the hard work, dedication and professionalism demonstrated by each member of the Defence Team in the service of Canadians at home and abroad is an immense source of pride.

We also believe that we should never rest on our laurels. One of the top priorities for DND and the CAF is to find efficiencies and increase effectiveness through civilian-military collaboration and integration. We must therefore be prepared to recognize that the organizational, historical, cultural and functional distinctions between military and civilian personnel may affect integration and collaboration within the Defence Team, and then seek to understand the challenges and opportunities for optimizing this fundamental partnership.

For these reasons, we are pleased to introduce *The Defence Team: Military and Civilian Partnership in the Canadian Armed Forces and the Department of National Defence*. This timely volume is the first to systematically identify and analyze the key relational and organizational issues central to the partnership between military and civilian personnel in DND and the CAF. It moves through the historical evolution of the role of civilians inside National Defence to an analysis of the present-day civilian and military workforces, including the most recent research into the experiences and perceptions of our civilian and military personnel. The contributors to this volume also examine trust, leadership, culture, diversity, gender and identity, thereby incorporating historical, strategic, theoretical and empirical perspectives on many of the central aspects crucial to the efficiency and effectiveness of the Defence Team.

FOREWORD

This volume is intended to stimulate discussion and reflection of ways to further strengthen the Defence Team. Although the perspectives presented by the contributors are their own, we believe that this volume represents a substantial contribution to our understanding of military-civilian relations within the Defence Team. It will serve as an important resource for those seeking a greater understanding of the complementary roles that each member plays within Canadian defence, the considerations and strategies for optimizing the partnership between military and civilian personnel, and the potential of the Defence Team to continue to serve together admirably, ready to face the challenges of tomorrow, at home and abroad.

Thomas J. Lawson
General
Chief of the Defence Staff

W. Davern Jones
Acting Deputy Minister
of National Defence

ACKNOWLEDGEMENTS

The publication of this volume would not have been possible without the support of key people. First and foremost, our sincere thanks to Susan Truscott, Eugenia Kalantzis, Keith Stewart and Dr. Tzvetanka Dobreva-Martinova for recognizing the importance of research and analysis on military-civilian personnel collaboration and for encouraging and supporting the program of research in this domain. We are particularly grateful to Dr. Kelly Farley for his valuable guidance and instrumental feedback throughout the completion of this volume. We would also like to thank Major Gary Ivey for his generous advice. In addition, we would like to extend our gratitude to Lieutenant-Colonel Jeff Stouffer and Commander David Woycheshin for their early guidance and support on this project, and for setting us on the right path. Finally, we would like to thank Mélanie Denis for all of her guidance and support in navigating this project.

INTRODUCTION

MILITARY-CIVILIAN INTEGRATION IN CANADA'S DEFENCE ESTABLISHMENT

Irina Goldenberg, Angela R. Febbraro, and Waylon H. Dean

Canada's defence establishment is a unique organization, comprising two constitutionally independent and culturally distinct institutions: the civilian-led Department of National Defence (DND), headed by the civilian Deputy Minister of National Defence (DM), and the military-led Canadian Armed Forces (CAF), headed by the Chief of the Defence Staff (CDS). In practice, however, civilian and military personnel, collectively referred to as the *Defence Team*, are highly integrated with one another. About two thirds of DND's full-time civilian workforce is actually employed in the military structure, and several thousand CAF military personnel perform departmental functions inside DND.[1] In fact, many DND civilians are supervised by military managers and some civilians manage CAF personnel.[2] Thus a significant number of civilians and military members work side by side and under one another's supervision in a variety of contexts, including on bases, on operations, in military academic settings, in defence research centres and at National Defence Headquarters.

On the one hand, these highly integrated workforces allow the defence establishment to draw upon the complementary expertise of both military and civilian personnel. As stated in joint messages by Canada's DM and CDS, "it is the unique military-civilian relationship that makes the Defence Team itself so successful."[3] On the other hand, there are some fundamental differences between military and civilian personnel. The two workforces are governed by two separate personnel management systems: civilian personnel, as part of the Public Service Commission of Canada, are governed by the *Public Service Employment Act* and by the collective agreements relevant to their occupations within DND;[4] military personnel are governed by the Code of Service Discipline in the *National Defence Act*.[5]

Moreover, the two parts of the Defence Team also have very distinct cultures, reflecting the different histories, values, roles and policies of defence civilians and CAF members. These differences in attitudes, perceptions and behaviours can affect the partnerships and work culture between these two groups of personnel.[6] Integrating military and civilian cultures can be challenging, for example, because many military personnel have spent much of their careers on bases, and may find it difficult to assimilate into the more bureaucratic and civilian-oriented culture of National Defence Headquarters. Similarly, civilian personnel can find it difficult to adapt to the more hierarchical, command-oriented military culture.[7] Such cultural and organizational differences can affect collaboration and integration on the Defence Team, resulting in missed opportunities to maximize operational effectiveness.[8]

Whatever the potential challenges, the fundamental importance of a well-integrated Defence Team has been clearly recognized by military and civilian leaders in Canada and is well documented in high-level strategic documents. The vision statement in the *Canada First Defence Strategy* – the government's twenty-year plan for National Defence – is for "Canada to have a first-class, modern military that will work in partnership with the knowledgeable and responsive civilian personnel of the Department of National Defence."[9] Similarly, the *Defence Priorities and Elements*, a guiding strategic document that delineates DND's mission, areas of focus and desired results, states that aligning civilian and military workforces is one of DND's six core priorities and, moreover, that optimal alignment of the military and civilian workforces is a precondition for the successful execution of the other Defence Priorities.[10] Statements emphasizing the integrated Defence Team – as opposed to the individual institutions – are also common in organization-wide messages.[11]

Despite the challenges posed by civilian-military integration and senior leadership's strong commitment to it, very little research has been conducted in this area.[12] A request through The Technical Cooperation Program (TTCP)[13] by the editors of this volume, for example, returned very little research on civilian-military relations in defence organizations. In fact, the TTCP representatives who received the request informed us that they would be interested in any research we uncovered. To address this gap, two of the editors of this volume initiated a North Atlantic Treaty Organization (NATO) Research Task Group[14] to systematically examine key aspects related to civilian-military personnel integration from an international perspective. Indeed, the standing up of this group is timely, because other defence organizations are making similar moves toward deeper integration of their civilian and military workforces, as evidenced by recently introduced terms analogous to the Defence Team, including the "Whole Force Concept" in the UK, "One Defence Team" in Sweden, and the "Total Defence Workforce" in New Zealand.[15] Of note, interest on behalf of CAF and DND leadership in evidence-based information about military-civilian relations on the Defence Team also provided the impetus for the development of the Defence Team Survey (discussed in Chapter 4 of this volume).

All of this speaks to the timeliness of the present volume. It is paramount that we understand the unique nature of integrated Defence Teams and the factors that enable optimal military-civilian collaboration. In the hope of furthering that goal, this volume presents a multifaceted analysis of the key contextual, organizational and relational issues influencing integration and collaboration between military and civilian personnel in DND and the CAF. The chapters provide a comprehensive historical, conceptual and empirical overview of this topic. The volume is aimed at a diverse audience, including Defence Team personnel, senior leaders in DND and the CAF, human resource professionals, military managers of civilian personnel and civilian managers of military personnel, as well as a more general audience interested in work group and organizational diversity.

In Chapter 1, Daniel Gosselin provides an historical overview of the key events, political motivations and policy documents that have transformed the role of civilian public servants in DND from junior support staff into senior-level management. Gosselin follows the progressive prominence of civilians in DND through the reorganization of defence stemming from the Royal Commission on Government Organization in the 1960s, the realignment of the roles of senior military and civilian leaders and the creation of the National Defence Headquarters brought on by the Management Review Group in the early 1970s, and the effect of the 1979 Task Force on Review of Unification of the Canadian Armed Forces and the 1994 *Defence White Paper*. Finally, the author examines the changing roles of civilians in light of the post 9-11 operational focus and transformation of the Canadian military brought about by former CDS General Rick Hillier. Gosselin shows how these government initiatives increased the responsibilities and influence of the deputy minister and senior civilian public servants, and discusses the impact of these changes at National Defence Headquarters on civil-military relations. Gosselin argues that, although many DND civilians are still junior staff – what he calls "foot soldiers in coveralls" – senior public servants have increasingly played a "watchdog" role for the federal government's exercise of civil control over the military institution.

In Chapter 2, Alan Okros examines the strategic- and corporate-level relationship among politicians, senior members of the CAF, and senior public servants in DND inside National Defence Headquarters. Drawing on two contemporary models of civil control of the military, he asks and attempts to answer the four principal questions about the roles of civilians and military members through a civil-military relations framework: Who exercises control? What is controlled? Whose priorities take precedence? and Whose expertise is brought to bear? Okros suggests that these four issues can either result in beneficial tensions characterized by constructive debate of complex issues or they can lead to divisive conflicts. The quality of the civil-military partnership depends on both the nature of current leadership and on mutual understanding between the military and civilian parties. Indeed, he contends that each side's understanding – though not necessarily adoption – of the other's priorities, key objectives and unique professional perspectives is the key to informed decision making and optimal work culture within the Defence Team.

Chapter 3 presents the demographics of the military and civilian workforces in DND and the CAF between 2003 and 2013. In the first part of the chapter, Lise Arseneau and Amy Cameron examine how the demographics of the two workforces have changed as a result of force expansion, budgetary growth and restraint, and the changing priorities of National Defence over the last decade. The authors also cover the distribution of civilian and military personnel across National Defence's functional capacities. In the second part of the chapter, the authors introduce a practical approach for determining the optimal composition of the Defence Team, given the importance of ensuring the best possible distribution of military and civilian roles and expertise across DND and the CAF.

Understanding how civilian and military personnel perceive their partnership and their work in the unique military-civilian environment is important for developing policies that foster that partnership. In Chapter 4, Irina Goldenberg presents selected results from the Defence Team Survey, which was the first large-scale empirical examination of the views, attitudes and experiences of DND civilian and CAF military personnel about the unique work dynamics within the Defence Team. Administered to large random samples of both military and civilian members, the survey assessed issues such as the quality of relations and communication between military and civilian personnel, the effects of military supervision on civilian personnel (and vice versa), and the effects of the military rotational cycle (e.g., postings and deployments) on the work of civilian employees. The empirical data presented in this chapter reinforce and help to further contextualize the information provided in the rest of the volume.

In Chapter 5, Allan English examines how changes in the Canadian military's organizational culture have shaped relations with the civilian side of the Defence Team. English argues that military leaders have often sought to change the culture of the CAF to make the organization more effective and responsive to contemporary needs. But neither military culture nor its connection to military effectiveness is well understood. As a result, English suggests, leadership has tended to oscillate between two models of military effectiveness: the inward-looking traditionalist model, which focuses on developing the military ethos and the fighting spirit, and the outward-looking modernist model, which focuses on a professionalism aligned with trends in the broader Canadian society. English suggests that extreme versions of each of these models have led to problems in the CAF. Leadership's espousal of extreme modernism in the 1990s led to the so-called Decade of Darkness, while the recent resurgence of the traditional model in the doctrine of "operations primacy" may betoken a move toward the opposite extreme. In the absence of clear answers on the culture-performance connection, English argues that the safest course for leadership is to have its officers acknowledge and leverage the strengths – especially with respect to finance and management – that the civilian culture brings to the Defence Team. Indeed, military and civilian members of the Defence Team may have more in common with respect to their management culture than appearances would suggest. These commonalities can provide a basis for overcoming cultural and organizational differences, thereby facilitating effective collaboration.

Moving from organizational culture to the value of cultural awareness, Chapter 6 by Karen Davis explores the role of cultural intelligence (CQ) in leader development and how CQ can contribute to the success of the Defence Team. Davis argues that developing leaders who understand how culture influences both themselves and others is important for the CAF and the defence organization as a whole. Thus, she explains what CQ is and how it can be used to further mutual understanding and cooperation within the Defence Team. She further argues that many aspects of CQ are mirrored by the Canadian Forces Leadership Institute's Leadership Development Framework (LDF) and, therefore, CQ can be understood as an extension of the LDF. Importantly, Davis argues that the values and ethics common to the professional identities of civilian defence employees and CAF members can bridge the collaborative gaps in the Defence Team. Indeed, an understanding of CQ can be leveraged to guide *both* military and civilian leaders as they develop strategies for effective collaboration within the Defence Team.

Ritu Gill and Megan Thompson argue in Chapter 7 that trust between partners is necessary for effective teamwork. The authors draw upon the organizational trust literature, lessons learned from past interagency collaborations, and their own innovative research to illuminate how interagency trust is fostered, and they offer strategies for developing and maintaining trust and provide insight into how trust can be repaired after a trust violation. Gill and Thompson suggest that the highest level of trust occurs among parties who share a collective identity rooted in clear objectives, a shared workload, equal ownership, effective communication, and a sharing of information and physical workspaces. They argue that these insights into how to build, maintain and repair trust may also be useful for military and civilian personnel on the Defence Team.

Although military and civilian personnel within the Defence Team share a common mandate under the Minister of National Defence, these two groups are likely to form unique social identities that will impact their relationship.

INTRODUCTION

Drawing on social identity theory, Irina Goldenberg, Waylon H. Dean and Barbara D. Adams discuss in Chapter 8 the importance of identity and its influence on intergroup dynamics within the Defence Team. The authors contend that military personnel are likely to have a stronger and more salient social identity than their civilian counterparts. These different social identities can affect team relations and organizational integration, which can in turn affect organizational outcomes. Goldenberg, Dean and Adams discuss ways by which social identity may be managed, and even harnessed, to facilitate optimal integration and collaboration between military and civilian personnel.

In Chapter 9, Justin Wright examines the pros and cons of alternative training delivery, especially its effects on the formation of the identity of military recruits. Alternative training delivery – which includes outsourcing military occupational training to civilian educational institutions – is often cheaper and may even be academically superior to military occupational training in some cases. But it may also have implications for the socialization of recruits and the development of their military identity, because the military training system has long been a vehicle for socializing recruits. Wright argues that the civilianizing effect of outsourced training may be exaggerated and, thus, that the benefits to be had from outsourcing seem to outweigh the risks. Moreover, he suggests, recruits' exposure to civilian training may enhance the military's ability to communicate, collaborate and share a common identity with their civilian partners within the Defence Team.

Finally, in Chapter 10, Angela R. Febbraro explores the influence of gender in the Defence Team context. Given differences in the demographic profiles of the military and civilian Defence Team counterparts (i.e., the relatively greater proportion of women among DND civilians), previous research indicating that gender may define the experiences of organizational personnel, and the paucity of research examining gender within defence organizations specifically, Febbraro suggests that a gender-based analysis of the Defence Team may raise new questions and reveal hidden complexities in Defence Team integration. Drawing on the few existing empirical studies of gender in defence organizations and theoretical work on military culture and social identity, Febbraro makes a case for the influence of gender on Defence Team dynamics. She concludes that taking gender diversity into account is necessary for building a strong Defence Team and suggests several avenues for future research.

In sum, the contributors to this volume have advanced our understanding of these uniquely integrated workforces, the important roles that both military and civilian institutions play within the Canadian defence partnership, and of the factors that promote effective integration and collaboration within the Defence Team. We hope the analyses in the following chapters will further our understanding of the multifaceted and interconnected nature of the military and civilian partnership, and help to inform future discourse and the evolution of the military and civilian partnership within the Canadian Defence Team.

ENDNOTES

1　　Department of National Defence, *Report on Plans and Priorities 2010-11*, Part 3 Estimates, http://www.tbs-sct.gc.ca/rpp/2010-2011/inst/dnd/dnd01-eng.asp. The 2011 transformation report presents this extent of integration as of March 2010.

2　　Cynthia Binnington, "Civilian HR Management in DND/CF" (presentation, Defence Resources Management Course, Ottawa, ON, November 6, 2008). Department of National Defence, *Report on Plans and Priorities 2012/2013*.

3　　E-mail sent over Defence Wide Area Network entitled "Joint DM-CDS Message on National Public Service Week," June 9-15, 2013.

4　　Treasury Board of Canada Secretariat, Office of the Chief Human Resources Officer, retrieved from http://www.tbs-sct.gc.ca/pubs–pol/hrpubs/coll–agre/siglist-eng.asp.

5　　Director General Military Personnel, *CFJP 1.0 Military Personnel Management Doctrine*, Canadian Forces Joint Publication B-GL-005-100/FP-001 (Ottawa, ON: Department of National Defence, 2008).

6　　Irina Goldenberg and Filsan Hujaleh, *Partnership Between Military and Civilian Personnel in Defence Organizations: An Annotated Bibliography*, Director General Military Personnel Research and Analysis Technical Memorandum 012-020 (Ottawa, ON: Defence Research and Development Canada, 2012).

7　　Julie Coulthard and Irina Goldenberg, *Civilian and Military Personnel Work Culture and Relations in DND/CF*, Director General Military Personnel Research and Analysis Technical Memorandum 2011-008 (Ottawa, ON: Defence Research and Development Canada, 2011).

8　　André Fillion, "The Integration of Defence Civilians within the Defence Team: How Far Can We Go?" (research paper, Canadian Forces College, North York, ON, 2007); B. Van Vianen, "Managing Civilians in the Canadian Forces" (research paper, Canadian Forces College, North York, ON, 2007).

9   Department of National Defence, *Canada First Defence Strategy*, 3, http://www. forces.gc.ca/assets/FORCES–Internet/docs/en/about/CFDS-SDCD-eng.pdf.

10   These Defence Priorities also "represent areas where Defence will direct additional effort in order to address gaps in capability and capacity, and where broader government direction dictates that greater action be taken" (Department of National Defence, Report on *Plans and Priorities 2010-11*, 1). These priorities also form the foundation for the business planning cycle for the development of the Reports on Plans and Priorities (RPP). The priorities are represented in a multi-year format reflecting the long-term nature of actions necessary to achieve them. (Department of National Defence, *Report on Plans and Priorities 2010-11*).

11   E-mail sent over the Defence Wide Area Network to DND and CAF personnel regularly address the "Defence Team," instead of each group or one group. For example: "Message from the VCDS–Champion of the Defence Youth Network," December 4, 2013; "Joint DM/CDS Message on the launch of the Defence Connex networking space," December 9, 2013; "Message from the Senior Associate Deputy Minister on the close of National Public Service Week 2013," June 14, 2013; "Message from the new Deputy Minister," May 13, 2013.

12   It also bears mentioning that in being assigned to Assistant Deputy Minister (Human Resources – Civilian) Irina Goldenberg saw that many of the personnel issues affecting DND employees and managers were ultimately issues with integration into the military organization (e.g., culture, military supervision). Similarly, the decision over the employment of civilian personnel often affected the work and personnel considerations of the military organization.

13   For more on the TTCP, see http://www.acq.osd.mil/ttcp/.

14   Specifically, the Science and Technology Organisation Human Factors and Medicine Panel Research Task Group 226 (NATO STO HFM RTG-226) on Civilian and Military Personnel Work Culture and Relations in Defence Organisations; this international research group consists of ten nations: Canada (lead nation), the United States, the United Kingdom, the Netherlands, Belgium, Germany, Switzerland, Sweden, Estonia and Turkey.

15   On the "Whole Force Concept," see Ministry of Defence, *The New Operating Model: How Defence Works*, 58, available at http://www.raf.mod.uk/rafbrizenorton/ rafcms/mediafiles/28AA36D7–5056–A318–A83E819FCEDCF008.pdf; on the "Total Defence Workforce," see New Zealand Ministry of Defence, *Defence White Paper 2010*, available at http://www.defence.govt.nz/reports-publications/defence-white-paper-2010/ chapter6-people-centred-nzdf.html.

CHAPTER 1

THE UNARMED SERVANTS OF THE STATE: THE EVOLVING ROLE OF CIVILIANS IN NATIONAL DEFENCE[1]

Daniel Gosselin[2]

Civilian control of the armed forces
is not civil service control of the armed forces.[3]

– General Rick Hillier, Chief of the Defence Staff, 2005-08

Contrary to claims made by critics,
the part played by senior bureaucrats in formulating defence policy
and in holding the military accountable to civilian authority
is both necessary and in line with statute law.[4]

– Philippe Lagassé, University of Ottawa

The role of civilians inside the Department of National Defence has evolved dramatically over the past fifty years. In the early 1960s, civilian public servants were employed almost exclusively in junior trades and administrative positions in DND. Over the years, public servants were brought in to add civilian expertise to manage and administer more complex defence programs and to enhance the capacity of the military to deal with the central agencies and processes of the government. Indeed, government after government since then has moved civil servants into more and more senior positions inside DND, eventually creating an integrated military-civilian strategic defence headquarters. Although governments have seldom publicly expressed it, the reason for integrating and elevating civilians within DND has always been primarily to strengthen civil control over the military.[5] This objective has largely been realized now that senior civil servants within DND can challenge the military and assist the defence minister with controlling military activities.[6] Over the last fifty years, therefore, while the majority of civilians in DND continue to be employed as "foot soldiers in coveralls," in junior support staff, research and administrative positions, senior public servants have taken a more prominent role as "watchdogs" of the military.

This chapter examines the role of civilian public service employees inside national defence, focusing on the pivotal events, phases and studies that have shaped the expanding role of civilians since the early 1960s, in what is nowadays called the Defence Team. This examination is broken down into six parts, corresponding broadly to the different phases in the evolution of the role of civilian public service employees within DND. I begin with the work of the 1960 Royal Commission on Government Organization, which influenced the reorganization of Canadian defence in the 1960s and 1970s. In the second part, I review the influence that the unification of the three armed services in the mid-1960s had on the role of civilians in National Defence.[7] I next review the work of the Management Review Group (MRG) of 1971-72, which led to the creation of National Defence Headquarters (NDHQ) and the realignment of the roles of senior military officers and civilian defence officials. In the fourth part, I examine the 1979 Task Force on Review of Unification of the Canadian Forces, which raised several concerns from military members about the "civilianization" of the defence establishment in the wake of the creation of NDHQ.

The fifth part of this chapter covers the 1990s, a decade marked by unprecedented change in defence in the aftermath of the Somalia Affair, the 1994 *Defence White Paper* and deep defence budget cuts, which included initiatives to contract out, to re-engineer defence activities and to reduce the size of headquarters by half. Over the decade after 9-11, defence underwent another unprecedented change. Public servants across DND became heavily engaged in supporting a Canadian military absorbed in high-intensity combat operations in Afghanistan and multiple operations elsewhere. In 2005, moreover, General Rick Hillier became Chief of the Defence Staff and initiated a major transformation of the Canadian military, aimed primarily at restoring its operational focus. The transformation targeted both the functions of NDHQ and the strategic governance of the armed forces and DND – and, by extension, the role of civilians inside the national headquarters. I explore these post-9-11 changes in the last part of this chapter.

THE 1960 ROYAL COMMISSION ON GOVERNMENT ORGANIZATION

One of the events that would significantly shape the views of future governments and ministers of defence toward more integration of civilians within Canada's defence establishment was the Royal Commission on Government Organization – known as the Glassco commission, after its chairman, J. Grant Glassco. Appointed by the Diefenbaker government in 1960, the commission was mandated "to inquire into and report upon the organization and methods of departments and agencies of the government of Canada."[8] Since managerial efficiency in government was the main interest of the commission, the role of civilians within the department was examined carefully by the commissioners.

The Department of National Defence was singled out because of its size, the range of its activities, the magnitude of its budget, and its unique composition.[9] Further, the commission acknowledged that "the composition of the department is unique, consisting as it does of two elements, military and civilian differing in status, rank structure, and terms of employment, although they function as an entity."[10] In *Report 20*, the commission specifically focused on defence: the commissioners commented on the basis and structure of the defence organization, on its governance (in particular the role of senior civilian officials and military officers), and on defence human resources policies and practices. All these aspects touched on the role of civilians inside the department.

The Glassco commission first examined the role of the DM. Acknowledging that the DM of DND is different from the DMs of other departments because "the general oversight and direction vested in the DM...is exercised subject to the limitations set out in the *National Defence Act*," the commissioners nevertheless found his functions "too narrowly circumscribed," with the result that the defence minister did not receive the staff assistance required to discharge his responsibility for the direction of the Canadian defence establishment.[11] It is also clear that the commissioners looked at the DM as being the civilian official responsible for providing independent defence advice, and as the essential person inside the machinery of government whose task it was to assist politicians with overseeing the activities of the military and to ensure effective civil control of the armed forces. While the commissioners acknowledged that the minister "may rely primarily on the Chiefs of Staff Committee for advice and on questions of military effectiveness" because "it is natural he should do so," it remains that,

> the military character of this group raises doubts as to the reality of civilian control if the minister places excessive reliance upon it. There is thus a need for a strong staff group which is essentially civilian in character, outside the framework of the management of the Armed Forces.[12]

It is important to note that the department had two structures in 1962: one under the direction of the DM, concerned with administration, finance and procurement, and another organized functionally under the control of the chiefs of staff of the three services, dealing with operations and training.[13] The Glassco commission also criticized the weakness of the committee structure of decision making and proposed a more robust departmental staff group, one that would be strengthened in its role relative to the three services. A strong, unified DM group would be in a better position to take a more comprehensive view of defence organization and administration, opined the royal commissioners, and it was expected that the DM would be able to rise above tri-service rivalry when advising the minister on defence issues.[14]

In reviewing civilian and military roles, and departmental manpower policies and practices, the commission noted that of the 50,000 civilians in the department "the vast majority are employed as tradesmen or in junior administrative positions, mostly in a support role in non-combatant functions," while "the senior positions are filled almost exclusively by Service officers." The royal commissioners questioned, as well, why thousands of military personnel were employed in supporting activities, and they were at a complete loss to understand the significant civilian employment differences that existed among the three services.[15] They viewed the existing arrangements as a highly inefficient way to conduct defence business, questioning "whether it is in the national interest to employ such a large number of uniformed personnel in tasks that could be performed by civilians at less cost."[16] The costs and benefits of civilian public servants versus uniformed members in the defence establishment would be a common refrain that surfaced again and again over the next forty years.

The lack of civilians in the higher administrative echelons of the department concerned the commission for several reasons. First, they believed that civilians could perform many of the senior public administration tasks of the three services more efficiently. Downplaying military experience and expertise, the commission argued that civilians should be employed "even in such fundamentally military staff functions as those dealing with plans and operations." Increasing the number of civilians in senior positions would also provide more opportunities to combine the different backgrounds and expertise of civilians and military officers in the highest levels of the department, stated the commissioners, even predicting that it would "contribute to better [defence] performance."[17] In short, civilians would bring in different perspectives on defence issues, add expertise in specific public administration and management areas, and even provide a much-needed internal challenge function in areas where none existed before.

Third, the commission pointed out that the lack of civilians in several areas of the department did not provide an opportunity to develop promising civilian officials for the higher echelons of the organization. By having civilians working in the military sphere of work, continued the commissioners, public servants would gain greater familiarity with defence matters, and this "would reduce the tendency – to which civilians are all too prone – to regard military affairs as professional mysteries comprehensible only to the military mind." It would certainly better prepare them to serve in senior executive positions later in their careers, thus benefitting the defence establishment as a whole.[18]

The commissioners were careful to note the legal restrictions placed on public servants who worked in DND, and they certainly realized that their recommendation to increase significantly the role of civilians inside the department would be viewed with scepticism and apprehension by a military that was jealously guarding its autonomy and independence.[19] The object of their policy recommendations was clearly intended to integrate the civilian and military elements of the department and to prevent the segregation of civilian and military elements into two separate organizations, "between which antagonisms can too easily develop." Still, conscious of how their recommendations might be perceived by the military and the three services, the commissioners added a reassurance:

> It is important that civilians employed in senior administrative posts in the Services should not be looked upon as having a duty *to control or check Service activities.* Their sole function should be to assist the Services and provide continuity in administering programmes, bringing an additional viewpoint and sometimes special skills to bear, and serving as partners and co-workers with the Service officers.[20]

Unless the government directed reforms from the highest levels, few expected the role of civilians in the department to change. The Glassco commission's work was certainly widely quoted in the 1960s and early 1970s, but, as events proved, and for reasons discussed below, its recommendations would not lead to immediate, significant changes in the administration of defence policy in Canada. Nevertheless, over time, the Glassco commission would have a formative impact on government operations, bringing "a sort of managerial revolution in the bureaucracy," as one expert on public administration characterized the influence of the commission twenty-five years later.[21]

The findings and recommendations of the commission were important, and they would provide a degree of authority to those who wanted to reform defence.[22] One of those who would exploit the work of the commission to great effect was the young and ambitious Paul T. Hellyer, Minister of National Defence in the newly elected Liberal government in early 1963. He embarked on the most radical set of reforms to the Canadian military since the early 1900s.

UNIFICATION OF THE CANADIAN ARMED FORCES

Minister Hellyer began his mandate to modernize and reorganize Canada's defence establishment in 1963. His main challenge was controlling the increasing costs of defence, especially for a government that was becoming more inclined to spend on social programs.[23] As a result, he initially relied on the conclusions of the Glassco commission, "which had done such a splendid job of exposing the waste and extravagance resulting from duplication and triplication."[24] As well, a series of separate but interconnected events between 1957 and 1963 had created turmoil in Canada's defence policy, strongly influencing the new Liberal government to issue a new white paper on defence, to reorganize the military, and to strengthen the mechanisms of civil control of the Canadian military, all of which had the potential to influence the role of defence civilians.[25]

Hellyer's ideas first came to light with the 1964 *White Paper on Defence*, which contained several original concepts and set out the basic rationale for the unification of the armed forces. To the new minister, the solution to the defence budget challenges was straightforward: reduce the size of the defence organization and integrate the three armed forces service staffs under a single CDS and a single defence staff. In the white paper, the government frequently referenced the work and recommendations of the Glassco commission, mainly to justify the impending reforms focused on eliminating duplication and on increasing efficiency at defence.[26]

Two subsequent acts of Parliament to implement the government's agenda to restructure defence made scant mention of the role of civilians in DND.[27] However, as part of several important studies conducted between 1963 and 1966 to support his efforts for the reorganization of the military, the minister did commission a study to review policies for the employment of civilians within Canada's armed forces. Completed in early 1966, the minister's *Manpower Study* (Men) aimed to review the concerns raised by the Glassco commission regarding the wide disparity in service employment policies for civilians and to make recommendations for an effective civilian employment policy in a restructured Canadian military.[28] The study group's work was quite narrow in scope, and it limited its recommendations to the replacement of military personnel by civilians in four military occupations, mostly due to the essentially civilian nature of those occupations. There is no evidence that the recommendations of the study were ever implemented.

Hellyer had also acknowledged in the white paper that his success in maintaining effective civil control over the military – echoing the words of the Glassco commission – entailed that the DM be given greater responsibility for the resolution of defence issues, for exercising a review function over the organization and the administration of the defence establishment, and for assisting him in discharging his responsibilities.[29] He quickly backed away from this commitment, stating just a few months later in Parliament that "there is no need to change the legislation relating to the Deputy Minister," emphasizing instead the need to protect against civilian staff assuming "functions which are necessary to the military staffs in order that they can efficiently control their military forces and carry out their military responsibilities."[30]

By 1966, the issue of unification of the three military services had become highly controversial and had become a matter of public debate and open acrimony within parts of the armed forces, especially the Royal Canadian Navy, demanding the constant attention of the minister.[31] Confronted with a crisis of civil-military relations over much of his tenure as minister, Hellyer therefore devoted little effort to strengthening the DM staff. It is also clear that he never had any intention of amalgamating the armed forces with the department; integrating and unifying the military staffs was his main objective. The department under the DM thus remained relatively unchanged from 1953 through the early 1970s.[32]

By December 1967, when Hellyer left the defence portfolio, the role of civilians inside defence had changed very little, despite the studies and promises of the past seven years.[33] Hellyer certainly strengthened civil control, but this was achieved primarily through the creation of the position of the CDS, which simplified civil control for him, the revamping of the Defence Council, which he chaired, and by exercising a forceful and directive management style that left no doubt about who was in charge of the military and the department.[34]

In the early 1970s, Vernon Kronenberg, an Australian defence fellow, conducted a detailed study of the integration and unification initiatives of the 1960s. He argued that the Glassco commission failed to adequately understand how the lack of career structure and incentives for defence civilians had contributed to a lack of civilian expertise at defence headquarters, and how this lack of civilian expertise at the senior departmental levels in turn affected civil control of the military.[35] The commission saw control of the military in the more narrow sense of direct political control, in the way Hellyer exercised it with relentless determination during his tenure, and not in terms of what was required, organizationally and institutionally, to adequately exercise this oversight. To Kronenberg, this is one of the reasons that little change in the role of civilians occurred in the 1960s.[36]

Except for the creation of the Canadian Forces Headquarters (CFHQ) in 1966, which saw public servants who were working in the three service headquarters become part of an integrated Canadian military headquarters, Hellyer ignored nearly all the recommendations of the Glassco commission about civilians in defence, concentrating his efforts instead on restructuring the military. As Kronenberg astutely observed in 1971, "civilians in the department…have suffered a very long period of what appears to be not merely neglect, but incomprehension of the role that [they] can play in facilitating the department's business."[37]

This situation changed dramatically in 1971, however, when a civilian team from outside government, mandated by a new defence minister, returned with determination to the findings of the Glassco commission and proposed fundamental changes to the structure of defence management and decision making and to the role of senior defence civilians.

THE MANAGEMENT REVIEW GROUP OF 1971-1972

In 1971, the Trudeau government announced in a white paper on defence, *Defence in the 70s*, the creation of a Management Review Group to examine the organization and management of the entire defence establishment.[38] The review had been triggered by several defence problems and ministerial concerns, including difficulties with the management of major equipment procurement contracts, a lack of progress in responding to the Glassco commission, a perceived lack of responsiveness from the department to the Minister's and Cabinet's direction, and a lack of transparency with what was happening inside both the department and the CAF.[39]

In their report, *Management of Defence in Canada*, the MRG identified a litany of major concerns in the areas of management, planning, procurement, financial services, personnel administration and defence research. Three themes relevant to this chapter emerged from the report. The first was a need to increase dependence on civilians with the requisite professional expertise in order to manage more complex defence issues. The second was a strong belief that defence outputs could be improved with sound modern management techniques. And, more critically, the group believed that it was time to remove from the military the responsibility for formulating defence policy, for advising the defence minister on defence policy, and for managing military procurement, and to delegate these responsibilities to civilian assistant deputy ministers (ADMs).[40]

The MRG was convinced that two deep-seated factors were contributing to the mismanagement of defence: a flawed departmental organizational structure and outmoded but firmly entrenched attitudes in the senior echelons of the military and the department about defence management. It concluded that some of the managerial and administrative problems were caused by a lack of political sensitivity on behalf of senior military and civilian managers, a criticism centred on the inability of the department to adjust to changing priorities and values in Canada and to work effectively with the federal government's central agencies.[41]

While shallow in its depth of analysis in several areas, and in the appropriateness of some of the recommendations made (the report was considered too sensitive to be released at the time, and it was not made public until 1984), the review nevertheless confirmed to the minister that a number of serious defence management problems demanded action, namely, greater civil servant involvement in the administrative and management structure of DND.[42] The government's solution was to link the two headquarters, the CFHQ and the departmental headquarters, and to change the distribution of responsibilities between civilian and military officials.

The new NDHQ included the establishment of an additional assistant deputy minister, ADM (Policy), a civilian public servant who would be designated as the most senior ADM, and who would be "a politically sensitive civilian, with extensive experience in planning and coordination in the context of the activities of the federal government as a whole."[43] This move was clearly aimed at wrestling the development of defence policy away from the military and at providing a focal point for liaising with the central agencies of government. In the formulation of defence policy and advice to the minister and government, the MRG wanted to make a distinction between military and defence advice, and the creation of a defence policy group under the DM, the MRG argued, was the most direct way to bring it about.[44]

It must be noted that it was common practice at the time to appoint retired military officers to senior civilian positions; so the top echelons of both organizations, CFHQ and the DM staff group, were often filled with former senior military officers.[45] In the spirit of headquarters integration, however, it was decided that all civilian ADMs would have an associate DM at the rank of major-general or rear-admiral, because it was expected that ADMs would be civilians.[46]

The merging of the two headquarters was a radical step. The intent was to significantly alter the way Canadian defence was managed through an enduring organizational solution and to realign the responsibilities and accountabilities of civilian officials and military officers. The impact of this decision, unforeseen at the time of the amalgamation, remains significant for the CAF and DND forty years later.

NDHQ AND CIVILIANIZATION OF THE MILITARY

The integration of CFHQ and the departmental headquarters in 1972, which resulted in military and civilian staff working side by side, immediately brought into greater focus the role of senior defence civilians.[47]

Colonel Paul Manson (who would become CDS in 1986) penned an article in 1973 in the *Canadian Defence Quarterly* portraying the early days of the restructuring in as positive a light as possible. He came to the conclusion that the closer integration of civilians – experts in defence management – with the military had become "inevitable" and that the separation of military and civilian functions that existed until then was no longer suitable. He foresaw the closer civilian-military working relationship in headquarters as streamlining decision making, improving coordination, and facilitating the advancement of defence issues with the central agencies. "The old division between civilian and military staffs has disappeared," declared Manson, adding that "many of the new positions in the new structure can now be filled either by a member of the armed forces or by a civilian member of the Department." Manson acknowledged that this new structure would provide the CDS with "more civilian advice in command matters than heretofore, which is surely a good thing in the changing world of the seventies."[48] Even though the headquarters was less than one year old, Manson had observed that the relationship with Treasury Board had already improved as a result of the new integrated structure.[49]

Prescient in his analysis, the future CDS could see several potential problems looming. Manson anticipated difficulties arising with the "apparent introduction of civilians into the military command structure at NDHQ," with the division of responsibilities between the deputy chiefs and the ADMs, and with "a tendency towards bipolarity, that is, for elements of the organization to polarize around the CDS and the DM along military and civilian lines."[50]

Echoing a statement that the Glassco commission had made a decade before about the potential growing influence of civilians, Manson took the time in his article to caution those who were concerned that it "would be wrong to suppose that this [closer civilian-military relationship] reflected a need to impose tighter civilian control of the military in Canada, because that control is already absolute."[51] Without the benefit of the MRG report (which had not been released publicly), Manson was perhaps unaware that, on the contrary, the decisions made by the government in 1971 to create NDHQ, to strengthen the role of the DM, and to shift important responsibilities away from the military (such as defence policy, materiel, and procurement) was driven largely by a need for the government and the minister to exercise, in a more effective and active way, day-to-day oversight, monitoring and control of the military.

Manson's article would turn out to be one of the very few positive assessments of NDHQ to ever come out, especially one written by a senior military officer. The chairman of the Defence Research Board had a more critical opinion of the merging of the two headquarters, calling it "an act of mayhem committed in the name of administrative madness."[52] The rearranging of the CFHQ and departmental headquarters chairs had not even been completed in early 1973 when another restructuring took place, and the criticism of the new organization started immediately. Concerns over the "overly centralized, overly staff-ridden," and excessively civilianized organization would grow in the 1970s and 1980s, and continue for over twenty-five years.[53]

Critics complained frequently about the 1972 reforms, pointing chiefly to Hellyer and his unification project as the event that set the conditions for the creation of NDHQ, forgetting, as years went by, that several defence mismanagement issues in the early 1970s had pushed the government to the NDHQ solution.[54] The most commonly heard argument criticizing NDHQ was that the changing role of civilians and military officers had led to a blurring of the responsibilities of civilian officials and military officers, to increased civilianization and bureaucratization in defence, and to an excessive reliance on management and business methods. Many decried that those factors contributed to a progressive loss of operational focus in the CAF and a corresponding erosion of the military ethos.[55] Throughout the 1970s and 1980s, concerns were raised that officers were acquiring skills and an orientation characteristic of civilian administrators or even political leaders, contributing to a decline in military professionalism.[56] At NDHQ, "civilianization" was used to denote the change of culture taking place, in particular that military policies, regulations and decisions were becoming generally based on civilian and public service concepts, values and interests.[57]

As expected, the issue of civilianization of the CAF was one of the central issues that emerged from the report of the Task Force on Review of Unification of the Canadian Armed Forces in 1980. Commissioned by the defence minister during the short-lived Conservative government of 1979-80, and composed of both civilians (inside and outside government) and uniformed members, it was mandated with examining the merits and disadvantages of the unification of the CAF, together with an analysis of the command structure. The task force interviewed nearly one thousand serving members, and it was told that the CAF had adopted civilian norms and standards to an unacceptable degree.[58] The perception, as one author characterized the feeling at the time, was that the CAF "had lost control of their own headquarters," and that public servants were exercising undue influence over matters that were exclusively military in nature.[59]

Upon careful consideration, the task force concluded that the perception that existed in the CAF may have been based on an incomplete understanding of those in the field about the nature and functioning of NDHQ, "attributable to the composition of the Defence Management Committee which is perceived to be dominated by civilians."[60] While senior civilians may have been more visible by 1979 in their roles in the integrated NDHQ, the reality is that there had been no influx of civilians in the 1970s – the numbers of senior military and civil service personnel in defence had in fact contracted slightly since 1967.

Admiral Robert Falls, CDS between 1977 and 1980, commented in 1978 that, with the creation of NDHQ in 1972, the CDS and his senior commanders at NDHQ began losing their control over the CAF. Falls lamented that strengthening the DM's staff as a means of enhancing civil control by the political executive provided public servants "a degree of authority over military affairs without responsibility for military accountability or performance."[61] Defence analyst (and retired military officer) Douglas Bland, who devoted considerable time to studying defence administration, wrote in *Chiefs of Defence* in the mid-1990s that the "integration of the NDHQ civilian and military staff [in 1972] has heightened, not lessened, the conflict between the two elements in the headquarters and…created institutional ambiguity where none [existed]."[62]

Critics of the national headquarters have not only been historians, defence commentators and former military officers. Civilians complained equally about military officers and their management incompetence. Former Deputy Minister C. R. "Buzz" Nixon declared in 1982 in a presentation at the Canadian Forces College that NDHQ was inappropriately staffed by military officers who were incapable of managing well in the Ottawa environment, and that "military parochialism," or friction between the services within the military, was impeding the success of several projects and ideas in Ottawa.[63]

Harriett Critchley, a political scientist who was a member of the 1980 task force, argued in an analysis of the NDHQ governance that, on the contrary, the military in the 1980s had greater influence than before, over a broader range of issues and at a higher level, by virtue of its increased membership in a large number of senior committees (especially after the commanders of the three environments were added to several senior NDHQ committees in the early 1980s).[64] Still, the criticism of NDHQ and the role of civilians in it did not abate. "Over the years," wrote military historian David Bercuson in 1996, at the height of the Somalia Inquiry, "the power and influence of the DM have increased while those of the CDS have declined," leading him to conclude that the "merging of military and civilian advisors at NDHQ has been disastrous."[65]

It can be argued, however, that the apparent "civilianization" of military values and norms in the 1970s and 1980s emerged not solely because of the amalgamation of CAF and departmental headquarters, but because of several other factors at work at the time, including increased job specialization in society, a decline in the importance of the combat fighting ability of the CAF, the introduction into the military of civilian and business management principles, and bureaucratic rationalization in the federal government at large.[66] These elements were all noted after unification of the three services in 1968, but became a more significant concern after the creation of NDHQ in 1972. As one study found, as early as 1978, the broad institutional change taking place in the military (i.e., civilianization) merely reflected societal trends, which were affecting the military organizations of other Western democracies in a similar way.[67]

This failure to fully appreciate the reasons for the apparent heightened influence of civilians at NDHQ, which persisted both inside and outside the CAF, meant the controversy would not fade over time. In fact, it would culminate in the mid-1990s when NDHQ integration would be critically re-examined as part of several reviews conducted for the preparation of a new white paper on defence and during the Somalia Inquiry.

THE 1994 DEFENCE WHITE PAPER AND THE SOMALIA AFFAIR

The beating death of a Somali teenager by Canadian soldiers during a United Nations peacekeeping mission in 1992 set off several investigations, inquiries and studies into the incident and the Canadian military, and it triggered a series of important reforms that impacted not only the Canadian military but the defence department as well. At the same time, with the end of the Cold War and the expectation of a peace dividend, the government aggressively targeted defence in its efforts to eliminate the federal deficit.[68] The end result was a significant reduction of the civilian (and military) defence establishment and the introduction of new approaches to providing defence services, such as re-engineering work processes and contracting out existing defence activities. These efforts created significant turmoil in the department and brought into question the role of the 33,600 defence civilians from several directions.[69]

Testifying in September 1994 to the Special Joint Committee of the Senate and House of Commons (SJC), which was looking into a new defence policy, Deputy Minister Robert Fowler (who by then had been DM at DND for over five years) tabled a document entitled "The Organization of Canadian Defence," which had been prepared at the request of the SJC to outline the responsibilities of the DM and the CDS and the role of NDHQ. It also specifically addressed the criticism of the current headquarters and, in particular, the unique contribution of defence civilians:

> This integrated headquarters has been in existence for over 20 years. The close civil–military relationship brings together an exceptionally wide range of knowledge, skills and perceptions – all of which contribute to defence management that is comprehensive, efficient and effective...

> A number of observers have called for the separation of the civilian and military branches of the Department.... In the main, however, they argue that the present arrangement encourages civilian "interference" and "politicizes" the military.

> In fact, the integrated headquarters exists precisely because, at the strategic level, political imperatives, economic considerations, and operational issues are inseparable. Operations, capital equipment programs, and other Departmental activities have political and economic contexts that must be addressed. Beyond matters that one might call "departmental," the inescapable reality is that DND and the CF must also carry out government-wide policies and programs with respect to social change, bilingualism, and open government.

> An integrated military-civilian headquarters does this more effectively and efficiently, drawing as it does on the different but complementary skills of the military and civilian staffs. Uniformed personnel are able to provide their unique expertise on military questions, but they are not as experienced as civilians in dealing with political considerations, governmental compromise, and public finances. Beyond this, while actions at the strategic level impact on the operational level (and vice versa), civilian involvement does not compromise the chain of military command in operations.[70]

Having heard "conflicting testimony of whether this [integrated headquarters] arrangement is appropriate for the needs of the Canadian Forces," the SJC could not come up with a recommendation for the government, suggesting instead a more detailed study.[71] The 1994 *Defence White Paper*, released a few months later by the Chrétien Liberal government, made an effort to affirm that the civilian workforce was an integral component of the Defence Team.[72] Despite its critical role, the government planned to reduce the number of civilian employees to 20,000 in five years. The white paper directed the military and the department to reduce all headquarters dramatically (the reduction target was initially set at 33%, then increased by the minister to 50%) and to put in place a new command structure.[73] But the government ignored the advice of the SJC and instead strongly validated the need for a civilian-military NDHQ, before anyone had serious thoughts about "reversing the civilian-military integration of National Defence Headquarters."[74]

Faced with dwindling budgets, successive and substantial personnel cutbacks, and significant pressure from the government's central agencies to reform the management and administration of defence, the department and the CAF increasingly adopted business practices to be able to implement the policy direction and the budget reductions. This meant accelerating the centralization of resources, the re-engineering of processes, and the privatization of non-core defence functions to achieve more efficiency. While the defence budget was being cut, the Canadian military was facing an increased operational tempo, deploying more frequently and in more dangerous situations, as "peacekeeping" operations were undertaken around the globe.

Defence developed a five-year plan containing several elements, including downsizing (especially of headquarters), management renewal, and alternative service delivery (ASD), which all impacted the role of civilians in one way or another. ASD was the term for a "systematic search for new and better ways of providing government services," but everyone saw it for what it was: privatization, or the contracting out of non-core defence activities.[75] For many defence civilian employees, the irony of this exercise was that they had to conduct cost-benefit analyses of their own jobs, which not only questioned their role inside defence, but could provide the rationale for eliminating their positions.

This era reached its high-water mark in 1995 with the Management Command and Control Re-Engineering (MCCR) initiative, when private sector management practices and re-engineering (by re-organizing along process lines versus functional lines) tended to dominate most defence processes, and an obsession with "do more with less" surfaced, distorting defence decision making and negatively affecting relations between the military and public servants.[76] In the end, as the Auditor General of Canada stated in his annual report in 1999, numerous errors were made in implementing ASD, and its results were definitely mixed. To most defence employees and many in the military, however, the experiment was a failure, and it created frustration, cynicism, low morale, and a lingering suspicion of this type of initiative – one that remains to this day.

In 2003, Minister of Defence John McCallum launched the Advisory Committee on Administrative Efficiency to identify $200 million in internal efficiency savings. Ironically, the committee found that contractors were generally more expensive than public servants or military personnel, and that "there is significant potential for savings by replacing this contracted 'hidden' workforce with public servants."[77] It seemed that contracting out the work of public servants was not a panacea for defence efficiency. The committee found many problems with NDHQ (loss of strategic focus, bureaucratic process-driven culture, transactional issue-management approach to business), but they did not directly associate these problems with the division of roles and responsibilities between civilians and military officers at headquarters.

While downsizing and re-engineering was taking place, the Somalia Inquiry of 1995-97 was unfolding and making national headlines. The Somalia commission did not examine the role of civilians in any detail, although it laid blame on both the military and public servants for what happened in Somalia. It confirmed the conclusion others had reached, namely, that the "hierarchy of authority in...NDHQ," especially between the CDS and the DM, had "become blurred and distorted." The commission therefore recommended that responsibilities be clarified to prevent civilian officials from interfering in uniquely military matters, and it cautioned that the "notion of civil control of the military should not be confused with control exercised by public servants," stressing that "[c]lear, unambiguous lines of accountability and responsibility should be in the forefront of factors to be considered in any revision of the organization of national defence."[78]

The Somalia commission, which focused primarily on examining matters related to the deployment and employment of the Canadian military in Somalia, strongly implied in its report that senior civilian public servants had intruded in military affairs, operational issues and the military chain of command, and that this interference had contributed to a series of ill-advised decisions regarding the deployment of the Canadian Airborne Regiment.[79]

General John De Chastelain, CDS when the Somalia deployment decision was made in the fall of 1992, was questioned quite extensively on the division of responsibilities between the CDS and the DM and, in particular, on the "danger" that the integrated headquarters had contributed to a blurring of the functions between the DM and the CDS. De Chastelain was unequivocal in his answer on this matter, stating that the CDS and the DM worked well, arguing instead that "the danger is greater by the separation of the two functions, particularly at the strategic level and at National Defence Headquarters," where the integrated military-civilian mix facilitates a "strategic understanding and the strategic provision of advice to the ministers and to Cabinet of defence issues."[80] In fact, continued De Chastelain, the integrated civilian-military headquarters existed precisely because, at the strategic level, political imperatives, economic considerations and operational issues were found to be inseparable, repeating the words Deputy Minister Fowler had offered to the SJC two years before.[81]

In the end, the Somalia commission did not go as far as recommending a separation of the military and civilian structures at NDHQ, as some were strongly advocating, or for any change to the fundamental role of civilians, although it recommended that the *National Defence Act* (NDA) be amended to "expressly prohibit the deputy minister from assuming the powers or prerogatives of the minister as regards the authority to direct the CDS in any matter concerning the 'command and administration of the CF.'"[82] It was tempting for outsiders not understanding the DM–CDS joint governance, and for those who wanted to break apart NDHQ, to blame interference and undue influence in policy and operations decisions by senior public servants for some aspects of the Somalia fiasco; however, we know today that it was primarily a command and leadership failure of the Canadian military, on many levels.

The commissioners had originally been mandated to look at the actions and decisions of both the Canadian military and DND to determine whether there had been failures in leadership, with the intent of examining the decisions not only of officers, but also of top civilian staff at NDHQ, including the DM. By early 1997, however, with a federal election looming, the government grew concerned about the direction of the commission and decided to cut the inquiry short, before those aspects of decision making could be investigated fully.[83]

Minister of National Defence Doug Young observed in his 1997 *Report to the Prime Minister on the Leadership and Management of the Canadian Forces* that there "is a great deal of misunderstanding and misinformation about how our national headquarters works."[84] However, Young "categorically defended the importance and legitimacy of having senior bureaucrats involved in managing Canada's defence affairs,"[85] and summarily dismissed any notion of returning to a pre–1972 construct for NDHQ:

> Civilians must have a significant role in the national structures of every democracy. There are, of course, many ways of structuring complementary civilian and military work relationships. No one model is perfect. Everywhere, however, the effectiveness of the system rests on cooperation and consultation at all levels – not on totally separate structures working on the same things at the same time often at cross purposes and in ignorance of one another.[86]

Having affirmed the critical role of civilians at NDHQ, Young chastised the military for not adequately preparing its officers – especially general and flag officers – to "operate effectively" in an integrated civil-military headquarters:

> It is all the more important, therefore, that all military officers – especially at senior levels – have a solid and in-depth understanding of the role and functions of the Department, government in general and the central agencies in particular. They must also have a solid appreciation of the roles of civilians at National Defence Headquarters and be well prepared to perform staff functions in the integrated headquarters.[87]

Young acknowledged the concerns expressed about a blurring of the military and civilian accountabilities at NDHQ, and directed that the authority, responsibility and accountability of the CDS, DM and senior staff be clarified.[88]

In early 2005, the government announced the appointment of General Rick Hillier as the new CDS. Hillier's strong leadership, unbounded confidence and strategic focus changed the balance of the relationship between civilians and the military like no CDS in recent years. The national headquarters is still feeling the effects of the influence of Hillier.

THE TRANSFORMATION OF 2005 AND THE AFGHANISTAN WAR

The 2005 *Defence Policy Statement* (DPS) highlighted a new vision for the Canadian military, including a commitment to increase the defence budget, expand the forces and transform their capabilities. Uncharacteristically for a Canadian defence white paper, the DPS provided much detail on the transformation of operational capabilities and the command and control structure; nonetheless, the document was mute on the department and the role of civilians. This silence, combined with a minister and a DM who were supportive of the changes proposed by Hillier, gave the strong-willed CDS the latitude he needed to assert his authority and to quickly pursue important changes to NDHQ to better position the headquarters to support Canadian military operations in general, and the impending war effort in Afghanistan in particular.[89]

Scarred by the legacy of the 1990s, especially the aftermath of the Somalia Affair, and the multiple verdicts that suggested the Canadian military had lost its operational focus and military ethos, Hillier moved quickly to transform NDHQ and to strengthen the decision-making role of the military on matters affecting operational issues.[90] Hillier never publicly stated his agenda, though it is clear that in pushing for an operational focus and a command-centric approach to decision making, he wanted to restore to the military some responsibilities for operational issues that he believed should be decided by military officers and not by senior public servants. As such, the increased focus on actual combat operations in Afghanistan – especially after the move of the Canadian battle group to Kandahar in 2006 – provided him the opportunity to reinforce the importance of military professional expertise in Canada. Hillier had been frustrated by the tendency of civilian politicians and bureaucrats to discount military advice and expertise, and the Afghanistan operations were increasing the status, power and influence of military advisors, especially those like Hillier who had present-day operational experience to back up their rhetoric.[91]

Hillier moved aggressively to implement the changes, justifying the speed of change by the need to be prepared to command and support the Afghanistan campaign. He established a new command structure with four operational commands and formed a new Strategic Joint Staff (SJS) to assist him with strategically commanding the armed forces.[92] As part of this initiative, he even attempted, without success, to reassign the operational policy directorate (commonly referred to as J5 Policy) from ADM (Policy) to the SJS. With the creation of Military Personnel Command in 2007, he also increased the separation of military personnel from civilian human resource administration, returning to an organizational model pre-dating the creation of NDHQ. For all intents and purposes, Hillier was creating an operations-focused CFHQ inside NDHQ. In all this, the DM, Ward Elcock, facilitated Hillier's efforts to develop and implement his transformation policies and initiatives.[93]

Despite the significant publicity surrounding Hillier's efforts, which was at times negative, the fundamental role of civilians in DND during this period changed little, except that their efforts were now focused on supporting the Canadian military in several demanding operations, at home and abroad, including a combat mission in Afghanistan.[94] Defence civilians responded at all levels of the organization with pride, energy and dedication to support the military, whether working inside the CAF to help generate the units and capabilities needed for deployment overseas or inside NDHQ to assist with the planning and execution of operations. The high operational tempo, unprecedented in recent memory, gave everyone an opportunity to exercise their roles, and the responsiveness of NDHQ validated the view that the restructured military-civilian integrated headquarters could function very effectively in both peace and war.[95]

In his change of command speech as CDS in July 2008, Hillier warned the audience, which included the Prime Minister and several dignitaries, about attempts by senior civil servants ("field marshal wannabes," as he labelled them) to assume a bigger role in directing the day-to-day operations of Canadian military forces in the field. "Civilian control of the armed forces is not civil service control of the armed forces," stated Hillier loudly.[96] Although he did not make the distinction at the time, it is clear that Hillier's criticism was not directed at defence civilian officials, but rather at bureaucrats in the central agencies and other departments who wanted more influence and control over the CAF contingent in Afghanistan.[97] Inside defence, there was no doubt in anyone's mind that Hillier strategically commanded the Canadian military with a firm grip, and that the "field marshal wannabes" were sitting behind desks at the Privy Council Office across the Rideau Canal, and not at 101 Colonel By Drive.[98] In his tenure as CDS, Hillier also frequently appealed to the public, enhancing the perception of the CDS as the individual who spoke not only for the men and women in uniform, but on matters of national strategy and policy.[99]

In his 2009 memoirs, *A Soldier First*, released just over a year after he left as CDS, Hillier asserted that Conservative Defence Minister Gordon O'Connor had offered to separate the CAF from DND to bring clarity to the military and civilian roles inside defence. Hillier had dismissed the offer at the time, since the relationship that he had established with Deputy Minister Elcock allowed him to continue his transformation of the Canadian military. In hindsight, however, Hillier changed his mind, coming to the conclusion that "separating the Canadian Forces completely from the government bureaucracy in Ottawa may be the best way to ensure it remains effective."[100]

Hillier was no doubt passionate in his view and had the best interest of the nation in mind, but it is very difficult to envisage how the Canadian military could work effectively in Ottawa, and in domestic and overseas multinational operations, if it were functionally separated from the Department of National Defence. He was right to protect the sanctity of the military chain of command, such that orders and direction to the military come from senior military commanders, but he was off the mark in not acknowledging the role of civil servants in assisting elected officials with strengthening defence accountability and maintaining civil control of the military. As Lagassé observed correctly in 2010, in his comprehensive study *Accountability for National Defence*, "senior bureaucrats play a legitimate and necessary role in helping to keep the military accountable to cabinet, and vice versa."[101] While the legitimacy of civil control of the military in Canada has never been in doubt, the extent and the manner in which this oversight and control are exercised, especially by senior bureaucrats on behalf of politicians, has often been contentious.

CONCLUSION: WATCHDOGS OF THE MILITARY

During the 1950s and 1960s, a large majority of civilian public servants in Canadian defence were employed in junior trades and in clerical and administrative positions. Following the recommendations of the Glassco commission in 1963, and in particular the merging of the CAF and DND headquarters into NDHQ in 1972, defence civilian employees gradually expanded their roles, bringing administration and managerial expertise to specialized functions in middle manager and senior executive positions.

The major shifts in the roles and responsibilities of public servants in DND occurred over fifty years, achieving three main objectives. The first was to create a stronger DM group, including civilian staff who could take a comprehensive view of defence issues and administration in order to better assist ministers of national defence in performing their functions. Along with the growth of the federal government, the second was bringing needed civilian expertise to manage and administer more complex defence programs and to enhance the capacity of the military to deal vertically and horizontally with the central agencies and processes of the government. The third purpose was to assist the government and politicians in exercising oversight of the CAF and strengthening civil control of the military. Many of the initiatives by the government were clearly intended to increase the responsibilities, authority, power, and influence of senior civilians, in particular those of the deputy minister.

The large majority of civil servants in Canadian defence today remain highly dedicated "foot soldiers in coveralls," with 64% of defence civilian employees working within military organizations.[102] They work diligently inside units and formations of the CAF, providing essential support to ensure that the CAF can carry out its missions daily. With the high CAF operational tempo of the past ten years, they have proven their value. As for the senior civil servants working in NDHQ, they are certainly not the "field marshal wannabes" that General Hillier spoke of in 2008. The robust command structure that now exists in the CAF, from the tactical to the strategic level, with the CDS commanding at NDHQ with support from a robust joint staff, ensures that orders to CAF units come from military commanders in the chain of command – as is stipulated in the *National Defence Act*. Civilian public servants certainly participate in the process, on many levels, but military commanders make the decisions, and they are accountable for them.

The creation of NDHQ in 1972 definitely changed the respective roles of civilians and military officers in the senior levels of the department. This is precisely what the successive governments and several defence ministers intended to do with the reforms of the 1960s and 1970s. The changes brought civilian defence bureaucrats into the process of military policy and decision making for several reasons: to increase administrative efficiency in defence, to create an internal challenge function, to shift defence policy away from the military – emphasized with the creation of the Policy Group – and to strengthen bureaucratic oversight and control.

The concept of a merged headquarters and a single military-civilian defence staff, as instituted in 1972, has certainly not proven to be the solution to all the concerns identified at the time. Over the years, it has profoundly impacted the culture of the officer corps, as many have decried; but it can also be argued that it has transformed the culture of public servants working at defence.[103] While the Somalia Affair and budget reductions and downsizing of the 1990s brought turmoil in Canadian defence, with NDHQ being the most frequent target of criticism for the problems of defence, Minister Young unambiguously clarified the role of senior civilians in DND and put to rest any notion of returning NDHQ to a pre-1972 construct. In short, as this chapter has argued, government after government has seen the importance of maintaining the integration of civilian public servants with military officers in one strategic defence headquarters, often justifying NDHQ on reasons of efficiency rather than on the need to enhance accountability and civil control of the military.

The changing role of civilians employed at the highest levels of the department over the last fifty years must be understood within the context of the changes that took place in government, maturing civil-military relations, and in the evolution of the responsibilities of the DM group. As defence ministers and others proposed and implemented changes over the years to the responsibilities of the DM, the role of defence civilians, especially in the top echelons of NDHQ, inescapably evolved in parallel. More recently, the enactment of the *Federal Accountability Act* in 2006 conferred more authority on the DM, rendering the DM legally answerable to Parliament for the proper use and allocation of departmental finances. To a degree, this law has brought more clarity to the role and responsibilities of the DM. At the same time, however, Hillier's transformation of the headquarters, the conflict in Afghanistan, which led to a greater distinction between the military and civilian roles in NDHQ for operational issues, and the changing responsibilities of the DM have all contributed to accentuating the CDS-DM polarization that Colonel Manson had predicted and feared in 1973. Over the years, there has been much criticism of the alleged heightened power and influence of senior civil servants within DND; it remains, however, that it would be very difficult to envisage how the CAF could work effectively in Ottawa if it were functionally separated from the department.

There is a clear expectation from the current government, as there was from the Glassco commission in 1963 and the Management Review Group in 1972, that the growing presence, authority and influence of senior public servants inside defence will allow them to critically probe and to challenge military advice, recommendations and even decisions. Recent assertions of inadequate civilian oversight of major procurement programs, leading to cost overruns, may provide greater justification for strengthening even further the role of civilians in defence. The associate minister of national defence stated, as recently as May 2013, that DND had acknowledged the need to reform internal decision making and to "institute a formal mechanism to enable a greater capability and challenge function much earlier in the process [of aligning capabilities to strategic goals]."[104] While there was no mention of who would perform this "challenge function," it can be expected that the responsibility for strengthening challenge mechanisms inside the department will rest with the DM.

Because civilians in DND continue to bring professional expertise in policy development, public administration, resource management and in government decision-making processes, they have over time become "watchdogs" of the military. However, as civil-military relations expert Philippe Lagassé noted correctly a few years ago in a major study of accountability for national defence, the changing role of public servants must be seen within the context of defence accountability at large, rather than strictly as an assertion of civilian supremacy or political control over the military.[105]

Ultimately, as former CDS General Gerry Theriault stated in the mid-1990s, the organization of national defence and, in particular, the role of senior civilians within NDHQ, has a crucial impact on civil-military relations in Canada, affecting not only how the different groups – politicians, military officers, and public servants in defence and elsewhere in government – interact, but also the quality and relevance of the military and defence advice provided to the government.[105] Those considering future changes to the role and organization of senior civilians in Canada's defence establishment must be mindful of this reality.

ENDNOTES

1   This expression and the title are adapted from Peter Feaver's well-known expression from his work *Armed Servants: Agency, Oversight and Civil-Military Relations*, paperback edition (Cambridge, MA: Harvard University Press, 2005).

2   I am grateful to the following individuals for their helpful suggestions and comments in reviewing earlier drafts: Dr. Joel Sokolsky, Dr. Allan English, Dr. Ross Pigeau, Major-General Mike Hood, Captain (Navy) Craig Baines, Captain (Navy) Sean Cantelon, and Captain Michel Gosselin.

3   CTV Newsnet, "Hillier Speaks from the Ceremony," July 2, 2008, at http://www.ctv.ca/CTVNews/CanadaAM/20080702/Hillier_retire_080702/. No longer accessible.

4   Philippe Lagassé, *Accountability for National Defence*, IRPP Study No. 4, March 2010, 5.

5   As the reader will note immediately, issues of civil–military relations and frameworks of civil control of the military underlie many of the ideas and themes discussed in this chapter. However, for brevity, I have decided to leave this discussion aside and focus more exclusively on the evolution of the role of civilians inside defence.

6   In democracies, civilian direction is meant to imply direction by elected civilians. Both the adjectives "civil" and "civilian" control are used alternately in the literature with a distinction seldom made; however, the U.S. literature of recent years uses almost exclusively the expression "civilian" control. The Somalia Inquiry of 1995-97 made a distinction between the two: "In Canada, as in most liberal democratic states, civil control of the military means the control of the armed forces by civilians elected to Parliament acting in accordance with statutes passed by that legislative body. This principle is distinctly and conceptually different from the notion of civilian control of the military, which may mean control by anyone not enrolled in the armed forces, such as public servants." Except for

specific citations, the term "civil" will be employed throughout this chapter to refer to the civil authority (politicians). See Gilles Létourneau, *Dishonoured Legacy: The Lessons of the Somalia Affair*, Report of the Commission of Inquiry into the Deployment of Canadian Forces to Somalia (Ottawa: Public Works and Government Services Canada, 1997), 162; and, Douglas Bland, "A Unified Theory of Civil-Military Relations," *Armed Forces and Society* 26, no. 1 (Fall 1999): 10.

7   The term "integration," prior to the 1970s, referred to the amalgamation of the headquarters, commands and support establishments of the three services, while preserving the services themselves as separate institutions. "Unification" means the establishment of a single military service (the Canadian Armed Forces) in place of the army, navy and air force. After 1972, integration often referred to the merging of the CAF headquarters with the departmental headquarters, to create NDHQ, as it is known today.

8   Royal Commission on Government Organization [Glassco Commission], *Report, Vol. 1* (Ottawa: Queen's Printers, 1963), as quoted in Douglas L. Bland, ed., *Canada's National Defence, Volume 2, Defence Organization* (Kingston, ON: Queen's University, School of Policy Studies, 1998), 21.

9   Glassco commission, *Report, Vol. 4* (Ottawa: Queen's Printers, 1963), *Report 20: Department of National Defence*, 61; and Bland, Volume 2, 21.

10   Glassco, *Report 20*, 61.

11   The DM was limited to the traditional functions, such as the preparation of the annual budgetary estimates, the control of the expenditures appropriated to the department, the review of contract requests from the three services, the determination of the civilian personnel establishments, the formulation of construction programs and the audit of stores. Glassco, *Report 20*, 74-6. See also A. W. Johnson, "The Role of the Deputy Minister: III," *Canadian Public Administration* 4, no. 4 (1961): 363-73.

12   Glassco, *Report 20*, 76. Of note, the use of the term "staff group" in 1963 referred specifically to the DM's civilian staff.

13   On the organization of the department, see R. L. Raymont, *The Evolution of the Structure of the Department of National Defence, 1945-1968*, Report to the Task Force on Review of Unification of the Canadian Armed Forces (Ottawa, Department of National Defence, 1979), 26-27 and Chart 2b.

14   Douglas L. Bland, *The Administration of Defence Policy in Canada 1947 to 1985* (Kingston, ON: Ronald P. Frye, 1987), 126; and Glassco, Report 20, 77.

15   For instance, 54% of Air Material Command consisted of uniformed personnel, while the Navy managed with only 5%. The remainder was civilian employees (Glassco, *Report 20*, 83-4).

16   Glassco, *Report 20*, 81-2.

17   Glassco, *Report 20*, 65-6, and 78-9.

18   Glassco, *Report 20*, 78-9.

19   Bland, *Administration of Defence Policy*, 126.

20   Glassco, *Report 20*, 79 (emphasis added).

21   Donald J. Savoie, *Governing from the Centre* (Toronto: University of Toronto Press, 1999), 203.

22   Bland, *Administration of Defence Policy*, 31.

23   Daniel Gosselin and Craig Stone, "From Minister Hellyer to General Hillier," *Canadian Military Journal* 6, no. 4 (Winter 2005–2006): 6-7.

24   Paul T. Hellyer, *Damn the Torpedoes: My Fight to Unify the Canadian Forces* (Toronto: McClelland and Stewart, 1990), 36.

25   On the events, see Jon McLin, *Canada's Changing Defence Policy 1957-1963: The Problem of a Middle Power in Alliance* (Baltimore, MD: John Hopkins Press, 1967), 3; J. L. Granatstein, "The Defence Débâcle, 1957-1963," in *Canada 1957-1967: The Years of Uncertainty and Innovation*, ed. J. L. Granatstein (Toronto: McClelland and Stewart, 1986), 101-38; and Peter T. Haydon, *The 1962 Cuban Missile Crisis: Canadian Involvement Reconsidered* (Toronto: The Canadian Institute of Strategic Studies, 1993).

26   "White Paper on Defence, March 1964," in *Canada's National Defence, Volume 1: Defence Policy*, ed. Douglas L. Bland (Kingston, ON: Queen's University School of Policy Studies, 1997), 92.

27   Bill C-90 (May 1964) amended the *National Defence Act* (NDA) to create the office of the CDS, while Bill C-243 (December 1966), the *Canadian Forces Reorganization Act* (informally referred to as the "Unification Act") was the government's legislation that amended the NDA to eliminate the three services and create one unified military force. See Bland, Administration of Defence Policy, 37–53.

28   Commodore R. L. Hennessy, *Report of the Minister's Manpower Study (Men)* (Ottawa, ON: Department of National Defence, 1966); in particular, see Chapter 16, "Civilian Personnel." A previous study on officers had been conducted the year before.

29   "White Paper on Defence, March 1964," in Bland, *Volume 1*, 93. In his memoirs, written nearly 25 years after he left defence, Hellyer made scant mention of the proposal to increase the role of the DM. See Hellyer, *Damn the Torpedoes*, 42.

30   Paul Hellyer, House of Commons, *Debates*, 8 May 1964, 3068, and Bland, Administration of Defence Policy, 46.

31   Daniel Gosselin, "The Storm over the Unification of the Armed Forces," in *The Insubordinate and the Non-Compliant: Case Studies of Canadian Mutiny and Disobedience, 1920 to Present*, ed. Howard G. Coombs (Toronto: Dundurn, 2007), 309-43.

32   D. G. Loomis, "The Canadian Forces and the Department in War and Peace," Supporting Paper to NDHQ Study S3/85 (Ottawa, ON: Department of National Defence, 1985), 43; see in particular the discussion at 70-8.

CHAPTER 1

33   Peter Kasurak, "Civilianization and the Military Ethos: Civil-Military Relations in Canada," *Canadian Public Administration* 25, no. 1 (Spring 1982): 120, contends that "unification also significantly altered the role of civilians within NDHQ." Kasurak is incorrectly linking the creation of NDHQ (which he erroneously dates to 1968) with integration and unification. Loomis, in his NDHQ Study S3/85, confirms that Kasurak is mistaken in his interpretation.

34   The reconstructed and re-energized Defence Council under the chairmanship of the minister was composed of the CDS, the DM, and the chairman of the Defence Research Board, who provided military, bureaucratic, and scientific advice to the minister. Subordinate officers to the CDS frequently attended the meetings. Douglas L. Bland, *Chiefs of Defence: Government and the Unified Command of the Canadian Armed Forces* (Toronto: The Canadian Institute of Strategic Studies, 1995), 74. On the strengthened role of the Defence Council for decision making, see Hellyer, *Damn the Torpedoes*, 89-90 and Vernon Kronenberg, *All Together Now: The Organization of the Department of National Defence in Canada 1964-1972* (Toronto: Canadian Institute of International Affairs, 1973), 108.

35   See the discussion in Kronenberg, *All Together Now*, 61-6.

36   Kronenberg provides another reason: the force of personalities at the top. Between 1955 and 1960, the DM was the former vice-chief of the air staff, Air Marshal Frank Miller, who went on to become Chairman of the Chiefs of Staff Committee in 1960, and first Chief of the Defence Staff in 1964 (until 1966). Dominant as he was, Miller did little to foster greater use of civilians. Kronenberg, *All Together Now*, 65.

37   Kronenberg, *All Together Now*, 67. Although *All Together Now* was published in 1973, Kronenberg wrote in 1971 the thesis that formed the basis for the book.

38   *Defence in the 70s*, in Bland, *Volume 1*, 172.

39   C. R. "Buzz" Nixon, having just left as DM at defence, listed during a speech in 1983 six major ministerial concerns that led to the minister initiating the MRG (the two other concerns included the minister having to constantly adjudicate advice received from the CDS and the DM and duplication of functions between the CDS and the DM); see Loomis, "The Canadian Forces and the Department in War and Peace," 93-4, and also, J. L. Granatstein and Robert Bothwell, *Pirouette: Pierre Trudeau and Canadian Foreign Policy* (Toronto: University of Toronto Press, 1990), 236-43

40   *Management of Defence in Canada – Report in Brief* (Ottawa, ON: Department of National Defence, 1972), in Bland, *Volume 2*, 167-72.

41   Management of Defence in Canada, in Bland, *Volume 2*, 168, and 185–200 for a complete list of symptoms identified by the MRG.

42   On the flawed analysis and conclusions of the MRG, see Bland's analysis, in *Volume 2*, 163-4, and Bland, "Institutionalizing Ambiguity: The Management Review Group and the Reshaping of the Defence Policy Process in Canada," *Canadian Public Administration* 30, no. 4 (Winter 1987): 527-49.

43   This ADM was initially identified to as ADM Strategy, Policy and Plans, but was quickly shortened to ADM (Policy) by fall 1972 (*Management of Defence in Canada*, in Bland, *Volume 2*, 212 and 219-20).

44   The MRG did not use the terms "military" and "defence" advice, as such. Rather, they argued that strategic studies should not be limited to military threats, but should incorporate national security threats in the broadest sense, and since at the strategic level there is "no such thing as a 'purely military' requirement, but only alternatives with varying risks, costs, and military involvement," there is a need for a group inside the department to present alternative policies and objectives to the minister and the government (ibid., 220).

45   See the discussion in Kronenberg, *All Together Now*, 5-6.

46   Over time, some of the ADMs, namely Personnel and Materiel, were filled by either military officers or senior civilians. This practice continued until the 1990s. As of 1972, NDHQ included the following senior appointments: Vice Chief of the Defence Staff, Deputy Chief of the Defence Staff Operations, Deputy Chief of the Defence Staff Support (eliminated in 1973), and five ADMs: Evaluation, Finance, Materiel, Personnel, and Policy. See testimony of Minister Edgar Benson, Special Committee on External Affairs and National Defence, 28 March 1972. This practice continued until the 1990s.

47   See Paul Manson, "The Restructuring of National Defence Headquarters," *Canadian Defence Quarterly* 3, no. 3 (Winter 1973–74): figures 1 and 2, 9-10. Manson wrote the paper while at the National Defence College. He had been the executive assistant to the CDS immediately before, and thus had a front-seat perspective on the impact of the merger at the top echelons of NDHQ.

48   Ibid., 10 and 13.

49   One of the main reasons was likely that the new DM, Sylvain Cloutier, had come from Treasury Board and the Department of National Revenue, and expressly at the Prime Minister's request (Granatstein and Bothwell, *Pirouette*, 242).

50   Manson, "The Restructuring," 12-4.

51   Ibid., 9.

52   Quoted in Bland, *Chiefs of Defence*, 93.

53   On early concerns, see E. M. D. Leslie, "Too Much Management, Too Little Command," *Canadian Defence Quarterly* 2, no. 3 (Winter 1972-73): 30-2; and J. E. Neelin and L. M. Pederson, "The Administrative Structure of the Canadian Armed Forces: Over-Centralized, Overly Staff-Ridden," Canadian Defence Quarterly 4, no. 2 (Summer 1974): 33-9. On continuing concerns, see Kasurak, "Civilianization and the Military Ethos," 108-29; Bland, "Institutionalizing Ambiguity," 527-49 and *Chiefs of Defence*, 27-74, passim.

54   The line of reasoning is that if Hellyer had been less single-minded about the unification initiative, and had implemented some of the key Glassco commission recommendations (as he has committed to do in the 1964 white paper), the department and CFHQ would have been in a better position to deal with the issues that surfaced in the late 1960s (especially the development of the defence program), and there likely would have been no need for the government to commission an independent review group, such as the MRG. Bland discusses these aspects in passing in *Administration of Defence Policy*, 59-63, 126-7, and 200-1. Forty years later, Hellyer contends that he "would have fallen on his sword" if the government had ordered him to integrate CFHQ with the department (see Hellyer as quoted in Lewis Mackenzie, "Rick Hillier's Right, So Back Off," *Globe and Mail*, August 1, 2005, A11).

55   See, in particular, Kasurak, "Civilianization and the Military Ethos," 108-29. David Bercuson, *Significant Incident: Canada's Army, the Airborne, and the Murder in Somalia* (Toronto: McClelland & Stewart, 1996), also discusses this theme at 72-4.

56   Létourneau, *Dishonoured Legacy*, 157.

57   Bland, *Volume 2*, 249. There are several meanings for the term *civilianization* in defence. Civilianization is usually meant in three contexts: increased number of civilians in key positions affecting defence; the belief that CAF members have adopted civilian norms and standards to an unacceptable standard; and, undue influence of civilians over matters that are (or should be) exclusively military in nature (see also Kasurak, "Civilianization and the Military Ethos," 109-10).

58   *Task Force on Review of Unification of the Canadian Forces*, Final Report (Ottawa: Department of National Defence, 15 March 1980), in Bland, Volume 2, 258-342.

59   Kasurak, "Civilianization and the Military Ethos," 112.

60   Task Force on Review of Unification, in Bland, *Volume 2*, 337.

61   Admiral Robert Falls, as quoted in D. G. Loomis, "The Impact of the Integration, Unification and Restructuring of the Functions and Structure of National Defence Headquarters," Supporting Paper to NDHQ Study S1/85 Report (Ottawa: Department of National Defence, 1985), 130.

62   Bland, *Chiefs of Defence*, 161 and discussion in Bland, "Institutionalizing Ambiguity," 527-49.

63   Bland, *Chiefs of Defence*, 163 and 170.

64   W. Harriet Critchley, "Civilianization and the Canadian Military," *Armed Forces & Society* 16, no. 1 (Fall 1989): 117–36.

65   Bercuson, *Significant Incident*, 72-4.

66   Létourneau, *Dishonoured Legacy*, 157-8.

67   See Charles Cotton, Rodney K. Crook, and Frank C. Pinch, "Canada's Professional Military: The Limits of Civilianization," *Armed Forces & Society* 4, no. 3 (May 1978): 365-89.

68   *1994 Defence White Paper* (Ottawa, ON: Department of National Defence, 1994), Chapter 7, "Implementing Defence Policy."

69   Much of this effort was also part of what is now referred to as the "new public management," aimed at reshaping how governments operate. For a more comprehensive discussion about Canadian defence, see David Detomasi, "The New Public Management and Defense Departments: The Case of Canada," *Defense & Security Analysis* 18, no. 1 (2002): 51-73.

70   Robert Fowler, "The Organization of Canadian Defence" (Ottawa, ON: Department of National Defence, 1994), a document prepared for the Special Joint Committee of the Senate and House of Commons that was conducting hearings for the preparation of the

1994 *Defence White Paper*. The document was later tabled in 1996 by Deputy Minister Robert Fowler as Exhibit P-105 for his testimony to the Somalia Inquiry. In his testimony, Fowler implied that the document was a departmental document, and that it had been endorsed by the CDS.

71 Pierre De Bané and William Rompkey, *Security in a Changing World*, Report of the Special Joint Committee on Canada's Defence Policy (Ottawa, ON: Parliamentary Publications Directorate, 1994), 44.

72 1994 *Defence White Paper*, in Bland, *Volume 1*, 352.

73 The target established was to reduce headquarters personnel from 14,000 to 7,000 by 1999. *Fact Sheet: Management, Command and Control Re-engineering* (Ottawa, ON: Department of National Defence, November 1995), 1.

74 1994 *Defence White Paper*, in Bland, *Volume 1*, 348.

75 Auditor General of Canada, *Report of the Auditor General of Canada 1999*, Chapter 27: National Defence Alternative Service Delivery (Ottawa, 1999), 27-7, and also Michael Rostek, "A Framework for Fundamental Change? The Management Command and Control Re-Engineering Initiative," *Canadian Military Journal* 5, no. 4 (Summer 2004-05): 65-72.

76 Rostek, "A Framework,"68–9; see also, *MCCRT Historical Report* (Ottawa, ON: Department of National Defence, 1997).

77 Department of National Defence, *Achieving Administrative Efficiency* (Ottawa, ON: Department of National Defence, August 2003), "Executive Summary," iv-xiii, and 70. The committee recognized at the same time that some of the contracted functions are less expensive than using public servants, or that contractors are often the only option (such as selected medical services), 70-1.

78 Létourneau, *Dishonoured Legacy*, 16, 52; and Lagassé, Accountability for National Defence, 36.

79 Létourneau, *Dishonoured Legacy*, 6-7.

80 The first "danger" quotation is from the commission counsel when questioning General De Chastelain. Neither General De Chastelain, CDS between 1989 and January 1993, nor Lieutenant-General Paul Addy, the DCDS between June 1992 and January 1993, who were both intimately involved in advising the government on the deployment decision, and were both served by the commission a Section 13 Notice under the Inquiries Act for potential misconduct, laid any blame or responsibility on to the DM or ADM (Policy) during their testimony to the commission (and subsequent written objection by Lieutenant-General Paul Addy). See Lieutenant-General Addy's testimony of February 19, 1996, in Vol. 48 of the *Hearing Transcripts of the Somalia Inquiry*, and in particular the *Written Submission on Behalf of Lieutenant-General Paul Addy*, made by Greenfield & Barrie, Barristers and Solicitors, April 1997; and the testimony of General De Chastelain, February 20, 1996, in Vol. 49, in particular 9825-45. Even Bercuson, highly critical of the integrated NDHQ structure, does not mention the negative influence of the DM with respect to operations in *Significant Incident*.

81   The DM at the time, Robert Fowler, strongly echoed the statements made by De Chastelain (testimony of Robert Fowler, February 20, 1996, in Vol. 50, in particular 10160-5).

82   Létourneau, *Dishonoured Legacy*, 1421. This conclusion by the commissioners is interesting considering that Douglas Bland was advising the commission, and even prepared a study on NDHQ recommending fundamental changes to the structure of the HQ; see Douglas Bland, *National Defence Headquarters: Centre for Decision* (Ottawa, ON: Public Works and Government Services, 1997). Bland had been advocating a return to the CFHQ days for nearly 15 years by then. See his arguments and rationale in "White Paper on Defence," *Canadian Defence Quarterly* 20, no. 3 (December 1990), 30.

83   Létourneau, *Dishonoured Legacy*, 116.

84   Douglas M. Young, *Report to the Prime Minister on the Leadership and Management of the Canadian Forces* (Ottawa, ON: Department of National Defence, 1997), 30.

85   Lagassé, *Accountability for National Defence*, 36.

86   Young, *Report to the Prime Minister*, 29.

87   Young, *Report to the Prime Minister*, 31.

88   Douglas Young, "Authority, Responsibility and Accountability: Guidance for Members of the Canadian Forces and Employees of the Department of National Defence," as part of the *Report to the Prime Minister*.

89   Philippe Lagassé, "A Mixed Legacy: General Rick Hillier and Canadian Defence, 2005-08," *International Journal* (Summer 2009): 617-8. See also Rick Hillier, *A Soldier First: Bullets, Bureaucrats and the Politics of War* (Toronto: HarperCollins, 2009), 397, 406, 418, 427, and 469.

90   On how much the 1990s affected Hillier and his views of the military and bureaucracy, see Hillier, *A Soldier First*, passim.

91   Lagassé, "A Mixed Legacy," 617.

92   See Gosselin and Stone, "From Hellyer to Hillier," for a more complete discussion.

93   Lagassé, "A Mixed Legacy," 617; and Joel Sokolsky and Philippe Lagassé, "A Larger 'Footprint' in Ottawa: General Hillier and Canada's Shifting Civil-Military Relationship, 2005–2008," *Canadian Foreign Policy* 15, no. 2 (2009): 16-40.

94   See, for instance, Lawrence Martin, "In Defence, the Civilian Side in on the Slide," Globe and Mail, September 7, 2006; and Eugene Lang and Janice Gross Stein, *The Unexpected War: Canada in Kandahar* (Toronto: Viking, 2007), 260-1.

95   E-mail communications between the author and General Walter Natynczyk, May 28, 2013.

96   CTV Newsnet, "Hillier Speaks from the Ceremony," 2 July 2008, at http://www.ctv.ca/CTVNews/CanadaAM/20080702/Hillier_retire_080702/. No longer accessible. See also

Murray Brewster, "Hillier Warns Against Civil Servants Directing Military Operations," *Globe and Mail*, October 11, 2010.

97   Hillier, *A Soldier First*, 411–27.

98   The Afghanistan Task Force, led by a deputy minister, was operating from the Privy Council Office. It was responsible for interagency/departmental coordination and cooperation on Canada's diplomatic, deployment and aid mission to Afghanistan. The largest portion of NDHQ is located at 101 Colonel By Drive.

99   Lagassé and Sokolsky, "A Larger 'Footprint' in Ottawa," passim.

100   Hillier, *A Soldier First*, 427.

101   Lagassé, *Accountability for National Defence*, 57.

102   Department of National Defence, *Report on Transformation 2011* (Ottawa, ON: Department of National Defence, 2011), 16. The data on civilians is from 2010.

103   On the culture of the officer corps, see Gerry Theriault, "Democratic Civil-Military Relations: A Canadian View," in *The Military in Modern Democratic Society*, ed. Jim Hanson and Susan McNish (Toronto: Canadian Institute for Strategic Studies, 1996), 9. General Theriault was CDS between 1983 and 1986.

104   Kerry-Lynne Findley, transcript of breakfast keynote speech at CANSEC 2013 (Ottawa: Department of National Defence), May 30, 2013.

105   Lagassé, *Accountability for National Defence*, 29. For a more complete discussion on civil control, see Peter D. Feaver, *Armed Servants: Agency, Oversight, and Civil-Military Relations* (Cambridge, MA: Harvard U. P., 2003), 54-95, and Richard H. Kohn, "How Democracies Control the Military," *Journal of Democracy* 8, no. 4 (1997): 140-53.

106   Theriault, "Democratic Civil-Military Relations," 10.

CHAPTER 2

CIVIL-MILITARY RELATIONS:
THE BROADER CONTEXT

Alan Okros

Canada relies on a fully integrated military-civilian defence structure, with almost fifty years having passed since the major changes brought about by integration of the three services (1964), namely, the unification of the Canadian Armed Forces (in 1968) and the creation of a single National Defence Headquarters in 1972.[1] Surprisingly, it is only in recent years that attention has been paid to the organizational issues arising from these "mil-civ" dynamics. In fact, the use of the Defence Team concept to refer to a military-civilian partnership under Canada's Minister of National Defence was only articulated in 1992 and has generally received ambivalent support in departmental survey research.[2] Moreover, it is possible that weak support for the Defence Team may have been exacerbated by recent public commentary, such as the criticisms of the civil service levelled by now-retired Chief of the Defence Staff General Rick Hillier.[3] Conversely, there are numerous examples of military and civilians members coming together as a team, particularly when special circumstances required extra effort.[4] As a result, debate continues as to the appropriate roles and responsibilities for each.[5]

This chapter presents a broad overview of the underlying principles that inform the more practical questions of formal roles and informal relationships between military members and civilians working in national defence. My primary focus is the strategic or corporate level at National Defence Headquarters – or what is often referred to as the political-military or "pol-mil" interface.[6] In other words, I examine the relationship among the politicians who form the government of the day, senior members of the Canadian Armed Forces, and senior civilian members of the Public Service in the Department of National Defence. I begin with the two contemporary models of civil control of the military from the civil-military relations literature, highlighting the issues, tensions and differing perspectives that arise around four key issues: Who exercises control? What is controlled? Which priorities dominate control decisions? and What expertise is brought to bear on the issues?

CIVIL CONTROL OF THE MILITARY

The civil-military relations (CMR) literature has developed around the question of how a country can have a military strong enough to defend it without having the military control it. Particularly since the end of the Cold War, the debate over civil-military relations has re-emerged among military analysts in both liberal-democratic societies and those attempting to establish such regimes.[7] Theoretical work has focused on the relationship between the military, its host society and its government, and this focus helps explain aspects of the relations among politicians, military personnel and civilian bureaucrats.

The early statements of CMR were those of Samuel Huntington, a political scientist, and Morris Janowitz, a sociologist, both of whom based their observations on the United States' military profession in the Cold War conscription era. In positions that are by now well known among scholars of armed forces and society, Huntington saw the military as set apart from its host society in a number of ways. He depicted civil and military spheres as separate areas of activity, with the military remaining a politically neutral arm of government, amenable to political direction and civilian control, and only providing advice in narrow areas of specific military expertise.

Janowitz, on the other hand, saw the military institution as deeply embedded in its host society and dependent on society to effectively perform its responsibilities. In addition to his argument that the military had to reflect the values of liberal-democratic societies, he thought that the military should take a more active role in providing advice to government. While he did not see the military profession usurping political roles, he believed that officers' expertise should include an understanding and appreciation of the social and political context and that senior military leaders should have a voice in government decisions that affect the armed forces. The Janowitzian model fits contemporary civil-military relations in Canada, and his central ideas are clearly reflected in the CAF's *Duty with Honour: The Profession of Arms in Canada.*[8]

The CMR literature provides a sound basis for reflecting on theoretical issues surrounding civil control of the military and, from that, the relations between members of DND and the CAF in Canada. But a number of issues arise when theory is put into practice. Below I identify four significant practical problems, and I show how and why these problems influence the military-civilian Defence Team partnership.

CONTROL BY WHOM? THE DM-CDS DIARCHY

The CAF's Janowitzian understanding of CMR entails that there is a role for senior military leaders in government decision making. In the Canadian context, Douglas L. Bland has argued that military leaders share responsibility for civil-military decisions related to defence, and that this requires regular interaction between government officials and military leaders – a concept reflected in *Duty with Honour.*[9] As Bland notes, however, confusion arises in the Canadian context over who is meant by the "government officials" who exercise "civil control."[10] Under CMR theory, the expressions refer to members of the elected government which, in Canada, means the Prime Minister, Cabinet and the Minister of National Defence. In other words, "civil control" in CMR theory means political control of the military by elected members of the government, and pointedly not control by civilian government employees.

In the Canadian context, however, the line between political control and control by civilian government employees is blurred by the diarchal structure of National Defence. The division of authority between the civilian Deputy Minister of National Defence and the Chief of the Defence Staff results in a blurring of accountabilities, because senior members of the DND and the CAF both engage in defence decision making. Several of the most senior positions in the defence establishment (called level ones), for example, report to both the CDS and the DM.[11] Indeed, the 2006 *Federal Accountability Act* has exacerbated the confusion of roles by making the DM the "accounting officer" to Parliament. This increase in the DM's responsibilities has resulted in additional blurring of accountabilities between the CDS and the DM.[12]

Several attempts have been made to articulate the responsibilities of the CDS and the DM and, hence, the responsibilities of their subordinates in the CAF and DND.[13] The following statement by DND attempts to explain the DM's responsibilities:

> Both civilian and military personnel are accountable to the Deputy Minister, through their Environmental Chief of Staff or Group Principal, for the exercise of delegated statutory, policy and administrative authorities related to the management of funds, public service employees, property and other resources... . The responsibility and accountability of military staff to the Deputy Minister for the exercise of financial, administrative or civilian human resources authorities does not mean that the Deputy may issue orders to military personnel; nor does the issuing of directives by the Deputy somehow "civilianize" members of the Canadian Forces.[14]

Of course, this guidance invites the following question: When is direction a military order (the prerogative of the CDS) and when is it a managerial decision (which either the DM or CDS can take)? The military view is that any decision related to operations should be taken solely by the military chain of command. Yet almost all of these decisions involve "funds, property or other resources," bringing them under the authority of a senior civilian.

Military leaders understand that they must follow appropriate regulations and obtain requisite approvals. But the point of principle often applied is that only a member of the CAF should have the power to approve or deny, not a public servant. Because the DM is the accounting officer to Parliament, however, both sides of the diarchy will be involved in a range of areas where those in uniform believe civilians should not be. The limitation on decisions made by the Armed Forces Council (AFC) is a case in point. The AFC is the senior military body of the CAF with a mandate "to advise the Chief of the Defence Staff on broad military matters pertaining to the command, control, and administration of the Canadian Forces and to help the CDS make decisions."[15] Yet the proviso on the council's advisory mandate that "there be no resource implications"[16] in its decisions is one that is not always stated and often not understood by CAF members.

The military might wish for "pure" military control, with the CDS providing the final approvals for all decisions affecting any aspect of military operations. But many in DND take the opposite view, given the obligations inherent in the DM being the departmental accounting officer. When civilian members of DND are responsible for managing funds, property, or other resources, it is no surprise that they see themselves as having a very clear and important role in providing managerial oversight of CAF decisions. A challenge here is that the DM or the DM's senior staff can easily overstep boundaries and interfere in the normal business of the CAF – especially when the DM is a dynamic or forceful individual.[17] Either way, the DM-CDS diarchy and the overlapping roles it creates can easily lead to tensions between the two sides of the Defence Team.

CONTROL OVER WHAT? THE "POWELL DOCTRINE" LIVES ON

In adopting a Janowitzian approach to CMR, the Canadian defence establishment is committed to the principle that senior officers should have some say in political decisions that have important consequences for the military. But even when a CMR model takes for granted control of the military by the elected government, the question remains, when theory is put into practice, "Control over which types of decisions?" The idealized view of the military is that soldiers are the experts in military affairs; hence, the politicians should provide strategic objectives and then step aside while the admirals and generals plan and execute military operations (with public servants supporting the military decision makers). The contrasting perspective, represented in the slogan "War is too important to be left to generals," is that politicians – and, by implication, civilian members of their staffs – must take part in decisions that will direct military decisions at the strategic, operational and even tactical levels.[18] While neither view quite fits the division of roles in the Canadian defence establishment, there is little consensus within defence over which decisions belong in the political domain and which are the prerogative of the military, and even less over who should have the final say on which matters.

This question is not confined to the Canadian military, of course, and one U.S. general's answer has gained ground among senior military members north of the border. In the lead-up to the 1991 U.S.-led United Nations mission to force Iraqi troops out of Kuwait, General Colin Powell, then U.S. Chair of the

Joint Chiefs of Staff, articulated what he saw as the requisite conditions for committing the U.S. military to war. His principles were fairly straightforward and had been stated by military theorists for centuries, with the two key pre-conditions being that all other political means to resolve the issue have been exhausted and that the nation should provide all necessary resources to ensure military success, including clear political support and the generation of national will. In articulating these principles, however, Powell made strong public statements that were interpreted by many as suggesting that the military had the right to "insist" that these pre-conditions be met before "agreeing" to any mission. As a result, the "Powell Doctrine" entered professional military discourse as the appropriate role of the military when providing advice to politicians.[19]

The impact of the Powell Doctrine on the U.S. military's interpretation of appropriate civil-military relations was one of the issues examined in the comprehensive "gaps" research (i.e., gaps between civil and military views) conducted by Peter Feaver and his colleagues at the Triangle Institute for Security Studies (TISS) in 1998.[20] When asked to specify the proper role of the military leadership in decisions to commit the military abroad on seven key factors, with responses *be neutral, advise, advocate,* or *insist,* a majority of senior U.S. officers endorsed *advocate* or *insist* on several of the items. In 2001 to 2003, this research was replicated with senior CAF officers attending a program at the Canadian Forces College, with very similar results. As the authors of the final report stated,

> Responses on the "Powell Doctrine" items regarding the proper role of senior military leadership tended to echo what the TISS researchers concluded was a worrisome norm within the military elite cohort that the military should advocate or insist on key issues including: selecting kinds of military units (68% of Canadians endorsed "insist" vs. 63% in the US), developing an "exit strategy" (53% of Canadians chose "insist" vs. 52% in the US) and setting rules of engagement (48% of Canadians endorsed "insist" vs. 50% in the US)....Like their American colleagues, civilian Canadians' opinions were more closely aligned with civil control theory in viewing the military as being generally neutral or as simply providing advice regarding whether to

intervene, deciding what the goals should be, and generating public support for the intervention.[21]

This research shows that both U.S. and Canadian officers see a difference between purely political issues and what they deem to be military ones. A significant percentage endorsed the correct response of *be neutral* or the somewhat acceptable *advise* regarding decisions to intervene, establishing political goals and generating public support. However, in endorsing *insist* on items related to determining the kinds of military units, defining the military goals, developing an exit strategy and setting the rules of engagement, a significant proportion of military respondents indicated that it should be the military, not politicians, who have the final say on the conduct of operations. In short, this research provides clear evidence of wide support for the military worldview where the politicians decide when to go to war and the generals decide how to conduct it.

It is worth pointing out that the Powell Doctrine appears to extend beyond questions of war and operations for the CAF leadership. Decisions surrounding major equipment purchases provide a clear example of the military approach: The military should define the requirements, Cabinet should decide how much money will be allocated, and the military should be the one to pick the right equipment for the job. Similarly, the history of adjusting personnel policies to align military human resources practices with evolutions in the broader society shows a consistent pattern of the CAF assuming the prerogative to decide if, when and how policies should be amended, with changes most often made only when forced on the CAF by the courts.[22]

A military's desire to exercise control over decisions affecting the conduct of missions, the selection of equipment or the management of personnel all fit under the rubric of professional self-regulation.[23] All professions seek a high degree of autonomy over the central functions deemed critical to their primary purpose. While the focus in other professions, such as medicine and law, is entrance standards, qualifications, standards of practice and the regulation of codes of conduct, the military's overriding focus is operational effectiveness. As a result, the CAF seeks to exercise control over the factors that lead to success on operations. These factors extend across a broad range of mission-planning and force-generation activities, including using intentional socialization to instil shared values, beliefs and identity; conducting extensive collective training to create cohesive, motivated teams; and, ensuring structure and clarity through doctrine, regulations and specific directions, such as rules of engagement. In contrast, the Public Service is best seen as a "weak" profession in that it does not place as much emphasis on professional self-regulation.[24] As a result, it can be difficult for civilians to understand the rationale for the degree of control the military seeks to exert over particular functions.

In sum, civil control of the military in CMR theory means control by members of the elected government, not by civilian bureaucrats. In the Canadian context, however, differentiation among elected officials, the CAF and DND civilians are easily blurred because of the DM-CDS diarchy and, in particular, the role of the DM as the departmental accounting officer.[25] Even when the dynamic is between senior military leaders and politicians, and even when the military maintains the appropriate apolitical orientation, tensions and significant differences can arise out of the practical division of responsibilities in Canada's defence establishment. The desire for professional autonomy over key facets of the profession helps explain why a military seeks a high degree of control over those issues that it sees as critical to operational effectiveness and mission success. And the fact that there is not a comparable emphasis within the Public Service can lead to a misunderstanding by DND civilians about the rationale for the military approach to controlling certain decisions.

CONTROL BASED ON WHICH PRIORITIES? COMPETING NUMBER ONE PRIORITIES

The third locus of tension is the different priorities and objectives that govern the parties that administer National Defence and make defence policy. At the strategic level, decisions must be based on three broad factors: an understanding of the political dynamics and the agenda of the government of the day; consideration of the pan-governmental objectives of the "machinery of government" (i.e., the central agencies); and the specific role, mandate and missions of the particular department or agency. While all three perspectives are likely to be taken into consideration, the CAF and DND can interpret priorities in different ways and, thus, disagree on how important issues should be understood and addressed.

Understanding the dynamics between DND and the CAF means recognizing the different roles and considerations of government that inform how each of the two communities understands their responsibilities or, more accurately, how each prioritizes competing responsibilities. For instance, the government of the day must attend to multiple considerations, including fulfilling all legal obligations, accounting to Canadians for the business of government, serving as the national guardian of the social good, advancing the agenda upon which they were elected, and (always) focusing on being re-elected. While the purely political aspects related to the government's agenda and getting re-elected are fairly obvious, it is worth recalling how these perennial political concerns create tensions between the CAF and DND before moving on to the less obvious sources of tension, the government's legal obligations, accountability, and serving the social good.

With respect to political expediency, consider that national defence is a major commitment of resources, which includes decisions about military equipment procurements, real property holdings, the numbers of civilian employees and military members, the nature of contractual arrangements and ongoing purchases for everything from "guns to butter." Naturally, military leaders would like to ensure that every dollar spent goes to optimizing military operational effectiveness. But the government will always want to ensure that every dollar spent achieves the greatest political benefit (or, conversely, attracts the least political baggage). This tension helps explain strong differences of opinion on the relative weight to be given to operational factors and political implications for everything from major equipment purchases to base closures.[26]

A second perennial factor specific to DND is that the government of the day is really only prepared to commit funds for the roles and tasks that it assigns to the CAF – in other words, for the actual missions of today.[27] As a profession, however, the military assumes a responsibility to anticipate plausible future roles and missions; thus the military profession sees the need to invest time, effort and money in building capacities for the missions of tomorrow (even when the government of the day has not articulated these future requirements). Allocation of resources and the development of departmental business plans are therefore acute sources of tension, because it is here that the priorities of CAF leaders and their DND colleagues can come into conflict.

The federal government's legal, fiscal, and other social responsibilities will also strongly influence decisions made by the DM, inviting clashes over priorities between DND and the CAF.[28] With the passing of the *Financial Administration Act* and the *Public Service Modernization Act*, accountability has become heavily focused on ensuring value for money and requiring multiple layers of approvals and audits for financial transactions. Extensive processes for managerial oversight of expenditures elevate accountability over effectiveness, resulting in lengthy approval processes and considerable effort being expended on addressing constant audits, verifications and requirements for business cases and justifications of decisions taken (the high levels of approvals now required for relatively minor hospitality expenses serves as a good example).

Similarly, and in the name of the social good, the federal government has undertaken to ensure that the government workforce proportionately represents key Canadian demographics and that workplace practices reflect certain social values – objectives reflected in the *Official Languages Act* and the *Employment Equity Act*.[29] The focus on social responsibilities – particularly with regard to DND's Public Service workforce being required to reflect the society it serves – leads to an increased emphasis on equity and parity, with a strong reluctance to take decisions that may set precedents.[30]

These foci inform the roles and responsibilities of the central agencies, bringing DND along with them: the Prime Minister's Office, the Privy Council Office, the Treasury Board Secretariat and the Department of Finance. As stated in the Parliamentary Library publication on the central agencies, their roles and responsibilities are often not well understood:

> The term [central agency] is generally used to designate organizations that have a central coordinating role. These organizations work across government departments to provide advice to the prime minister and Cabinet and to ensure policy coherence and coordination on their behalf. Central agencies have either formal or informal authority over other departments and often direct their actions. Line departments, on the other hand, provide services directly to Canadians and do not have the authority or mandate to direct other departments in their operations.[31]

While the central agencies ensure coherence across government, those discharging senior responsibilities within line departments, such as DND, must balance multiple, often competing priorities in fulfilling their duties. For the Defence Team, a particular challenge is that the military would prefer to work under the principle of unity of command (a single line of authority exercised with a philosophy of "the buck stops here") and can have difficulty recognizing multiple lines of authority and accountability. As an example, the Assistant Deputy Minister (Human Resources – Civilian) has several masters: this ADM is responsible to the Treasury Board for discharging the government's responsibilities as the Public Service employer; to the DM as the Accounting Officer for Defence; to the CDS (because 64% of DND civilian Public Service employees work in CAF units and formations),[32] as well as being accountable to other organizations, such as the Public Service Commission, when exercising delegated authorities for Public Service appointments. Ensuring coordination and coherence across departments naturally results in extensive regulation and a strong preference for standardized, one-size-fits-all approaches.

In short, there are two inherent tensions between DND and the CAF around resource allocation, because of their two very different sets of priorities – priorities that must be balanced by the Defence Team. The first is the balance between military effectiveness and political expediency when making major decisions involving equipment, base locations, infrastructure, or even the local purchasing of goods and services. The second involves balancing the allocation of time, effort, and money between carrying out the missions of today and building the capacities for the missions of tomorrow. So whose priorities win out? Suffice to say that the influence of the central agencies on major decisions has resulted in a strongly centralized, bureaucratic, and often slow-moving structure, with a preference for standardized approaches to the management of many functions.

CONTROL BASED ON WHOSE EXPERTISE? LIFERS AND ACCIDENTAL TOURISTS

As *Duty with Honour* explains, every profession applies a theory-based body of knowledge to the complex issues it must resolve. Professionals will also frame problems in their own way, apply their own intellectual processes to examine these problems, and draw on collective expertise developed over many years of professional practice to develop solutions.[33] It follows that DND and CAF professionals will interpret defence issues in ways that reflect their different areas of expertise. This fact invites the fourth and final question regarding the meaning of civil control of the armed forces, namely, "Control based on whose expertise?" I will look at this question, first, through "wicked problems" and whether and how the different military and civilian career development models are suited to dealing with them. Second, I look at the clash between the military's preference for a professional ideology and the government's preference for a bureaucratic ideology.

Originally the term "wicked problem" referred exclusively to a social issue that is difficult to comprehend, let alone to define or to solve.[34] "Social messes" like crime, illicit drug use, climate change, poverty, weapons of mass destruction or child soldiers are just some of the many wicked problems that are rarely ever well understood or defined.[35] Indeed, how the problem is framed and understood strongly influences how it is addressed; conversely, how success is defined determines how the problem is understood. Further, solutions to wicked problems are not right or wrong, but better or worse. Nor is there a finite range of alternative solutions: solving one wicked problem may mean creating a new one. And wicked problems tend to evolve over time, making them difficult to solve definitively.

One of the key features of wicked problems is that the scientific approach to them – i.e., using sequential steps, assumed objectivity and logic to define, analyze and solve the problem – does not work. Wicked problems require more than a resource management strategy that harnesses multiple agencies and groups. Such problems must be understood as an intellectual endeavour involving the four C's: complexity, chaos, contradictions and counter-intuitive solution sets. Needless to say, the complexity of Canada's defence establishment means that many of the problems the Defence Team faces will be wicked ones. Confusion can therefore arise when either or both CAF and DND professionals apply the wrong approach to understanding and addressing the wicked problems they face.

Unfortunately, the dominant intellectual approaches of both public administration professionals in DND and military operational planning professionals in the CAF are based on the scientific management model, which is unsuited to dealing with issues involving the four C's.[36] The weaknesses of the CAF's professional development system in generating effective institutional leaders were clearly identified in a comprehensive study conducted by retired Lieutenant-General Mike Jeffery.[37] Jeffery states that "there is an unstated but implicit belief within the CF that any good officer, with suitable operational and command experience can, with time, be a good strategic leader."[38] In the following excerpt from his report, Jeffery summarizes how and why this is a false assumption:

> Over a career this operational culture reinforces the perspective of the military way of thinking and acting. Exposure to other points of view or other cultures is for the most part limited and too often insufficient to have a lasting impact….The result is a strategic leader operating completely outside their frame of experience, performing at best in a suboptimal manner and reducing the effectiveness of the organization….For some the shock is too great and they never truly adapt.[39]

The two main conclusions from Jeffery's study are that senior military officers need additional exposure to alternate points of view and increased experience working in the "secondary" areas, which he identifies as defence policy, personnel, resource management and force development. As I pointed out in the last section, policy, personnel and resource management are key areas in which CAF leaders must collaborate with senior members of DND; hence, the weaknesses in military professional expertise that Jeffery identifies are in precisely those areas that military-civilian partnership is most critical. To state the problem another way, the weakness of the CAF's professional development system is that it can create "accidental tourists" who attempt to address complex portfolios – like defence policy, personnel, and resource management – with limited preparation.

There is no comparable study of civilians working at the senior levels in DND. Yet the amendments to the career systems in the Public Service and the philosophy adopted in the 1990s suggest that there are likely to be similar problems – although with different causal factors. Between 1994 and 1997, the federal government conducted a program review in an effort to significantly reduce spending and, in particular, to reduce the cost of running government.

Key in this initiative were the use of the "partnership test" and the "efficiency test," which were used to determine whether a particular function should remain in government or be shifted elsewhere, and to determine whether there was a more cost-effective way to deliver what remained in government.[40] As reported by Jocelyne Bourgon, then Clerk of the Privy Council, a consequence was that the government "shifted its role from ownership and operations to core policy development and regulatory responsibilities."[41] The functions that remained within government departments (as opposed to those that were shifted to agencies, crown corporations, or private partnership) tended to be generic corporate activities related to broad pan-government policy, governance systems, regulatory duties and shared support functions, such as finance, human resources and information technology.

Since the functions of mid- and senior-level Public Service members had become generalized across departments, it was expected that management-level personnel could and should move across departments as a prerequisite to assuming the highest responsibilities, as ADMs and DMs. To support this new philosophy, three of the main Public Service-wide changes initiated during this period were increased mobility, the adoption of competency-based human resource practices and a shift from job security to employability strategies.[42] These initiatives (along with the unsuccessful Universal Classification System initiative) were designed to open the government's internal labour market by making it easier for members of the Public Service to move from one functional area or department to another.

The new focus on lateral transfers based on broad, generalized competencies enabled individuals to hopscotch across government. But they did so at the expense of developing the depth of expertise that their predecessors had acquired by working in the same department or functional area. Although some "lifers" remained in DND – particularly in areas like the Materiel Group and Defence Research and Development Canada – a significant number of those assuming director or director general responsibilities in DND have come through the revolving door of interdepartmental moves. No doubt, those who parachute into departments or organizations under the new system bring valuable knowledge about the broad government agenda, about how to interpret the directions of the central agencies and how to develop integrated solutions to cross-cutting problems. But applying this expertise in a military context can present real challenges. The complexities of DND and their CAF counterpart's very different focus, assumptions and methods of framing complex problems can easily lead to a variation of the accidental tourist's culture shock that Lieutenant-General Jeffery described in CAF leaders.

The second question regarding whose expertise should count in key decisions pertains to the underlying philosophy of how business is conducted, which I examine through E. Friedson's comparison of professional and bureaucratic ideologies.[43] The professional ideology is focused on socially institutionalized outcomes, is ruled by values determined by expert association and draws on a shared vocational ethic to ensure that the desired social good is achieved in a manner consistent with professional norms. The bureaucratic ideology is focused on control, is ruled by management and draws on regulatory systems to ensure that work is conducted according to set rules. As practised by government, the bureaucratic approach strongly emphasizes hierarchical control mechanisms, including detailed regulations, formal levels of approvals, and coordinating governance structures, which are all designed to ensure that appropriate steps have been taken to verify that funds are expended and results are obtained in a manner consistent with the principles of effective management. These requirements result in a highly formalized and often time-consuming approach. (It was the bureaucratic ideology that retired General Hillier criticized in his comments about the civil service mentality referred to earlier.)

Among the many differences between the bureaucratic and professional approaches, two help explain some of the tensions or misunderstandings that can arise between the different ideologies at work in the CAF and DND. The first is the difference between rule-based and principle-based decision making. A key facet of professions is that the professional will engage in independent reasoning based on a set of internalized principles and values, with an emphasis on creativity, flexibility, and the initiative to determine the right thing to do in the circumstances. This stands in stark contrast with formal rule-based processes, which are dictated by others, and where the emphasis is on consistency, standardization and conformity in all circumstances.

The second difference between the bureaucratic and professional models is the relative importance accorded *position* and *expertise* in the two ideologies.

In hierarchical organizations power is vested in specific positions: those who occupy such positions are automatically given the authority to make decisions. Conversely, members of professions defer to those with the requisite expertise: specific office holders are not assumed to possess all the knowledge needed to reach the best decision. The emphasis on rule-based decision making by the incumbent of a position over principle-based decision making by the individual with the greatest expertise can lead to significant conflicts when these two ideologies are being applied by different members of the Defence Team.

CONCLUSION

The business of defence is conducted jointly by military members of the CAF and civilian members of DND working in partnership to achieve what the government of the day has directed, within the resources allocated, and in a manner that reflects Canadian values and earns the confidence and support of the citizenry. Nonetheless, differences of opinion and tensions can arise for a number of reasons. This chapter examined the corporate- and strategic-level reasons for tensions between the two sides of the Defence Team through four key themes borrowed from the CMR framework: Control by whom? Control over what? Control based on whose priorities? and Control based on whose expertise?

According to the CMR literature, the answer to the first question – Control by whom? – is political control by the elected government. As I argued, however, the DM-CDS diarchy inside national defence blurs the line between political control and civilian bureaucratic control. The locus of the tension is the DM's role as accounting officer to Parliament, which gives the DM and his civilian DND staff control over all defence decisions that involve "funds, property or other resources." As a result, civilian members of the Public Service in DND can and do control activities and decisions that the CAF views as solely its prerogative.

The second question is the practical one faced by all modern democratic governments: Over which decisions should the military have control? The military view – helped along by the influence of the Powell Doctrine – is that the government should set overall objectives, but that the military should decide on the means for achieving them. In contrast, governments are inclined to see the need for political direction all the way down to the tactical level. With respect to the everyday workings of the Defence Team, tension is most likely to arise around the CAF's desire for professional autonomy. The military profession will always seek to exercise a higher level of control over its members, its functions, and its equipment than will other Public Service professions. Hence, the CAF side of the Defence Team will always perceive its control over a broader scope of areas as critical to operational effectiveness and to mission success.

The third issue surrounded the different priorities of the CAF as a professional military, focused on the long-term defence of the nation and the priorities of DND as the accountant for the central agencies and the flag-bearer for the government of the day's agenda. Nowhere is the clash of priorities more evident than in decisions over resource allocation. First, the Defence Team must decide how to balance military effectiveness with political benefits when making major decisions involving equipment, base locations, infrastructure and even the local purchasing of goods and services. Second, allocating time, effort and money to conduct the missions of today must be balanced against building capacities for the missions of tomorrow. Balancing these multiple and often conflicting priorities can easily lead to sharp differences of opinion between the CAF and DND. Over time, I suggest, this problem of balancing priorities in major decisions has led to a strongly centralized, bureaucratic and often slow-moving structure, with a preference for standardized approaches to the management of many functions.

The fourth theme in the CMR framework explored here was the question of whose expertise is brought to bear in defence decisions. I suggested that this question is harder to answer in the Defence Team context than it appears. Given the complexity of Canada's defence establishment – the CDS-DM diarchy, the competing priorities at play, the military-civilian composition of the Defence Team, and the different professional ideologies at work – defence decisions are often wicked problems. Yet the career development models used by the Public Service and the CAF are not tailored to produce DND managers and CAF leaders capable of dealing with the complexity, chaos, contradictions, and counter-intuitive solution sets that are characteristic of the wicked problems the Defence Team faces.

Whether these four problems result in healthy tensions – with open, vigorous debate on complex issues – or in divisive conflicts and simmering feuds depends on the quality of leadership exercised and the personalities of the individuals involved. The effectiveness of the military-civilian partnership can also be influenced by each party's understanding of the other, including their understanding of each other's relative priorities, key objectives, and unique professional perspectives and worldviews. While it is possible to suggest a number of options to address the tensions that may arise, I will conclude with one recommendation. The most important skill for those who work in contexts where strong differences exist is to develop the ability to understand the other's point of view without necessarily adopting it. When the conditions are created where valid differences in views, understandings, expertise, priorities and principles can all be presented, considered and integrated, the net result will be more informed decision making and a respectful, professional climate. This, in turn, will ensure that the members of the Defence Team can continue to serve the nation in an effective manner.

ENDNOTES

1   See Gosselin, Chapter 1 of this volume.

2   For background information and research results on the D2000 initiative, see V. M. Catano, A. Day, and J. E. Adams-Roy, *Change and Renewal in DND: Results of the 1999 D2000 Survey*, Sponsor Research Report 99-16 (Ottawa, ON: Canadian Forces Directorate of Human Resources Research and Evaluation, 1999).

3   As reflected in the title, the clearest criticisms are contained in R. Hillier, *A Soldier First: Bullets, Bureaucrats and the Politics of War* (Toronto: Harper Collins, 2009); however, his views were also evident in media interviews and other public commentary. For additional analyses of General Hillier's public messaging, see A. Mowatt, *Rick Hillier: A Not So Silent Soldier* (paper produced in fulfillment of the National Security Programme, Canadian Forces College, 2009), retrieved from http://www.cfc.forces.gc.ca/259/282/283/mowatt.

4   Examples of "all one team" efforts in the recent past include civilian and military personnel at CFB Petawawa pitching in for the response to the 1998 ice storm, at the Naval Fleet Maintenance Groups preparing ships for short notice deployments to Haiti, and counter-piracy missions and Air Force technicians going the extra mile to support search and rescue missions and urgent air operations. For a specific illustration, see

J. Morin and R. Gimblett, *Operation Friction: Canadian Forces in the Persian Gulf* (Toronto: Dundurn, 1997).

5   Among other fora, the different perspectives are consistently evident in the National Security Programme leadership course seminar on the Defence Team. Participants represent four groups: two military (Canadian and international) and two Public Service groups (DND and other government departments; OGD). On some topics the sharp differences are evident between the defence military and civilians; for others, these emerge between the DND and OGD members of the Public Service; and, for others, these are all civilian versus all military. Aspects of these discussions inform this chapter.

6   It should also be recalled that, in addition to members of the Public Service, the civilian workforce extends to include non-public funds employees and may be considered to encompass contractors, particularly in cases where the contractors are embedded in defence organizations. A prime example of contractors who are integral to the business of defence are the two RCAF Flying Training Schools, 2 CFFTS and 3 CFFTS. For additional consideration of the larger issues related to the privatization of security, see C. Spearin, "The Changing Forms and Utility of Force: The Impact of International Security Privatization on Canada," *International Journal* 64, no. 2 (Spring 2009): 481–500.

7   The foundational works in this domain are S. Huntington, *The Soldier and the State* (Cambridge, MA: Harvard U. P., 1957) and M. Janowitz, *The Professional Soldier: A Social and Political Portrait* (New York: Free Press, 1961). For more recent extensions and reviews, see D. L. Bland, "A Unified Theory of Civil-Military Relations," *Armed Forces and Society* 26, no. 1 (Fall 1999): 7–26; A. Cottey, T. Edmunds, and A. Forster, "The Second Generation Problematic: Rethinking Democracy and Civil–Military Relations," *Armed Forces and Society* 29, no. 1 (Fall 2002): 31-56; J. Burk, "Theories of Democratic Civil-Military Relations," *Armed Forces and Society* 29, no. 1 (Fall 2002): 7-29 and P. D. Feaver, *Armed Servants: Agency, Oversight and Civil-Military Relations* (Cambridge, MA: Harvard U. P., 2005).

8   See F. C. Pinch, L. W. Bentley, and P. P. Browne, *Research Program on the Military Profession: Background Considerations* (Kingston, ON: Canadian Forces Leadership Institute, 2003) for additional discussion of the nature of civil-military relations in Canada and consideration of the implications for the profession of arms.

9   See again Bland, "A Unified Theory of Civil-Military Relations," 7-26 and Bland, "Patterns in Liberal Democratic Civil-Military Relations," *Armed Forces and Society* 27, no. 4 (Summer 2001): 525-40. For the CAF's perspective on the nature of interactions, see *Duty with Honour: The Profession of Arms in Canada* (Ottawa, ON: Canadian Defence Academy – Canadian Forces Leadership Institute, 2003), Chapter 3 and, in particular, Figure 3.1.

10   See D. L. Bland, "Who Decides What? Civil-Military Relations in Canada and the United States," *Canadian-American Public Policy* 41 (2000): 1-2.

11   As listed under the DND organization chart at http://www.forces.gc.ca/site/about-notresujet/org-eng.asp (accessed December 10, 2012) a total of six level ones report to both the CDS and the DM, including the second most senior CAF officer, the Vice Chief of the Defence Staff.

12   See A. Smith, *The Accountability of Accounting Officers Before Parliamentary Committees*, PRB 2008-18-E (Ottawa, ON: Library of Parliament, 2008) for a summary of the changes resulting from the 2006 *Federal Accountability Act*, and D. Savoie, *Court Government and the Collapse of Accountability in Canada and the United Kingdom* (Toronto: University of Toronto P., 2008) for an academic critique of the Act and general changes in parliamentary accountability in Canada and the U.K.

13   Contributing to the confusion, the formal departmental guidance, "Organization and Accountability," has not been updated to reflect the changes arising from the *Federal Accountability Act*, nor for significant re-organizations, such as reflected in the DND organization chart referenced earlier. The "Organization and Accountability Guidance" can found be at http://www.forces.gc.ca/admpol/Organization-e.html.

14   At http://www.forces.gc.ca/admpol/Organization-e.html (as of December 10, 2012).

15   As stated at http://www.forces.gc.ca/site/ocds-bcemd/afc-cfa/index-eng.asp (as of December 14, 2012).

16   Again, any decision that involves funds, property or other resources must be approved by the DM.

17   See D. L. Bland, *Chiefs of Defence: Government and the Unified Command of the Canadian Armed Forces* (Toronto: General Publishing, 1995) and S. Taylor and B. Nolan, *Tarnished Brass: Crime and Corruption in the Canadian Military* (Toronto: Lester Publishing, 1996) for comments on the personality clashes and dynamics between various DMs and CDSs in the 1980s and 1990s.

18   Two international illustrations of politicians overruling military commanders are found in the massacres in Rwanda and Srebrenica; see R. Dallaire, *Shake Hands with the Devil: The Failure of Humanity in Rwanda* (Toronto: Random House, 2003) for the first, and D. Rohde, *Endgame: The Betrayal and Fall of Srebrenica, Europe's Worst Massacre Since World War II* (Boulder, CO: Westview Press, 1997) for the second. A broader historical analysis is presented in E. A. Cohen, *Supreme Command: Soldiers, Statesmen, and Leadership in Wartime* (New York: Simon and Schuster, 2002).

19   See C. D. O'Sullivan, *Colin Powell: American Power and Intervention from Vietnam to Iraq* (New York: Rowman and Littlefield, 2009).

20   See P. D. Feaver and R. H. Kohn, *Soldiers and Civilians: The Civil-Military Gap and American National Security* (Cambridge: MIT Press, 2001).

21   A. C. Okros, S. Hill, and F. Pinch, *Between 9/11 and Kandahar: Attitudes of Canadian Forces Officers in Transition*, Claxton Paper no. 8 (Kingston, ON: McGill-Queen's Press, 2008), 31.

22   Among many illustrations and reports, the best illustration of this philosophy across a wide range of social policy issues was contained in the comprehensive review of CAF policies after the equality provisions (Section 15 of the *Charter of Rights and Freedoms*) came into effect. See Department of National Defence, *Charter Task Force: Final Report* (Ottawa, ON: Queen's Printers, 1986).

23   See A. C. Okros, "Rethinking Diversity and Security," in *Defending Democracy and Securing Diversity*, ed. Christian Leuprecht (London: Routledge, 2010) and also L. W. Bentley, *Professional Ideology and the Profession of Arms in Canada* (Toronto: The Canadian Institute of Strategic Studies, 2005).

24   While individuals in certain scientific and legal classifications and their respective unions commonly turn to external professional associations for guidance on professional practices, the Public Service per se does not present the characteristics of a shared and unique identity, a theory-based body of knowledge, or a coherent system to update professional norms, conduct and regulation. As an example, a recent broad guidance publication by the Clerk of the Privy Council contained only one brief declarative statement, "we are professional and nonpartisan," with no discussion of what this means or how it is achieved—see W. G. Wouters, *Blueprint 2020 – Getting Started – Getting Your Views* (Ottawa, ON: Clerk of the Privy Council, 2013). For a broad overview of issues, see D. Zussman and J. Jabe, *The Vertical Solitude: Managing in the Public Sector* (Ottawa, ON: Institute for Research on Public Policy, 1989). For a more recent discussion related to defence, see A. C. Okros, "Becoming an Employer of Choice: Human Resource Challenges within DND and the CF," in *The Public Management of Defence in Canada*, ed. Craig Stone (Toronto: Breakout Educational Network, 2009).

25   See Gosselin, Chapter 1 of this volume.

26   See P. Feaver, "The Civil-Military Problematique: Huntington, Janowitz, and the Question of Civilian Control," *Armed Forces and Society* 23, no. 2 (Winter 1996): 149–78 for a discussion of the political view of defence spending and tensions between politicians and military leaders.

27   See the Okros, Hill, and Pinch, *Between 9/11 and Kandahar* for additional discussion.

28   For a full presentation of the approach articulated by the Treasury Board Secretariat, see the Policy Framework at http://www.tbs-sct.gc.ca/pol/doc-eng.aspx?id=18790&section=text (accessed December 10, 2012).

29   Federal legislation may be broadly grouped into three domains: those laws that apply to all Canadians (*The Charter of Rights and Freedoms, Criminal Code, Canadian Human Rights Act*), the four presented here that apply to all components of the federal government, and those that contain specific provisions for the Canadian Armed Forces (i.e., the *National Defence Act*).

30   See, again, Okros, "Becoming an Employer of Choice" for additional discussion of these issues.

31   A. Smith, *The Roles and Responsibilities of Central Agencies*, PRB 09-01E (Ottawa, ON: Library of Parliament, 2009), 1.

32   Department of National Defence, *Report on Transformation 2011* (Ottawa: Department of National Defence, 2011), 16. The date is from 2010.

33   See A. C. Okros, J. Verdon, and P. Chouinard, *The Meta-Organization: A Research and Conceptual Landscape*, Defence Research and Development Canada – Centre for Security

Science Technical Report 2011-13 (Ottawa, ON: Defence Research and Development Canada, 2011) for additional discussion, and with reference to the academic links across ontology, epistemology and methods, or the original philosophical understanding of *episteme*, *techne* and *phronesis*. Each approach illustrates the unique ways in which knowledge is created, organized and applied.

34   The foundational work is H. W. J. Rittel and M. M. Webber, "Dilemmas in a General Theory of Planning," *Policy Sciences* 4 (1973): 155–69.

35   Characterizing wicked problems as "social messes" is intentional, of course, because such issues can have a widespread impact on societies, which is what makes them the responsibility of governments to address in the first place. In fact, one of the key drivers behind many governments' increased emphasis on "cross-cutting issues" or "whole of government solutions" is that many of their problems are wicked social messes. For a specific discussion of the implications of wicked problems for government, see Australian Public Service Commission, *Tackling Wicked Problems: A Public Policy Perspective* (Canberra, Commonwealth of Australia, 2007) and for a more general presentation of the emergence of new models of government to address issues such as these, see J. Bourgon and P. Milley, *The New Frontiers of Public Administration: The New Synthesis Project* (Waterloo, ON: Public Governance International, 2010).

36   As indicated in the title, Charles Lindblom described public administration as the science of muddling through in "The Science of 'Muddling Through'," *Public Administration Review* 19, no. 2 (1959): 79–88. For additional discussion of the conflicts between wicked problems and the scientific management model, see Okros, Verdon and Chouinard, *Meta-Organization*.

37   M. K. Jeffery, *The CF Executive Development Programme: A Concept for Developmental Period 5 of the CF Officer Professional Development System* (report submitted to the Commandant, Canadian Forces College, July 15, 2008).

38   Ibid., 16.

39   bid., 15–6; note, the author has taken the liberty of condensing over a page of text into a shortened presentation of the main narrative.

40   J. Bourgon, *Program Review: The Government of Canada's Experience Eliminating the Deficit, 1994-1999 – A Canadian Case Study* (Waterloo, ON: The Centre for International Governance Innovation, 2009), 15.

41   Ibid., 22.

42   Among others on the initiatives undertaken, see J. Stilborn, *Federal Public Service Renewal – The La Relève Initiative*, PRB 97-7E (Ottawa, ON: Library of Parliament, 1998).

43   Freidson also includes market ideology in his schema, which is not relevant in this case; E. Freidson, *Professionalism, The Third Logic: On the Practice of Knowledge* (Chicago: University of Chicago P., 2001).

CHAPTER 3

THE COMPOSITION OF THE DEFENCE TEAM

Lise Arseneau and Amy Cameron

The Defence Team is composed of military personnel in the Canadian Armed Forces and civilian personnel in the Department of National Defence, who work together to carry out the defence mandate.[1] This chapter presents a portrait of the current military and civilian workforces in DND and the CAF to provide context for the historical, conceptual and empirical discussions in the other chapters in this volume. The first part compares the demographic characteristics of the military and civilian workforces, based on data from the fiscal years 2003-04 through 2012-13[2] and explains how these demographic characteristics have changed during this ten-year period.[3] Given the importance of ensuring the best possible distribution of military and civilian roles and expertise across DND and the CAF, the second part of this chapter outlines a practical approach for determining the optimal composition of the Defence Team, along with the limitations of this approach.

OVERALL POPULATION OF THE DEFENCE WORKFORCE

Almost 125,000 military and civilian employees worked in DND and the CAF in fiscal year 2012-13. As shown in Table 3.1, the military component (comprising the Regular and Reserve Forces[4]) accounted for 78% of the total Defence Team workforce, while civilian personnel accounted for 22%. In the same year, the military workforce consisted of 69% Regular Force and 31% Reserve Force personnel, while the civilian workforce consisted of 92% indeterminate employees,[5] 3% term employees, 4% casual employees, and 1% student employees.

EMPLOYEE GROUP	POPULATION	PROPORTION
Regular Force	67,688	54%
Reserve Force (Primary Reserve)	29,973	24%
Civilians	26,844	22%
TOTAL	124,505	100%

TABLE 3.1: Military and Civilian Personnel Population, Fiscal Year 2012-13

In the last ten years, the Regular Force population has grown by more than 6,000 personnel, and the DND civilian population has grown by more than 4,500 personnel (Figure 3.1), yielding an overall relative growth of 10% in the Regular Force and 21% in the civilian workforce.[6] Both workforces increased each fiscal year between 2003-04 and 2010-11 and remained stable in 2011-12. The decline in the workforces in 2012-13 is a result of the federal government's Work Force Adjustment (WFA) directive, which applied to personnel across all governmental departments.[7] In order to provide more detail on the effects of these historical trends on the Defence Team, the civilian and military workforce demographics will include an examination of how they have changed between the fiscal years 2003-04 and 2012-13.

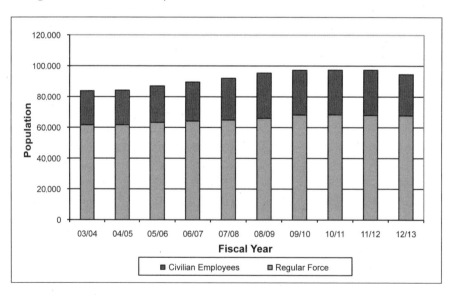

FIGURE 3.1: Military and Civilian Personnel Totals by Fiscal Year

CIVILIAN PERSONNEL IN THE DEPARTMENT OF NATIONAL DEFENCE

The civilian workforce in DND is unique in that about 60% work within a military structure[8] and 40% are directly supervised by a military manager.[9] The civilian workforce grew by 33% between fiscal years 2003-04 and 2011-12 as a result of several factors: force expansion, increased operational demands created by the Afghanistan missions and organizational changes resulting from the CF Transformation.[10] Nonetheless, the civilian workforce was downsized in the spring of 2012, resulting in a 9% decrease in the fiscal year 2012-13. The challenge will be to ensure that, despite the decrease, a high-performing civilian workforce is in place to deliver defence capability, now and into the future. In this section, the composition of the DND civilian workforce will be presented by employment tenure, employment classification, capability component and by gender, age and years of pensionable service.

Employment Tenure

The DND civilian population includes indeterminate, term, casual and student employees. The indeterminate tenure population accounted for 92% of the DND civilian workforce in fiscal year 2012-13 (Table 3.2).

EMPLOYMENT TENURE	POPULATION	PROPORTION
Indeterminate	24,742	92%
Term	833	3%
Casual	1,100	4%
Student	169	1%
TOTAL	26,844	100%

TABLE 3.2: DND Civilian Population by Tenure, Fiscal Year 2012-13

Figure 3.2 shows how the growth in the DND civilian population from 22,195 in 2004-05 to 29,111 in 2010-11 has been driven by the indeterminate tenure population, which increased by 46% (8,361 employees) during this time period. Meanwhile, the growth from 29,111 in fiscal year 2010-11 to 29,430 in fiscal year 2011-12 was driven by casual and student employees, whose numbers increased by 32% (392 employees). From fiscal year 2011-12 to fiscal year

2012-13, all tenures decreased. The indeterminate population decreased by 8% (1,904 employees) to 26,844, the term population decreased by 29% (346 employees) to 833, and the number of casual and student employees decreased by 21% (336 employees) to 1,269. Although the number of term employees decreased by 64% in the last ten years, they are a small group relative to indeterminate employees. The number of casual and student employees has fluctuated between the fiscal years 2003-04 and 2012-13, but their overall populations have remained roughly the same.

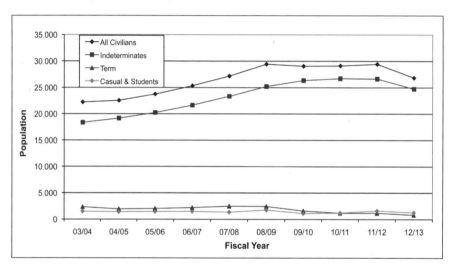

FIGURE 3.2: DND Civilian Population by Tenure and Fiscal Year

Employment Category

The civilian population in DND can be categorized by employment type: Administrative and Foreign Service, Administrative Support, Management, Operational, Scientific and Professional, Technical, and Other. The "Other" category consists of individuals in the Leadership Programs occupation group. Table 3.3 shows the population and proportion of the DND civilian workforce for the fiscal year 2012-13 categorized by employment category. The highest proportion of civilians belong to the Operational category (31%), followed closely by the Administrative and Foreign Service category (29%).

EMPLOYMENT CATEGORY	POPULATION	PROPORTION
Operational	8,369	31%
Administrative & Foreign Service	7,778	29%
Administrative Support	4,214	16%
Scientific & Professional	3,316	12%
Technical	2,977	11%
Management	149	1%
Others (i.e. Leadership Programs)	28	0.1%
TOTAL	26,831	100%

TABLE 3.3: DND Civilian Population by Employment Category, Fiscal Year 2012-13

In the last ten years, the Administrative and Foreign Service category has contributed the most to the growth of the civilian workforce (58%), with an increase of approximately 2,700 employees (Figure 3.3). Also in the last ten years, the Scientific and Professional category has grown by two thirds (adding 28% to the civilian population), while the Technical category has grown by one third (adding 16% to the civilian population). Still, the number of employees for all employment categories remained relatively stable in the fiscal years 2010-11 and 2011-12, and then decreased in 2012-13.

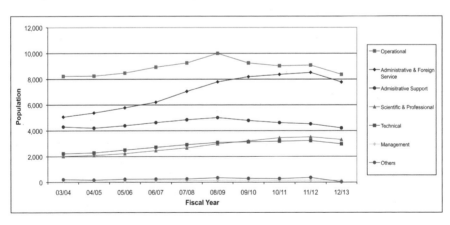

FIGURE 3.3: DND Civilian Population by Employment Category and Fiscal Year

Capability Component

The Defence Team workforce can be categorized by capability component, which is the main activity to which their work belongs.[11] There are 30 capability components in DND and the CAF.[12]

Table 3.4 shows the population and proportion of the 2012-13 DND civilian workforce by capability component with the highest number of employees. The "Other" category includes the remaining capability components: Joint Operations, Infrastructure and Environmental Functions and Department/Forces Executive. The majority of the civilian workforce works within the Naval Force, Army Force and Personnel Services capabilities (with about 60% of the civilian population divided equally across these capabilities), followed by 11% in Materiel Services and 8% in the Air Force.

CAPABILITY COMPONENT	POPULATION	PROPORTION
Naval Force	5,514	21%
Personnel Services	5,472	20%
Army Force	4,962	18%
Materiel Services	2,950	11%
Air Force	2,191	8%
Science & Technology	1,539	6%
Information Services	1,496	6%
Other	2,720	10%
TOTAL	26,844	100%

TABLE 3.4: DND Civilian Population by Capability Component, Fiscal Year 2012-13

Figure 3.4 shows the DND civilian population categorized by capability component from fiscal year 2003-04 to fiscal year 2012-13. During this period, the Personnel Services capability contributed the most to the growth of the civilian workforce (30%), with an increase of almost 1,500 employees. The Naval Force capability is second, contributing 29% (an increase of just over 1,400 employees) to the overall growth of the DND civilian population.

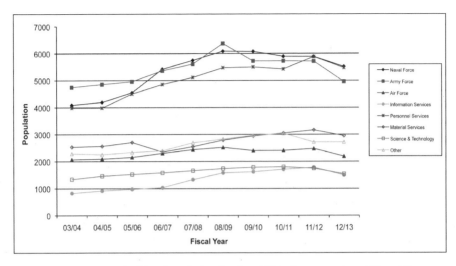

FIGURE 3.4: DND Civilian Population by Capability Component and Fiscal Year

Gender

In fiscal 2012-13, the male population was 15,765 (59%) and the female population was 11,073 (41%), proportions that have remained unchanged between the fiscal years 2006-07 and 2013-14. Since the 2003-2004 baseline year, female representation in the DND civilian population has increased slightly from 39%, and male representation has decreased slightly from 61%.

Age

Figure 3.5 shows the age profile[13] for the DND civilian population in fiscal year 2012-13. The average age is 46.9 years, which has increased slightly over the last ten years from 45.3 in 2003-04.

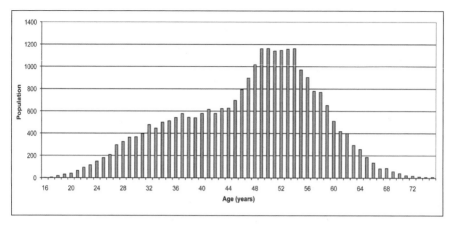

FIGURE 3.5: Age Profile of the Fiscal Year 2012-13 DND Civilian Population

Figure 3.6 shows the age structure of the DND civilian workforce in the fiscal years 2003-04 and 2012-13. In the last ten years, the number of civilian employees who are 55 years or older has increased from 17% (3,774 individuals) of the workforce in 2003-04 to 25% (6,614 individuals) of the workforce in 2012-13. Many of the individuals in this age group may be eligible to retire with immediate annuity.[14] However, the proportion of DND civilians between the ages of 35 and 49 years has dropped from 49% of the workforce in 2003-04 (10,843 individuals) to 39% of the workforce in 2012-13 (10,312 individuals).

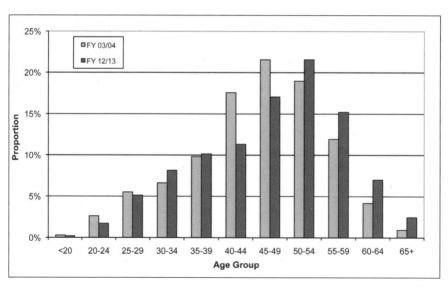

FIGURE 3.6: DND Civilian Population by Age Group in Fiscal Years 2003-04 and 2012-13

The change in age structure of the DND civilian population between the fiscal years 2003-04 and 2012-13 is partly due to the effect of the program review announced in the 1995 federal budget, which reduced the Public Service by approximately 45,000 positions. This led to the departure of many younger employees, along with many older and more experienced employees who accepted early retirement or early departure incentives. The result was a higher proportion of middle-aged employees who are now approaching retirement.[15] Further, the reduction created an age gap between experienced and new employees. Recruitment efforts beginning in 2007-08 have led to a slight increase in the proportion of employees aged 25 to 34 years, from 12% of the workforce in 2003-04 (2,694 individuals) to 13% of the workforce in 2012-13 (3,555 individuals).

Years of Pensionable Service

Figure 3.7 shows the profile by years of pensionable service[16] for the DND civilian population for the fiscal year 2012-13. The average number of pensionable years of service was 14.6 in 2012-13, which has remained almost the same as the average in 2003-04 of 14.2 years. Not many individuals have 14 to 19 years of pensionable service because of the Public Service reductions implemented since the 1995 federal budget.

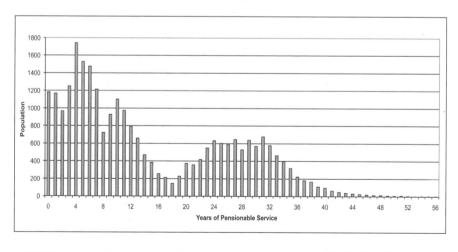

FIGURE 3.7: Profile by Years of Pensionable Service of the DND Civilian Population in Fiscal Year 2012-13

Retirements

The DND civilian workforce is aging, which means that a greater number of employees will be eligible to retire in the near future. In order to be eligible to receive an immediate annuity, an employee must be between 55 and 60 years of age with at least 30 years of pensionable service (55/30 rule), or 60 years of age or older with at least two years of pensionable service (60/2 rule).[17] In fiscal year 2012-13, 14% (3,777 individuals) were eligible to retire without penalty, including 9% (2,397 individuals) under the 55/30 rule and 5% (1,380 individuals) under the 60/2 rule. Although retirement can be used to reduce the overall size of the civilian population, corporate knowledge and experience can be lost in the process, which can in turn impact defence capability.

Attrition

The attrition rates[18] for the total DND civilian workforce and the indeterminate tenure population by fiscal year are shown in Figure 3.8. The attrition rate for the total civilian population is higher than that of indeterminate civilian employees because the total population includes term, casual and student employees whose positions are temporary and part-time (and, thus, this population includes more losses from the workforce). Generally, the attrition rate for the overall civilian workforce has been between 8% and 9%, except for fiscal 2009-10 when it reached a high of 11%. This was due to a significant loss in the number of term and casual employees that fiscal year. For the portion of the civilian workforce that has indeterminate tenure, the attrition rate has been approximately 6% since 2007-08. The high attrition rate in 2012-13 for the civilian workforce as a whole and for indeterminate civilian employees alone (8%) was caused by the implementation of Work Force Adjustment directives.

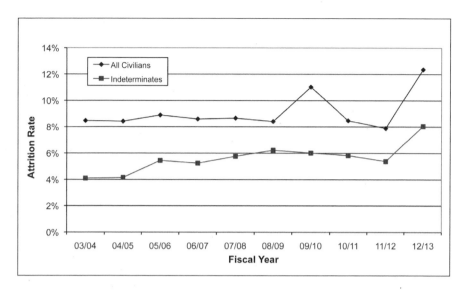

FIGURE 3.8: Attrition Rates for DND Civilian Population by Fiscal Year

MILITARY PERSONNEL IN THE CANADIAN ARMED FORCES

The focus of this section is the CAF's Regular Force population, which is the largest component of the CAF, and its personnel are enrolled for continuing full-time military service. In contrast, the Reserve Force includes personnel who serve on a temporary or part-time basis and may be activated when the military needs additional personnel.

The CAF is a single institution comprising the Royal Canadian Navy (RCN), the Canadian Army (CA) and the Royal Canadian Air Force (RCAF). The rank structure of the CAF has not changed over the last 20 years, with personnel divided into a hierarchy of numerous ranks of officers and non-commissioned members (NCM). There are demographic differences between officers and NCMs. Since 1997, for example, a university degree is required to be commissioned as an officer, resulting in officers generally being older than NCMs when they are hired. To understand the force structure of the CAF, then, we next examine some key demographic factors for officer, NCM and overall Regular Force populations.

Overall Population

Table 3.5 shows the composition of officers and NCMs in the Regular Force for fiscal year 2012-13. Officers account for 24% of the Regular Force population and NCMs for 76%.

REGULAR FORCE	POPULATION	PROPORTION
Officers	16,357	24%
NCMs	51,331	76%
TOTAL	67,688	100%

TABLE 3.5: Regular Force Population, Fiscal Year 2012-13

As Figure 3.9 shows, the overall population of the Regular Force has grown from 61,573 in fiscal year 2003-04 to 67,688 in fiscal year 2012-13. This increase was due to a commitment by the federal government in 2005-06 to support the growth of the Regular Force to 68,000 personnel by fiscal year 2011-12.[19] As the DND/CAF transitioned to a slower operational pace following the end of combat operations in Afghanistan, the federal government announced in the 2011-12 federal budget that the Regular Force strength will be maintained at its current strength of 68,000.[20]

During the last ten years, the officer population has grown by more than 2,200 personnel and the NCM population by more than 3,800 personnel. This corresponds to a relative growth of 16% for officers and 8% for NCMs.

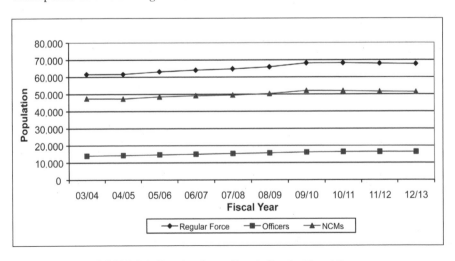

FIGURE 3.9: Regular Force Population by Fiscal Year

Career Fields

In fiscal year 2012-13, the Military Occupation Structure of the Regular Force population consisted of 37 officer and 64 NCM occupations. The CAF conducts the Annual Military Occupational Review to assess the overall health of each occupation and the courses of action necessary to maintain or improve the personnel state of each occupation.[21] As a result, future recruiting and production targets can be derived and modified on an annual basis. Although each occupation cannot be discussed in detail, the Regular Force occupations can be categorized by the 15 different career fields provided in Table 3.6. This table shows that there have only been slight changes in the proportion by career field between 2003-04 and 2012-13, even though there has been a relative growth of 10% for the Regular Force population during this time period.

CAREER FIELD	FY 2003-04		FY 2012-13	
	Population	Proportion	Population	Proportion
Air Operations	4,470	7%	4,678	7%
Air Operations Technical Support	6,327	10%	6,636	10%
Generals (officers only)	70	<1%	91	<1%
Facility Support (NCMs only)	1,517	2%	1,510	2%
Health Services	2,369	4%	2,737	4%
Human Resources Management	277	<1%	319	<1%
Information Management	5,043	8%	5,599	8%
Intelligence, Surveillance & Reconnaissance	1,808	3%	2,770	4%
Land Operations	13,160	21%	15,217	23%
Land Support	3,836	6%	4,416	7%
Naval Operations	3,445	6%	3,458	5%
Naval Technical Support	5,332	9%	5,364	8%
Operations Support	11,339	18%	11,687	17%
Specialist	2,426	4%	2,808	4%
Training	109	<1%	19	<1%
TOTAL	61,528	100%	67,309	100%

TABLE 3.6: Regular Force Population by Career Field, Fiscal Years 2012-13 and 2003-04 Compared

Capability Component

The Regular Force population can be categorized by the same capability components used to categorize the civilian workforce. Table 3.7 shows the population and proportion of the Regular Force in each capability component for fiscal year 2012-13. The Regular Force consists predominantly of the Army Force (35% of the Regular Force), the Air Force (20% of the Regular Force), and the Naval Force (19% of the Regular Force) capabilities.

CAPABILITY COMPONENT	POPULATION	PROPORTION
Army Force	23,937	35%
Air Force	13,363	20%
Naval Force	12,755	19%
Personnel Services	10,807	16%
Information Services	1,373	2%
Materiel Services	1,514	2%
Science & Technology	44	<1%
Other	3,893	6%
TOTAL	67,686	100%

TABLE 3.7: Regular Force Population by Capability Component, Fiscal Year 2012-13

Figure 3.10 shows the Regular Force population categorized by capability component from fiscal year 2003-04 to fiscal year 2012-13. The growth of the Regular Force population in the last ten years can be attributed to the increase in personnel in the Army Force (more than 2,800 new members) and Naval Force (2,500 new members). The contribution to the overall growth of the Regular Force during this period is 43% for the Army Force and 38% for the Naval Force capability. The Personnel Services capability contributed 24% to the overall growth of the Regular Force during this period, with an increase of more than 1,600 members. The populations for the remaining capability components have only changed slightly between 2003-04 and 2012-13, although there have been year-to-year fluctuations. The slight decreases in the Army, Air and Naval Force capabilities since 2010-11 are due to the federal government's commitment to maintain the Regular Force at 68,000 personnel.

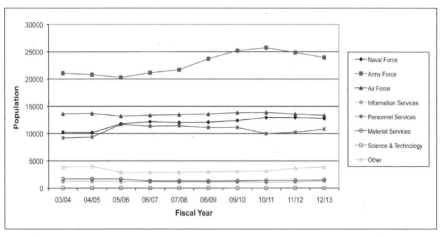

FIGURE 3.10: Regular Force Population by Capability Component and Fiscal Year

Gender

The female population in the Regular Force in fiscal year 2012-13 was 9,511 (14%) and the male population was 58,170 (86%), with female representation in the Regular Force increasing from 12% in 2003-04. For officers, female representation has increased slightly from 14% in 2003-04 to 17% in 2012-13. For NCMs, the proportion of female personnel has remained virtually the same over the last ten years: 12% from 2003-04 to 2005-06 and 13% from 2006-07 to 2012-13.

Age

Figure 3.11 shows the age profile[22] of the Regular Force population in fiscal year 2012-13. The average age is 35.1 years, which is almost identical to the average age of 35.0 years in 2003-04.

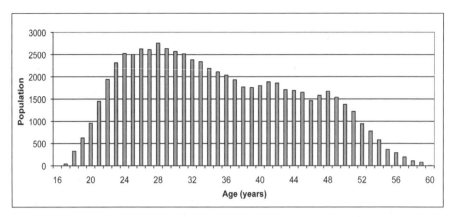

FIGURE 3.11: Age Profile of the Regular Force Population, Fiscal Year 2012-13

Figure 3.12 shows that the age structure of the Regular Force population has changed between fiscal years 2003-04 and 2012-13: the number of military personnel who are 45 years or older has increased from 13% (7,832 individuals) to 20% (13,843 individuals). However, the proportion of Regular Force members between the ages of 30 and 44 years has dropped from 59% (36,164 individuals) in 2003-04 to 45% (30,527 individuals) in 2012-13.

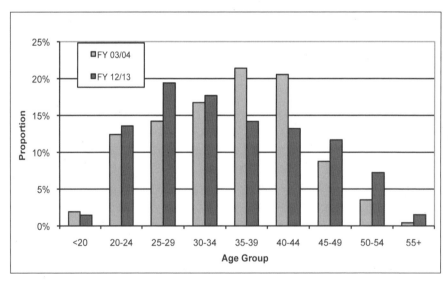

FIGURE 3.12: Regular Force Population by Age Group, Fiscal Years 2003-04 and 2012-13

Like the reductions of the DND civilian workforce that occurred in the mid-1990s, the Force Reduction Program was implemented in fiscal year 1994-95 to reach a Regular Force target strength of 60,000 personnel by 1998-99.[23] About 14,000 military personnel took early release or retirement during this period. This was followed by increased recruitment efforts after fiscal year 2006-07 to reach a Regular Force target strength of 68,000 by 2011-12. Figure 3.12 shows that there has been a moderate increase in the number of younger military personnel who are less than 30 years old from 29% in 2003-04 to 34% in 2012-13. The overall result of these various initiatives is an age gap between older and younger Regular Force members.

Years of Service

The profile by years of service (YOS)[24] for the Regular Force population in fiscal year 2012-13 is shown in Figure 3.13. The average number of years of service in 2012-13 was 10.8, which has decreased from an average of 13.1 in 2003-04. The effects of the Force Reduction Program are still being felt today in the Regular Force, with a lower number of individuals having 17 to 20 years of service. As of 2012-13, the average number of years of service for officers (12.6 years) is higher than for NCMs (10.2 years). But the years of service for both groups have decreased from 2003-04, when the average was 14.4 years for officers and 12.7 years for NCMs.

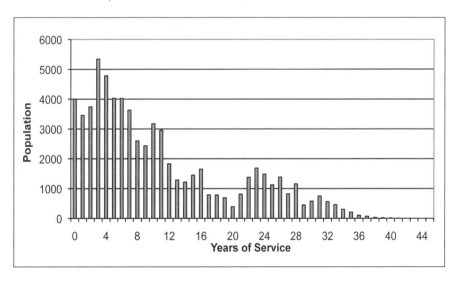

FIGURE 3.13: Profile by Years of Service of the Regular Force Population, Fiscal Year 2012-13

Attrition

Figure 3.14 shows the attrition rates for the Regular Force officer and NCM populations by fiscal year. The attrition rates all rose in fiscal year 2006-07 from the previous fiscal year and continued to increase in 2007-08. In 2008-09, the Regular Force attrition rate mirrored the previous year (at 9.1%), and then fell to 7.6% in 2009-10. The attrition rates have continued to decrease, coming in at 6.0% for the Regular Force in 2011-12, with 5.2% for officers and 6.3% for NCMs. The decline may be attributed to a combination of factors, such as changing Regular Force demographics, the period of economic and labour-market uncertainty since late 2008, and positive measures taken by the CAF to lessen voluntary attrition. In 2012-13, attrition rates for the Regular Force (6.6%) and NCMs (7.0%) rose slightly and remained steady at 5.2% for officers. Most Regular Force personnel who leave the CAF do so either before the end of their first year of service or once they have become eligible for a military pension (normally after 25 years of service).[25]

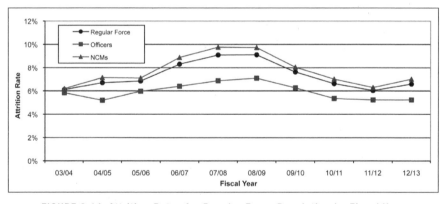

FIGURE 3.14: Attrition Rates for Regular Force Population by Fiscal Year

COMPARISON OF CIVILIAN AND MILITARY PERSONNEL DEMOGRAPHICS

An examination of the composition of the DND civilian and Regular Force workforces shows that these groups have followed similar trends:

- Both populations experienced significant reductions to personnel in the mid-1990s that continue to affect the demographics of the populations today.

- Both populations have grown in the last ten years to meet operational demands.

- The number of individuals eligible to retire from both populations is increasing.

- The Regular Force population's average years of service was 10.8 in fiscal year 2012-13, mirroring the average number of years that civilians had been with DND in the same year (i.e., 10.9 years, with the average being 11.5 years for the indeterminate population).

Despite the similarities that exist between the civilian and military workforces, there are some key differences in the two population's demographics:

- The Regular Force population had a much lower female representation at 14% in fiscal year 2012-13, compared to 41% for the DND civilian population.

- The DND civilian workforce contracted in 2012-13 as a result of deficit reduction efforts. But the Regular Force maintained (and will continue to maintain) its current strength of 68,000 personnel.

- The civilian workforce is older, with an average age of 46.9 years in 2012-13, compared to 35.1 years for the Regular Force population (although both groups have an age gap between younger and older members of their populations).

The civilian and military populations can also be compared by capability component, which provides insight into whether the ratio of DND civilian employees to Regular Force members differs by activity. Following are the four capability components where the proportions in fiscal year 2012-13 differed the most between the civilian and military workforces: Army Force (35% of the Regular Force, 19% of the civilian workforce); Air Force (20% of the Regular Force, 8% of the civilian workforce); Materiel Services (2% of the Regular Force, 11% of the civilian workforce); and Science and Technology (<1% of the Regular Force, 6% of the civilian workforce). By contrast, the proportions of civilian and military personnel were relatively more similar in the Naval Force (19% of the Regular Force, 21% of the civilian workforce) and in Personnel Services (16% of the Regular Force, 20% of the civilian workforce).

The next section of this chapter examines the military-civilian composition of the Defence Team in more detail and describes a methodology that can be used to determine whether the balance of civilian-to-military personnel is optimal for delivering defence capabilities.

FORCE MANAGEMENT: WORKFORCE SIZE AND COMPOSITION

It is important to optimize the composition of the Defence Team's military and civilian workforces for the defence mandate,[26] which is spelled out in the *Canada First Defence Strategy*: defend Canada, defend North America, and contribute to international peace and security.[27] National Defence is currently undertaking several workforce planning activities to bring the CAF and DND in line with these priorities:[28]

- Strategic Review, which is a comprehensive review of all departmental programs, with the intent of reallocating funding from low priority, low performing programs to higher priority programs.

- Strategic Operating Review, which is a one-time review of the cost of delivering programs and operations by the federal government, aiming to further improve the efficiency and effectiveness of the Government of Canada's operations and programs by fiscal year 2014-15, while ensuring ongoing annual savings.

- Development of the Regular Force Multi-Year Establishment Plan, which is a long-term, coordinated view of planned and approved changes to the Regular Force structure.

- Primary Reserve Employment Capacity Study, which is examining the distribution of full-time Primary Reserve employees across the department.

Further, personnel costs currently exceed the targets established by the *Canada First Defence Strategy*, and there are "increasing fiscal pressures related to eliminating the federal budget deficit; delivering savings identified under Strategic Review; and contributing to other public service cost cutting/ program efficiency exercises."[29] As a result of these funding cuts, leadership must determine how to transform and position the DND and CAF workforce for future success.[30]

Workforce planning and development, succinctly referred to as force management, is concerned with "getting the right number of people with the right set of skills and competencies in the right job at the right time."[31] Described below are the four main steps involved in the force management process.

The first step in workforce planning is determining workforce demand, which means defining the present and future needs of the workforce in terms of size (i.e., the total number of positions needed), composition (i.e., the proportions of military, civilian and contracted personnel) and job competencies (i.e., the backgrounds required by each position or group of positions). The second step is determining workforce supply, which means describing the workforce's current and projected state, given existing and predicted policies and practices (e.g., understanding current trends in hiring, attrition and retention). The next step, comparing demand with supply, identifies deficiencies and surpluses between the current workforce and the desired workforce, and then assesses options for addressing them. The final step, implement solutions, involves deciding on the solutions to be put in place, and then developing the processes, practices and monitoring tools needed to assure that the workforce is managed over time to meet requirements.

This four-step model is the basic framework for workforce planning and development. Although the process is simple enough to understand, applying it to the defence establishment has been a challenge for several reasons.[32] First, it is difficult to predict workforce demand given the challenges in predicting future threats and capability requirements in an evolving and dynamic security environment. Second, planning is complicated by the need to staff the large number of occupations and to accomplish the diversity of tasks carried out by the defence workforce, especially when there are different ways to get the work done. Some functions may only be carried out by military personnel, for example, while others are civilian specific, and still others can be carried out by military, civilian or contracted personnel.[33]

Which member of the workforce – civilian, military, contractor – carries out a role in defence is a further complication. The U.S. government, for example, recently civilianized a large number of jobs formerly performed by military personnel. However, the effects of this policy on the attitudes and behavioural intentions of military members and their civilian coworkers are not well understood.[34] Similarly, the New Zealand Defence Force (NZDF) recently initiated the Civilianisation Project, which was intended to reduce the number of military staff by converting military positions in the "middle" (i.e., logistics and training) and "back" (i.e., administrative and similar functions) into civilian positions, so that a higher proportion of military staff would be available for "front" positions (i.e., military deployment). According to a report by New Zealand's auditor general, however, the NZDF moved too quickly, without full consideration of the risks and the potential effects on staff. The result was decreased morale and increased attrition for both civilian and military personnel, ultimately reducing the capability of the NZDF.[35] This example illustrates the importance of understanding the unique and complex dynamics that permeate force management considerations and initiatives in defence organizations.

CONCLUSION

The Canadian defence establishment relies on the expertise of dedicated personnel in DND and the CAF – the Defence Team – to ensure its operational effectiveness. The workforce includes both military and civilian personnel who belong to two different cultural groups, but who must work together to effectively support the defence mission. The first part of this chapter examined the current and historical composition of the DND civilian and CAF Regular Force populations, and then compared the civilian and military workforce on demographic parameters. Compared to the Regular Force population, the DND civilian workforce is older (an average age of 46.9 years compared with 35.1 years in fiscal year 2012-13), has a greater female representation (41% compared with 14% in 2012-13), and has a higher proportion of employees working in the Materiel Services and Science and Technology capability components. On the other hand, a higher proportion of military than civilian personnel work in the Army capability (35% versus 18% in 2012-13) and the Air Force capability (20% versus 8% in 2012-13).

Although there are differences in the demographic profiles of the civilian and military workforces, both have experienced similar trends as a result of past and current federal government policy. In particular, the demographics of both the DND civilian and CAF Regular Force populations are still being affected by the significant reductions in personnel that occurred in the mid-1990s. Both the civilian and military workforces also experienced a period of growth between the fiscal years 2003-04 and 2011-12 as a result of increased operational demands. The most recent deficit reductions – announced in the 2012 federal budget – saw the Defence Team workforce enter a new phase, where the civilian population has been cut from almost 30,000 employees to just under 27,000 (2012-13), while the Regular Force will maintain its current strength of 68,000 personnel.

When the Defence Team enters a period of significant change – especially when facing considerable budgetary restraint – it becomes important to align the workforce with the highest priority activities. The last part of the chapter described the workforce planning and management process, which can be used to determine the optimal composition of civilian and military personnel. The methodology consisted of four main steps: (1) determine workforce demand, (2) determine workforce supply, (3) compare demand with supply, and (4) implement solutions. As we showed, however, applying this approach to the Defence Team is complicated by the uncertainty surrounding both future security needs and the effects of changes on the Defence Team. All the same, workforce planning and management will be required to ensure National Defence's vision of a "modern, first-class military that will be fully integrated, flexible, multi-role and combat capable, that will work in partnership with the knowledgeable and responsive DND civilian personnel."[36]

ENDNOTES

1   Department of National Defence, *Report on Plans and Priorities 2012-13* (Ottawa, ON: Department of National Defence, 2012), 5. Contractors are also hired by DND/CAF to fulfill tasks on a temporary basis. The composition of contractors in DND will not be discussed further in this chapter since limited data are available on the population.

2   All results are presented at the end of a fiscal year; for the remainder of the chapter, therefore, any reference to a fiscal year refers to March 31 of that year (i.e., fiscal year 2012-13 refers to the data as of March 31, 2013).

3   Readers might notice that when a population is broken down by a certain demographic characteristic, the totals differ from the overall population totals. This occurs because individuals who do not have a valid entry for the demographic characteristic under consideration are omitted from the calculations.

4   The Reserve Force is divided into four sub-components: Primary Reserve, Supplementary Reserve, Canadian Rangers, and Cadet Organizations Administration and Training Services. The Primary Reserve is the largest sub-component of the Reserve Force with approximately 30,000 members currently serving on either a full-time or part-time basis. The data presented in this chapter only include the Primary Reserves.

5   The Treasury Board classifies government employees by tenures of employment. An employee whose tenure has a fixed end date is classified as *determinate*; an *indeterminate* employee's tenure has no fixed end date. In simpler terms, an indeterminate employee is a permanent employee of the federal government (see Treasury Board of Canada Secretariat, Glossary of Terms and Definitions, v., "indeterminate employee," "type of employment," and "type of tenure," http://www.tbs-sct.gc.ca/pubs_pol/hrpubs/tbm_11a/2-eng.rtf).

6   The Reserve Force (Primary Reserves) decreased from 34,616 members in 2008 to 29,973 members in 2013.

7   Official documents related to the Work Force Adjustment can be found at the Treasury Board Secretariat's website, http://www.tbs-sct.gc.ca/lrco-rtor/wfa-rde/wfa-rde-eng.asp

8   Assistant Deputy Minister (Human Resources – Civilian), *Civilian Workforce Functional Planning Guidance* (Ottawa, ON: Department of National Defence, 2012), 3.

9   Irina Goldenberg, *Defence Team Survey: Descriptive Results*, Director General Military Personnel Research and Analysis Technical Memorandum 2013-026 (Ottawa, ON: Defence Research and Development Canada, 2013).

10   Assistant Deputy Minister (Human Resources - Civilian), *Civilian Human Resources Functional Assessment FY 2008-2009* (Ottawa, ON: Department of National Defence, 2007), 4.

11   Department of National Defence, *Equipment Management Team (EMT) Handbook*, Publication Number A-LP-005-000/AG-008 (Ottawa, ON: Department of National

Defence, 2004), 27, retrieved from http://dgmssc.ottawa-hull.mil.ca/MATKNET/NR/rdonlyres/4EF285BF-2080-48AF-BD75-89BEC4375667/0/HDBK_EMTpart01_v2_e.pdf.

12 Out of the 30 capability components in DND/CAF, 15 are capabilities and 15 are components of those capabilities.

13 Individuals younger than 16 years of age or older than 75 were omitted from the profile and were not included in the calculations for average age. Age is calculated as of March 31 of each fiscal year.

14 Public Servants are eligible to receive an immediate annuity if they leave the Public Service at age 60 or over, with at least two pensionable years of service, or at age 55 or over, with at least 30 pensionable years of service.

15 Department of Finance Canada, *Smaller Public Service*, Budget 1995 Fact Sheets 7, retrieved from http://fin.gc.ca/budget95/fact/fact_7-eng.asp.

16 Individuals with 57 or more years of pensionable service were omitted from the profile and were not included when calculating the average years of pensionable service. Pensionable years of service are calculated as of March 31 of each fiscal year.

17 Treasury Board of Canada Secretariat, *Your Pension and Insurance Benefits Guide* (Ottawa, ON: Treasury Board Secretariat, 2011), 6.

18 The attrition rates in this chapter are calculated based on a formula provided in S. Okazawa, *Measuring Attrition Rates and Forecasting Attrition Volume*, Director General Military Personnel Research and Analysis Technical Memorandum 2007-02 (Ottawa, ON: Defence Research and Development Canada, 2007), 31; specifically, attrition rates are calculated as the losses from the workforce in year M divided by the sum of the total workforce at the beginning of year m and one half of the total entries in year M.

19 Department of National Defence, *Canada First Defence Strategy*, 15.

20 Department of National Defence, *Report on Plans and Priorities 2012-13*, 59.

21 S. Latchman and G. L. Christopher, *DGMPRA Support to the Annual Military Occupation Reviews (AMORs)*, Briefing Note, May 22, 2009 (Ottawa, ON: Defence Research and Development Canada, 2009), 1.

22 Individuals younger than 16 years of age or older than 60, which is the Compulsory Retirement Age, were omitted from the profile and were not included in the calculations for average age.

23 Department of National Defence, *1994 Defence White Paper* (Ottawa, ON: Department of National Defence, 1994), 34.

24 Individuals with 46 or more years of service were omitted from the profile and were not included in calculations of the average years of service.

25 National Defence and the Canadian Forces, *Backgrounder: Recruiting and Retention in the Canadian Forces*, webpage modified May 4, 2010, retrieved from http://www.forces.gc.ca/en/news/article.page?doc=recruiting-and-retention-in-the-canadian-forces/hnps1uwf.

26   Assistant Deputy Minister (Human Resources – Civilian), *Civilian Human Resources Functional Assessment FY 2011-2012* (Ottawa, ON: Department of National Defence, 2011), 3.

27   Department of National Defence, *Canada First Defence Strategy*, 7.

28   M. Halbrohr, *Civilian Workforce Planning – Challenges and Opportunities*, Director General Military Personnel Research and Analysis Technical Memorandum 2011-030 (Ottawa: ON, Defence Research and Development Canada, 2011), 3.

29   Assistant Deputy Minister (Human Resources – Civilian), *Civilian Human Resources Functional Assessment FY 2011-2012* (Ottawa, ON: Department of National Defence, 2011), 3.

30   Assistant Deputy Minister (Human Resources - Civilian), *Strategic HR Plan 2012-2015* (Ottawa, ON: Department of National Defence, 2012), 3.

31   G. Vernez, A. A. Robbert, H. G. Massey, and K. Driscoll, *Workforce Planning and Development Processes: A Practical Guide* (Santa Monica, CA: RAND, 2007), 3.

32   S. M. Gates, C. Eibner, and E. G. Keating, *Civilian Workforce Planning in the Department of Defense: Different Levels, Different Roles* (Santa Monica, CA: RAND, 2006), 5.

33   Halbrohr, *Civilian Workforce Planning*, 3.

34   R. Kelty and D. R. Segal, "The Civilianization of the U.S. Military: Army and Navy Case Studies of the Effects of Civilian Integration on Military Personnel," in *Private Military and Security Companies: Chances, Problems, Pitfalls, and Prospects*, eds. T. Jager and G. Kummel (Netherlands: VS Verlag für Sozialwissenschaften, 2007), 213.

35   Lyn Provost, Controller and Auditor-General. *The New Zealand Defence Force: The Civilianisation Project*, January 24, 2013.

36   Assistant Deputy Minister (Human Resources – Civilian), *Strategic HR Plan 2012-2015* (Ottawa, ON: Department of National Defence, 2012), 1.

CHAPTER 4

WHAT DEFENCE TEAM PERSONNEL SAY: EMPIRICAL RESULTS FROM THE DEFENCE TEAM SURVEY

Irina Goldenberg

A complete understanding of civilian-military working relations in Canada's defence establishment must include the perspectives of members of the Defence Team themselves. This chapter presents selected empirical findings from the Defence Team Survey, which assessed the perspectives of civilian and military personnel in the Department of National Defence and the Canadian Armed Forces.[1] Both in scope and focus, this survey was unprecedented. Few empirical studies of military-civilian collaboration had been conducted, though there have long been anecdotal and incidental reports of integration considerations and challenges in the Defence Team. In order to fill this gap in the research and to determine the nature and prevalence of integration issues, the Defence Team Survey examined a range of factors unique to the Defence Team partnership, including the quality of military-civilian relations and communication, the effects of military supervision of civilian personnel (and vice versa), and the effects of the military rotational cycle on the work of civilian employees.

EMPIRICAL RESEARCH ON THE DEFENCE TEAM

Before the Defence Team Survey, very little empirical research had been conducted on working relations and dynamics between military and civilian members of the Defence Team. Yet several small-scale studies of civilian personnel designed to examine general personnel issues, particularly retention, discovered some challenges in military-civilian personnel collaboration and integration. For example, results of the 2007 *Civilian Well-Being and Retention Study*, based on 26 focus groups with civilian DND employees at CAF bases across the country, indicated concerns in this area and a need for further exploration.[2] In particular, it was found that civilian employees felt that military personnel received workplace advantages, that their skills and expertise were not recognized to the same degree as those of their military counterparts, that the military rotational cycle (i.e., postings and deployments) impacted their work, and that military managers at all levels lacked adequate training in the terms and conditions of civilian employment. The results of the *Canadian Forces Health Service Group Retention Study*,[3] again based on focus groups of civilian personnel (in this case in health-related occupations) at CAF bases across the country, corroborated these findings.

Anecdotal reports were also generally in line with these results. For example, in the context of exploring training for military managers and supervisors of civilian personnel, senior DND managers noted that there is a perception that military managers at all levels are not well-equipped to carry out civilian human resources responsibilities, although they emphasized that this perception required empirical validation.[4] Similarly, focus group studies at CAF bases indicated that some civilian employees expressed concerns with respect to the communication between union officials and CAF management, which was affecting the morale of some civilians, and that some civilians do not feel like respected members of the team.[5]

In short, all the evidence regarding working relations on the Defence Team was either anecdotal or incidentally derived from research that was not specifically designed to examine collaboration between military and civilian personnel. The degree and prevalence of considerations and challenges between the civilian and military workforces therefore required validation using representative samples of personnel. Moreover, the documented information came almost exclusively from civilian employees, and thus a more balanced perspective was needed that included the views of both the military and civilian personnel in the Defence Team. The Defence Team Survey was thus the first attempt to examine military-civilian personnel issues systematically, using large random samples of both military and civilian respondents.

METHODOLOGY

The Defence Team Survey was based on stratified random samples of CAF Regular Force personnel and indeterminate[6] civilian DND personnel. As is common with surveys of the Regular Force population, the military sample was stratified by rank and operational environment (i.e., land, sea, and air). In order to obtain a representative sample of indeterminate DND personnel, the civilian sample was stratified by years of service and occupational category. The survey was administered electronically between September and December 2012.

Military Sample

The survey was sent to 4,119 Regular Force CAF personnel. In total, 1,483 completed the survey, yielding an initial response rate of 36.0%. Unfortunately, technical difficulties with the survey link caused the connection to be terminated for many military respondents at a third of the way through the survey.[7] The researchers decided to use only the completed surveys, because the data were weighted by rank and environment for the military sample, and these variables were collected at the end of the survey. As a result, 663 completed surveys from military personnel were analyzed for this report. With this sample size, the overall margin of error is ±3.8% with 95% confidence, meaning that the results will be accurate 19 times out of 20 within a ±3.8% margin of error if the survey were to be repeated. Table 4.1 presents the demographic characteristics of the military survey sample and the Regular Force population of interest from which the sample was drawn, including rank, environment, YOS, age, gender and first official language (FOL).[8]

	Sample (n = 663)		Population (N = 56,490)	
	Number	Percentage	Number	Percentage
Rank[9]				
Junior NCMs	130	29.1	31,076	55.0
Senior NCMs	178	17.5	13,797	24.4
Junior Officers	166	35.3	6,618	11.7
Senior Officers	189	18.1	4,999	8.8
Environmental Uniform				
Royal Canadian Air Force	237	30.9	16,638	29.5
Canadian Army	347	52.4	30,270	53.6
Royal Canadian Navy	79	16.7	9,582	17.0
YOS				
1-4	23	5.3	11,240	19.9
5-14	176	36.3	24,342	43.1
15-24	194	27.4	11,521	20.4
25+	243	31.0	9,387	16.6
Age				
16-24 years old	13	3.0	5,144	9.1
25-34 years old	131	29.0	20,794	36.8
35-44 years old	218	32.5	17,100	30.3
45+ years old	271	35.5	13,452	23.8
Gender				
Male	540	79.4	48,744	86.3
Female	118	20.6	7,746	13.7
FOL				
English	464	72.3	41,103	72.8
French	180	27.7	15,387	27.2

TABLE 4.1: Military Sample and Population Demographic Characteristics

Civilian Sample

The survey was sent to 3,985 indeterminate DND personnel. In total, 1,149 personnel completed the survey, yielding a response rate of 28.8%. The overall margin of error is ±2.8% with 95% confidence, meaning that the results will be accurate 19 times out of 20 within a ±2.8% margin of error if the survey were to be repeated. Table 4.2 presents the demographic characteristics of the civilian survey sample and the DND population of interest from which the sample was drawn, including occupational category, YOS, age, gender and FOL.[10] As shown, the civilian sample is remarkably representative of the civilian population.[11]

	Sample (n = 1,149)		Population (N = 23,621)	
	Number	Percentage	Number	Percentage
Occupational Category				
Operational	177	30.0	7,206	30.5
Administrative Support	207	14.6	3,402	14.4
Administration and Foreign Service	342	30.7	7,157	30.3
Technical	229	11.7	2,753	11.7
Scientific and professional	142	12.5	2,930	12.4
Executive	52	0.6	143	0.6
YOS				
1-4	233	22.1	5,663	24.0
5-14	304	35.2	11,238	47.6
15-24	208	12.7	2,792	11.8
25+	401	30.0	3,778	16.0
Age				
16-24 years old	3	0.3	152	0.6
25-34 years old	90	10.6	2,845	12.0
35-44 years old	190	22.7	4,944	20.9
45+ years old	807	66.4	15,639	66.2
Gender				
Male	651	59.9	14,343	60.7
Female	483	40.1	9,278	39.3
FOL				
English	883	76.0	18,049	76.4
French	261	24.0	5,572	23.6

TABLE 4.2: Civilian Sample and Population Demographic Characteristics

MEASURES

The survey instrument comprised a range of items and scales used to assess key aspects of military-civilian work culture and relations (e.g., communication, intergroup respect), as well as attitudes and perceptions (e.g., perceptions of fairness) and key outcomes (e.g., organizational commitment). Whenever possible, an effort was made to use measures that had been published and validated in the scientific literature, as opposed to creating new scales and items for the survey. However, given the specificity of some of the issues of interest and the lack of existing research in this domain, a number of scales were created for the specific purpose of assessing military and civilian work culture and relations in defence organizations.[12]

Results

Extent of Interaction between DND and CAF Personnel

A series of questions assessed the extent to which military and civilian personnel work together and interact in DND and the CAF. Almost ninety percent of military (89.5%) and of civilian (89.4%) personnel indicated sharing their workplace with their Defence Team counterparts.

As Table 4.3 shows, 80.6% of military personnel who share a workplace with civilians indicated interacting with them on a daily basis.

Response Option	Number	Percentage	SE (%)
Daily	478	80.6	1.9
Several times a week	56	9.9	1.4
About once a week	18	3.4	0.9
About once every couple of weeks	17	3.9	1.0
About once a month	6	1.1	0.5
Less than once a month	3	0.3	0.2
Almost never	5	0.8	0.4
TOTAL	583	100.0	0.0

TABLE 4.3: "How much contact/interaction do you have with civilian personnel in your workplace?"

Similarly, Table 4.4 shows that 84.1% of civilian personnel who worked with military personnel indicated interacting with their military co-workers on a daily basis.

Response Option	Number	Percentage	SE (%)
Daily	856	84.1	1.3
Several times a week	88	7.7	0.9
About once a week	42	4.1	0.7
About once every couple of weeks	22	1.6	0.4
About once a month	9	0.7	0.3
Less than once a month	8	0.9	0.3
Almost never	6	0.8	0.4
TOTAL	1,031	100.0	0.0

TABLE 4.4: "How much contact/interaction do you have with military personnel in your workplace?"

Over 90% of military personnel indicated that their direct supervisor was military, whereas only 57.1% of civilian personnel were supervised directly by a civilian, with 42.9% being supervised by a military manager (Table 4.5).

	CAF Personnel			DND Personnel		
	Number	Percentage	SE (%)	Number	Percentage	SE (%)
Military supervisor	603	92.6	1.0	491	42.9	1.8
Civilian supervisor	57	7.4	1.0	657	57.1	1.8

TABLE 4.5: "Do you report directly to a civilian or a military supervisor?"

Perceptions of Importance/Value of Civilian Personnel

Civilian and military personnel were asked whether civilian employees are necessary and important to the success of the CAF mission, using a 6-point scale ranging from *strongly disagree* to *strongly agree*. As shown in Figure 4.1, both groups of personnel indicated that civilian personnel are necessary and important to the success of the CAF mission.[13] However, civilian personnel were somewhat more likely to evince these perceptions than their military counterparts, and they almost unanimously endorsed the importance of their role in this regard.

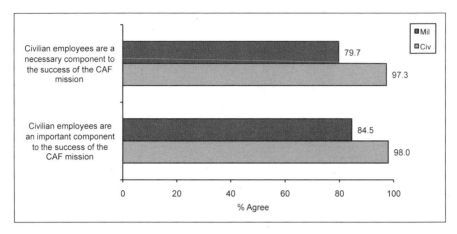

FIGURE 4.1: Role of Civilian Personnel in the Success of the CAF Mission[14]

WORK CULTURE AND RELATIONS BETWEEN MILITARY AND CIVILIAN PERSONNEL

Relationship Quality

Military and civilian respondents were asked a series of questions regarding the quality of their relations with one another on a 6-point scale, ranging from *strongly disagree* to *strongly agree*. As Table 4.6 shows, the majority of respondents from both workforces agreed that they have good relations with one another.[15] Further, military and civilian personnel's perceptions of the quality of their relationships were very similar to one another, although military personnel were slightly less likely than civilians to agree that "military and civilian personnel are focused on the same goals and mission," and to agree that "military and civilian personnel in my workgroup feel a responsibility to each other."

ITEMS	Civilian		Military	
	% Agree	SE (%)	% Agree	SE (%)
Military and civilian members treat each other equitably.	68.6	1.7	69.5	2.0
Civilian and military employees treat each other fairly in my workgroup.	75.1	1.6	78.0	1.8
Civilian and military personnel work together effectively as a team.	81.5	1.4	79.0	1.8
There is a productive partnership between military and civilian personnel in my workplace.	79.2	1.5	79.1	1.8
Military and civilian personnel have positive working relations with each other in my workplace.	79.6	1.5	80.5	1.8
Military and civilians get along well in my workplace.	84.3	1.4	84.9	1.5
Military and civilian personnel are focused on the same goals and mission.	79.7	1.5	68.5	2.0
Military personnel recognize the skills and expertise of civilian personnel.	74.9	1.6	-	-
Military and civilian personnel in my workgroup feel a responsibility to each other.	74.6	1.6	68.8	2.0
In my workplace military and civilian personnel get along well with one another.	85.9	1.3	87.1	1.3
The opinions of civilian employees are valued by military members.	71.6	1.7	-	-
Civilian personnel recognize the skills and expertise of military personnel.	-	-	74.6	1.8

TABLE 4.6: Relationship Quality

Communication

Military and civilian respondents were asked several questions regarding the quality of communication with one another on a 6-point scale ranging from *strongly disagree* to *strongly agree*. As shown in Figure 4.2, the majority of respondents from both workforces indicated having a high quality of communication with the other group.[16] However, over half of both military and civilian personnel indicated that they "sometimes feel that military and civilian employees are speaking different languages." Interestingly, the perceptions of military and civilian personnel with respect to quality of communication were extremely similar to one another.

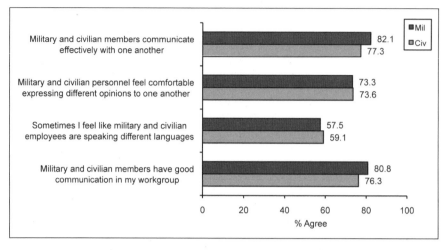

FIGURE 4.2: Quality of Communication[17]

WORKPLACE RESPECT

Both military and civilian respondents were asked to indicate the degree to which their Defence Team counterparts respect them in various ways within the workplace, using a 6-point scale ranging from *strongly disagree* to *strongly agree*. As Figure 4.3 shows, the majority of respondents from both workforces indicated feeling a high level of respect from the other group.[18] Further, military and civilian feelings of respect from their counterparts were extremely similar to one another.

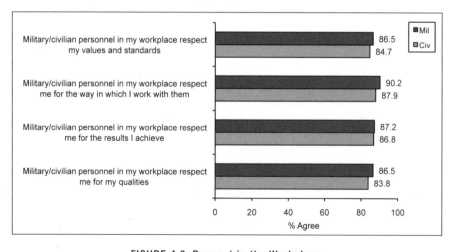

FIGURE 4.3: Respect in the Workplace

Inclusion

Military and civilian respondents were asked a series of questions regarding their perceptions of inclusion between the two workforces on a 6-point scale, ranging from *strongly disagree* to *strongly agree*. As shown in Table 4.7, the majority of both military and civilian personnel indicated that civilians make military personnel feel like part of the team in their work groups, but civilians were somewhat more likely to indicate that this is the case. Similarly, both military and civilian personnel indicated that military personnel make civilian personnel feel like part of the team in their workgroups, but military personnel were slightly more likely than civilian personnel to indicate that this was the case.

About two thirds of both groups agreed, however, that military personnel tend to communicate more with other military personnel, whereas civilian personnel tend to communicate more with other civilian personnel in their workplaces. Nonetheless, almost 80% of both groups indicated that military and civilian personnel socialize with one another at work.

On a less positive note, slightly more than half of civilian personnel indicated that "civilian personnel are often treated as though they are 'second-class citizens' by military personnel in the DND/CAF." This question was posed to follow up on previous focus group findings from several retention studies of civilian personnel that reported these sentiments.[19] Thus, this survey was used to assess the prevalence of this sentiment in a larger and more representative sample; and it did indeed confirm these observations.

ITEMS	Civilian		Military	
	% Agree	SE (%)	% Agree	SE (%)
Civilian personnel are often treated as though they are "second-class citizens" by military personnel in the DND/CF.	54.8	1.8	-	-
Military members tend to communicate more with each other than with civilian employees in my workplace.	68.1	1.7	60.4	2.1
Civilian employees tend to communicate more with each other than with military employees in my workplace.	60.2	1.8	61.4	2.1
Military personnel make civilian employees feel like part of the team in my work group.	74.1	1.6	84.1	1.6
Civilian employees make military personnel feel like part of the team in my workgroup.	86.0	1.3	71.2	1.9
Civilians and military members socialize together in my workplace.	79.1	1.5	77.9	1.8

TABLE 4.7: Inclusion

Senior Leadership Messages Supporting the Defence Team

Military and civilian respondents were asked several questions to assess their perceptions regarding senior leadership support and promotion of the Defence Team, using a 6-point scale ranging from *strongly disagree* to *strongly agree*. As Figure 4.4 shows, about three quarters of military respondents indicated that senior leaders make efforts to promote the military-civilian Defence Team and to emphasize the importance of military-civilian employee cooperation. A somewhat lower proportion of civilian personnel indicated that senior leaders promote the Defence Team and emphasize the importance of military-civilian employee cooperation. All the same, the majority of civilian respondents did indicate that this was the case. Further, 68.4% of military personnel and 56.8% of civilian personnel indicated that senior leaders do a good job of promoting the military-civilian Defence Team. Overall, civilian personnel were less likely than military personnel to indicate that senior leaders promote the Defence Team.

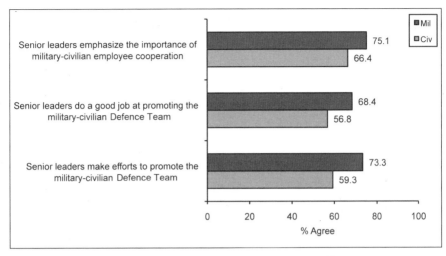

FIGURE 4.4: Senior Leadership Messages[20]

Supervision of Civilian Personnel by Military Supervisors and Supervision of Military Personnel by Civilian Supervisors

As noted above, about 43% of civilians indicated that their direct supervisor was a military member, and more than 7% of military personnel indicated that their direct supervisor was a civilian. In light of this, civilian respondents supervised by a military manager were asked a series of questions about their views regarding the nature and quality of this supervision – and similar questions were put to military members supervised by a civilian.

Supervision and Leadership of Civilians by Military Supervisors

As Table 4.8 shows, civilian personnel thought that improvements could be made with respect to the nature and quality of supervision that they receive from military managers. Most notably, about 83% of civilians supervised by military supervisors indicated that military managers are placed in positions of authority over civilians without receiving the training required to manage them properly. In the same vein, only about 55% indicated that military managers are able to manage civilian personnel effectively and that they are knowledgeable about civilian performance appraisals. Only about two thirds believed that military managers have a good understanding of civilian terms and conditions of employment. Similarly, a large proportion agreed that military managers are often confused about the role of civilian employees and do not make the most of what civilian employees have to offer.

On a more positive note, about three quarters of civilians indicated that military managers recognize civilian personnel's skills and expertise, and the majority indicated that military managers respect civilian terms and conditions of employment and support training opportunities for civilian employees.

ITEMS	% Agree	SE (%)
Military managers are often confused about the role of civilian employees.	68.5	2.7
Military managers don't make the most of what civilian employees have to offer.	69.1	2.7
Military managers are often placed in positions of authority over civilians without receiving sufficient training required to manage them.	83.2	2.1
Military managers are knowledgeable about the use of civilian performance appraisal systems and procedures.	55.1	2.8
Military managers support professional development opportunities for civilian employees.	65.8	2.8
Military managers support training opportunities for civilian employees.	70.8	2.7
Military managers recognize the skills and expertise of civilian personnel.	71.3	2.5
Military managers understand civilian terms and conditions of employment.	65.0	2.7
Military managers respect civilian terms and conditions of employment.	70.0	2.6
Military managers give preferential treatment to military personnel.	60.6	2.8
Military managers treat civilian and military personnel with equal fairness.	61.8	2.7
Military managers have a good understanding of civilian employees' personal obligations when assigning duties.	66.6	2.4
Military management makes me feel like a valued part of the team.	73.2	2.5
Military managers are able to manage civilian personnel effectively.	56.4	2.7

TABLE 4.8: Supervision and Leadership of Civilians by Military Supervisors and Managers

Supervision and Leadership of Military by Civilian Supervisors and Managers

As Table 4.9 shows, military personnel were somewhat more positive regarding supervision and leadership by civilian supervisors. In particular, most military personnel supervised by civilians indicated that civilians respect military terms of service, recognize the skills and expertise of military personnel, support the training and professional development of military personnel, make military personnel feel like a valued part of the team and are able to manage military personnel effectively.[21]

Nonetheless, there are some notable areas of concern. Like their civilian counterparts, about three quarters of military personnel indicated that civilian managers are placed in positions of authority over military personnel without receiving the training required to manage them, another two thirds indicated that civilian managers do not appreciate important aspects of military culture and are confused about the role of military employees, and only two thirds believed that civilian managers understand military terms of service. Taken together, it seems that improvements could be made on these issues, at least with respect to perceptions related to them.

ITEMS	% Agree	SE (%)
Civilian managers understand military terms of service.	62.1	7.0
Civilian managers respect military terms of service.	73.3	6.1
Civilian managers recognize the skills and expertise of military personnel.	79.0	5.8
Civilian managers support training opportunities for military employees.	78.6	5.9
Civilian managers support professional development opportunities for military employees.	82.0	5.5
Civilian managers are often placed in positions of authority over military personnel without receiving sufficient training required to manage them.	76.9	6.0
Civilian managers don't appreciate important aspects of military culture.	63.0	6.9
Civilian managers are often confused about the role of military employees.	67.0	6.6
Civilian managers give preferential treatment to civilian personnel.	36.3	6.9
Civilian managers are knowledgeable about the use of military performance appraisal systems and procedures.	55.5	7.0
Civilian managers treat civilian and military personnel with equal fairness.	75.8	5.3
Civilian managers make me feel like a valued part of the team.	71.7	6.5
Civilian managers are able to manage military personnel effectively.	67.6	6.6

TABLE 4.9: Supervision and Leadership of Military Personnel by Civilian Supervisors and Managers

Working in a Military Context

Given that working in a military context is unique to civilians in defence organizations, some of the potential consequences of civilians working in a military-civilian environment were explored. Civilian respondents were asked to indicate their degree of agreement with items assessing the effects of working in a military-civilian environment on their career development and training opportunities and about the effects on their work of the military rotational cycle (e.g., postings and deployments) on a 6-point scale ranging from *strongly disagree* to *strongly agree*.

As Table 4.10 shows, a large proportion of civilians indicated that working in a military context has had a negative effect on their career development. About half indicated that working in an organization with military personnel has affected their career opportunities, and six in ten indicated that DND offers fewer advancement opportunities than other government departments.

With respect to training, the majority of civilian personnel indicated that the training and professional development opportunities provided to military personnel make sense given their roles. However, about half of civilians indicated that they do not receive adequate training opportunities (in comparison with their military counterparts), and a third indicated that training for military members decreases the training available to civilian employees.

With respect to the effects of the military rotational cycle, 72.2% of civilians indicated that the frequent posting cycle of military personnel disrupts productivity in their workplace, and over half indicated that the rotational cycle of military managers and supervisors disrupts their work.

ITEMS	% Agree	SE (%)
Effects on Career Development		
Career opportunities for civilians are not affected by working in an organization with military personnel.	49.7	1.8
Career progression of civilians is limited in DND because the best positions tend to be given to military personnel.	53.2	1.8
The quantity of senior management positions designated for military personnel has limited my ability to progress to more challenging positions.	46.4	1.8
Priority hiring of former military members has limited my career progression.	42.5	1.8
There are fewer advancement opportunities at DND as compared to other federal government departments.	63.4	1.8
Careers of civilian personnel are limited because of positions given to former military members.	55.3	1.8
The most interesting assignments seem to be given to military personnel.	44.1	1.8
Effects on Training Opportunities		
Given our unique roles in DND/CAF, the training given to military and civilian personnel make sense.	77.6	1.6
Given our unique roles, the professional development opportunities given to military and civilian employees make sense.	72.9	1.6
Civilian employees receive an adequate amount of training opportunities compared to military members.	51.0	1.8
The training military members are given decreases the training opportunities available to civilian employees.	35.2	1.8
Effects of Military Rotational Cycle		
The frequent posting cycle of military personnel disrupts productivity in my workplace.	72.2	1.7
The rotational cycle of military managers and supervisors makes it difficult to do my work.	57.4	1.8

TABLE 4.10: Working in a Military Context

Key Employee and Organizational Outcomes

Respondents were asked to rate their job satisfaction, feelings of competence at work, and affective commitment to the organization on a 6-point scale ranging from *strongly disagree* to *strongly agree*, and to rate their work engagement on a 6-point scale ranging from *never* to *always*.[22]

As Figure 4.5 shows, both military and civilian personnel indicated high degrees of job satisfaction, work engagement, organizational commitment and feelings of competence. Mean scores between the two groups were similar on these important outcome variables.[23]

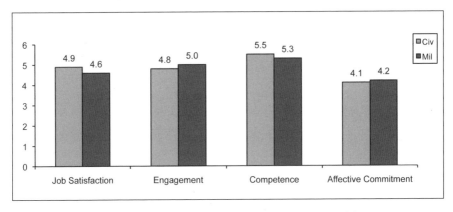

FIGURE 4.5: Job Satisfaction, Work Engagement, Feelings of Competence

As indicated in Figure 4.6, the majority of both military and civilian personnel indicated that they intend to remain in the CAF and DND. However, civilian personnel evinced slightly higher intentions to stay than their military counterparts.

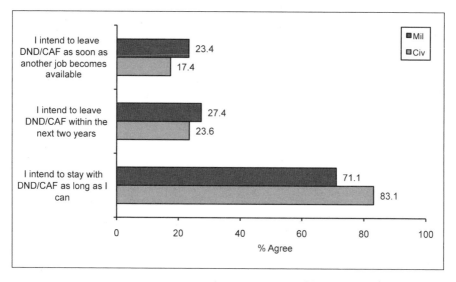

FIGURE 4.6: Retention Intentions[24]

CORRELATIONS BETWEEN MILITARY-CIVILIAN WORK CONTEXT AND RELATIONS VARIABLES AND OUTCOME VARIABLES

Correlational analyses were conducted to explore how the military-civilian work culture and the effects of working in a military-civilian environment relate to organizational outcome variables. The magnitude of these correlations may be interpreted as follows: $r = 0.10$ is a small correlation; $r = 0.30$ is a medium correlation; and $r = 0.50$ is considered a large correlation.[25]

As Table 4.11 shows, the perceived quality of relations between military and civilian personnel in DND and the CAF (e.g., perceived relationship quality, inclusion, communication, respect) was related to most of the important outcome variables, including organizational fairness, job satisfaction, work engagement, affective commitment and retention intentions for both military and civilian personnel. However, these work culture and relations variables were not related to self-reported competence for either military or civilian personnel. Similarly, perceptions of the quality of supervision by military supervisors (for civilians) and by civilian supervisors (for military personnel), as well as the degree to which senior leaders are perceived to support and promote the Defence Team, were related to important outcome variables (again, with the exception of self-reported competence). For civilian personnel, the perceived effects of working in a military context on career development and on training opportunities, as well as the effects of the military rotational cycle on one's work, were related to these important outcomes (again, with the exception of self-reported competence).[26]

Perceptions of organizational fairness and affective organizational commitment were the outcome variables most strongly correlated with aspects of military-civilian relations and work context, whereas correlations with job satisfaction, work engagement, and retention intentions were generally more moderate. Of note, these correlations were consistently stronger for civilian personnel, even though the military-civilian relations and work context were interrelated with key personnel and organizational outcomes for both military and civilian personnel.

	Organizational Fairness		Job Satisfaction		Work Engagement		Competence		Affective Commitment		Retention Intentions	
	Civ	Mil	Civ	Mil	Civ	Mil	Civ	Mil	Civ	Mil	Civ	Mil
Relationship quality	0.70	0.52	0.46	0.35	0.33	0.28	0.02	0.02	0.62	0.31	0.39	0.21
Inclusion	0.60	0.39	0.40	0.25	0.31	0.23	0.04	0.03	0.53	0.24	0.31	0.18
Communication	0.64	0.49	0.44	0.35	0.30	0.28	0.03	0.05	0.56	0.29	0.34	0.22
Respect	0.61	0.49	0.49	0.40	0.39	0.35	0.10	0.08	0.61	0.31	0.38	0.24
Leadership and supervision	0.70	0.46	0.45	0.27	0.33	0.21	-0.01	-0.03	0.60	0.25	0.41	0.22
Senior leadership messages	0.64	0.50	0.42	0.39	0.33	0.39	-0.004	0.06	0.55	0.44	0.37	0.33
Working in a military context – Career development	0.60	-	0.34	-	0.22	-	-0.02	-	0.48	-	0.32	-
Working in a military context – Effects on training opportunities	0.60	-	0.36	-	0.27	-	0.03	-	0.49	-	0.34	-
Working in a military context – Effects of military rotational cycle	0.27	-	0.19	-	0.15	-	0.03	-	0.26	-	0.17	-

TABLE 4.11: Correlations between Military-Civilian Relations and Work Context Variables and Outcome Variables

CONCLUSION

Understanding how civilian and military personnel on the Defence Team perceive their partnership is important for fostering that partnership and for contextualizing the other chapters in this volume. The Defence Team Survey provided an unprecedented look at this unique organizational dynamic, exploring a range of issues specific to collaboration between military and civilian personnel in Canada's defence establishment. This was an important initiative because it was a first systematic examination of these issues in a large sample of military and civilian respondents and, further, because it examined military-civilian relations and dynamics from the perspective of both military and civilian personnel.

The survey confirmed a high degree of interaction between military and civilian personnel in DND and the CAF. Almost 90% of civilian and military personnel work alongside their Defence Team counterparts, and over 80% of military and civilian personnel interact with each other on a daily basis. In addition, almost 43% of civilians are supervised by military members, while over 7% of military personnel reported directly to a civilian supervisor.

Many positive aspects were revealed about the collaboration and interaction between military and civilian personnel on the Defence Team. Civilians and their military peers both see civilian personnel as necessary and important to the success of the CAF mission. The work culture and relations between military and civilian personnel were found to be extremely positive. Each group reported good communication, perceptions of mutual respect, feelings of inclusion and high-quality relations with the other.

Overall, senior leaders were perceived to be promoting the Defence Team and military-civilian collaboration in DND and the CAF. There is still room for improvement in this regard, however, especially from the perspective of civilian personnel, who were less likely than military personnel to perceive that senior leaders promote the importance of the Defence Team.

Scores on important outcome variables were found to be high and were observed to be similar for both groups of personnel. Military and civilian personnel indicated that they perceive the organization to be fair overall, that they are satisfied with their jobs and engaged in their work, and that they are competent in their jobs. They also showed good affective commitment to the organization, and most reported that they intend to remain in DND and the CAF.

Despite the many positive findings, some potential areas for improvement emerged. One key area is the potential effects on civilians that may stem from working in a military context. Many civilian employees felt that working in a military context had a negative effect on their career progressions and training opportunities, and that the military rotational cycle disrupts their work. Many civilians also felt that military personnel treat them like "second-class citizens."

Supervision of civilian personnel (and vice versa) was also an area of concern. Many civilian personnel supervised by military managers (and vice versa) perceived that their supervisors did not appreciate their terms and conditions of service and their personnel appraisal systems. Many civilians also believed that military supervisors do not fully appreciate the roles of civilian personnel or fully capitalize on their skills and abilities.

These results suggest that military-civilian work relations and interaction are related to important employee and organizational outcomes, including perceptions of organizational fairness, job satisfaction, work engagement, organizational commitment and retention intentions. Personnel who see military-civilian collaboration in DND and the CAF more positively are more likely to be satisfied with their jobs, engaged in their work and committed to the organization than those who have less positive views of military-civilian collaboration. These associations are particularly strong for perceptions of organizational fairness and affective organizational commitment.[27]

Perceptions of competence were not related to the military-civilian work and relations variables assessed. The degree to which personnel feel they are competent and proficient at their jobs is not affected by their attitudes and perceptions regarding military-civilian personnel interaction, senior leaders' messages in support of the Defence Team, quality of supervision by military supervisors (for civilians) or quality of supervision by civilian supervisors (for military members). Further, civilian employees' feelings of competence in their jobs are not affected by working in a mixed military-civilian environment.

The quality of military-civilian relations and interaction were associated with key personnel and organizational outcomes, such as affective commitment for both military and civilian personnel, but these correlations were consistently stronger for civilian personnel than for military personnel. Of course, this is not particularly surprising because civilian personnel are a minority in DND and the CAF overall; in addition, civilian personnel are often understood to play a *supporting* role in the CAF's operational success.[28] Moreover, the proportion of civilian personnel directly supervised by military personnel is much larger than the proportion of military personnel supervised by civilian supervisors, which may also increase the importance of positive military-civilian work culture and relations for civilian personnel. Nevertheless, optimal military-civilian interactions, work culture and relations appear to be related to important employee outcomes for both workforces, which make them important considerations for the optimal personnel management of all members of the Defence Team.

In short, the results of this research support the need for a specific focus on the issues unique to the military-civilian personnel dynamic in order to optimize the partnership between these two workforces who must collaborate in the defence of Canada and its interests. Indeed, although outside the scope of this chapter, there are already many examples of DND and the CAF successfully managing integration and collaboration between military and civilian personnel.[29] These efforts are likely to further enhance the relations and working conditions of the Defence Team and ultimately to increase employee well-being and organizational effectiveness.

ENDNOTES

1   The material in this chapter presents selected content previously published in a more comprehensive internal departmental research report: Irina Goldenberg, *The Defence Team Survey: Descriptive Results*, Director General Military Personnel Research and Analysis Technical Memorandum 2013-026 (Ottawa, ON: Defence Research and Development Canada, 2013).

2   This study consisted of 26 focus groups with civilian DND employees at CAF bases across the country. See Brian McKee and Lisa Williams, *Civilian Well-Being and Retention Project: Qualitative Findings*, Director Personnel Applied Research, Sponsor Research Report 2007 (Ottawa, ON: Defence Research and Development Canada, 2007), 14.

3   This study was also based on focus groups of civilian personnel (in this case in health-related occupations) at CAF bases across the country. See Sylvie Lalonde, *Canadian Forces Health Service: Factors Affecting the Retention of Public Service Health Care Professionals in the Department of National Defence*, Director General Military Personnel Research and Analysis Technical Memorandum 2011-013 (Ottawa, ON: Defence Research and Development Canada, 2010).

4   Stephanie Poliquin, "Update of HR Content in CF Training" (presentation, Human Resources Management Team, Ottawa, Ontario, Canada, March 23, 2009).

5   Sylvie Lalonde, *Canadian Forces Health Service: Factors Affecting the Retention of Public Service Health Care Professionals in the Department of National Defence*, Director General Military Personnel Research and Analysis Technical Memorandum 2011-013 (Ottawa, ON: Defence Research and Development Canada, 2010). B. McKee and L. M. Williams, *Civilian Well-Being and Retention Project: Qualitative Findings*, Director Personnel Applied Research, Sponsor Research Report 2007-14 (Ottawa, ON: Defence Research and Development Canada, 2007).

6   The Treasury Board of Canada classifies government employees by tenures of employment. An employee who has been contracted with a fixed end date is classified as having a determinate tenure; an indeterminate employee's tenure has no fixed end date. In simpler terms, an indeterminate employee is a permanent employee of the federal government (see Treasury Board of Canada Secretariat, *Glossary of Terms and Definitions*, v., "indeterminate employee," "type of employment," and "type of tenure," http://www.tbs-sct.gc.ca/pubs_pol/hrpubs/tbm_11a/2-eng.rtf).

7   Repeated efforts to address this issue while the survey was still in administration were not successful.

8   The data were weighted by rank and environment in order to help correct for the demographic differences between the sample of respondents and the target population. The purpose of applying weights to samples is to make the sample more representative of the population of interest. This allows for better generalizations of the results to the target population.

9   Junior non-commissioned members (Jr NCMs) consist of the ranks between private/able seaman and master corporal/master seaman. Senior non-commissioned members (Sr NCMs) consist of the ranks between sergeant/petty officer 2nd class and chief warrant officer/chief petty officer 1st class. Junior officers (Jr Officers) consist of the ranks from officer/naval cadet to captain/lieutenant (Navy). Senior officers (Sr Officers) and above consist of the ranks major/lieutenant commander and higher.

10   The civilian sampling frame included 22,722 civilian employees after excluding 872 civilian employees with no e-mail addresses, three civilian employees with no information about years of service, five civilian employees with "unknown" as their occupation category, and 25 employees with "other" as their occupation category.

11   The civilian sample and the DND population of interest are similar. But the data were weighted by the stratification variables (YOS and occupational category) for the sake of consistency with the methodology used for the military sample and to further correct for demographic differences between the sample of respondents and the target population.

Note also that the means and percentages for the overall CAF and DND samples (meant to represent the total populations of Regular Force CAF and indeterminate DND personnel) are *estimates* of these respective populations; and because they are weighted, they are not direct representations of the mean scores and percentages reported by the survey respondents.

12   The survey instrument was developed using a variety of consultations and reviews. For the newly created scales, a workshop was held with defence scientists in Director General Military Personnel Research and Analysis to help refine the newly proposed items with respect to relevance, item validity, and item clarity. All items/scales were reviewed by a NATO Human Factors and Medicine Research Task Group – NATO HFM RTG-226, focusing on military–civilian personnel work culture and relations in defence organizations, and refined per the feedback of the members from this group of international subject matter experts. Meetings were held with Assistant Deputy Minister Human Resources – Civilian (ADM [HR-Civ]) managers with expertise in related civilian human resource areas, including Director Civilian Labour Relations, Director Diversity and Well-Being, and the manager of stakeholder engagement in Director of Change Management, who provided valuable feedback, and confirmed that the key areas related to civilian personnel working in a military context were covered in the instrument. Finally, a draft survey was submitted for review to the DND/CAF Social Science Research Review Board, and it was refined based on the feedback received from the board. Of note, two versions of the survey were developed—one for military personnel and one for civilian personnel. The versions are very similar, but are adapted for use with each of these two populations (i.e., terms military and civilian used as necessary; a small proportion of unique items in each version as applicable to each population). The items and measures used are described in detail in Goldenberg, *The Defence Team Survey*.

13   Throughout this chapter, where agreement is reported, respondents indicated *slightly agree* to *strongly agree*.

14   "Civilian employees are an important component to the success of the CAF mission," $SE = 0.5\%$ and 1.6% for civilian and military personnel, respectively. "Civilian employees are a necessary component to the success of the CAF mission," $SE = 0.6\%$ and 1.8% for civilian and military personnel, respectively.

15   Respondents indicated *slightly agree* to *strongly agree*.

16   Respondents indicated *slightly agree* to *strongly agree*.

17   "Military and civilian members have good communication in my workgroup," $SE = 1.6\%$ for both civilian and military personnel. "Sometimes I feel like military and civilian employees are speaking different languages," $SE = 1.8\%$ and 2.1% for civilian and military personnel, respectively. "Military and civilian personnel feel comfortable expressing different opinions to one another," $SE = 1.6\%$ and 1.9% for civilian and military personnel, respectively. "Military and civilian members communicate effectively with one another," $SE = 1.6\%$ for both civilian and military personnel.

18   Again, agree means respondents indicated *slightly agree* to *strongly agree*.

19   McKee and Williams, *Civilian Well-Being and Retention Project*; Lalonde, Canadian Forces Health Service.

20 "Senior leaders make efforts to promote the military–civilian Defence Team," SE = 1.8% and 1.9% for civilian and military personnel, respectively. "Senior leaders do a good job of promoting the military-civilian Defence Team," SE = 1.8% and 2.0% for civilian and military personnel, respectively. "Senior leaders emphasize the importance of military-civilian employee cooperation," SE = 1.8% and 1.9% for civilian and military personnel, respectively

21 The estimates of standard error are somewhat larger for these questions because responses were based on a relatively small number of respondents, since only 57 military respondents (10%) reported being directly supervised by a civilian supervisor.

22 Affective commitment refers to emotional connection to the organization. And it is the type of commitment most strongly related to other personnel and organizational variables, such as perceived organizational support and retention. It is also the type of commitment most emphasized in the Military Personnel Retention Strategy. See Chief of Military Personnel, *Military Personnel Retention Strategy*, Technical Report 5000-1 (Ottawa, ON: Department of National Defence).

23 The difference between the mean scores of civilian and military personnel on these variables were statistically significant: $t(1,202)$ = -5.18, $p < .001$, η^2 = .01 for job satisfaction; $t(1,266)$ = -2.65, $p <.01$, η^2 = .003 for engagement; $t(1,806)$ = -7.05, $p < .001$, η^2 = .01 for competence, $t(1,804)$ = 2.28, $p < .05$, η^2 = .002 for affective commitment. However, the effect sizes were extremely small and, therefore, these differences are interpreted as not meaningful.

24 "I intend to leave DND/CAF as soon as another job becomes available," SE = 1.3% and 1.9% for civilian and military personnel, respectively. "I intend to leave DND/CAF within the next two years," SE = 1.5% and 1.9% for civilian and military personnel, respectively. "I intend to stay with DND/CAF as long as I can," SE = 1.3% and 1.8% for civilian and military personnel, respectively.

25 J. Cohen, *Statistical Power Analysis for the Behavioral Sciences*, 2nd ed. (Hillsdale, NJ: Lawrence Earlbaum Associates, 1988).

26 "Effects of working in a military context" was not assessed for military personnel because, by definition, military personnel are assumed to work in a military context.

27 Of note, these findings are correlational, meaning that the variables are related. This does not necessarily imply that these relations are causal in nature.

28 See Chief of Military Personnel, *Military Personnel Retention Strategy*, retrieved from http://www.forces.gc.ca/en/about-org-structure/assistant-deputy-minister-human-resources-civilian.page. Modified July 24, 2013.

29 For example, all new and existing civilian managers and supervisors of military personnel are mandated to take the Managing Military Personnel course which aims to help civilian managers and supervisors understand environmental factors pertaining to the management of military personnel, the roles and responsibilities and issues related to chain of command, the management implications of the CAF career management cycle and procedures, as well as military terminology (Vice Chief of Defence Staff, 2010,

CANFORGEN 030/10 HR-CIV 09/001 211322Z). Similarly, the Managing Civilian Human Resources course is mandatory for all newly appointed military and civilian managers and supervisors of civilian DND employees and aims to familiarize these managers and supervisors with the range of HR disciplines related to civilians (e.g., classification, labour relations) and to provide clear understanding of manager responsibilities related to the supervision of civilians in DND (Vice Chief of Defence Staff, 2010, CANFORGEN 030/10 HR-CIV 09/001 211322Z). There are also three Defence Administrative Orders and Directives (DAODs) aimed at DND employees and CAF members who act as managers of DND employees provided to facilitate the management of civilians within DND. These include *Civilian Human Resources Management* (DAOD 5005-0), *Governance of Civilian Human Resources Management*, (DAOD 5005-1), and *Delegation of Authorities for Civilian Human Resources Management* (DAOD 5005-2). These resources indicate the DND's/CAF's recognition of the potential complexity of managing civilians in a defence organization. There are also a variety of ways in which senior organizational messages promote the Defence Team as well as the formation of a "super-ordinate" or shared Defence Team identify between military and civilian personnel – see Irina Goldenberg and Farhana Islam, *Theory and Research on Diversity in Work Groups and Organizations: Applications to Military and Civilian Personnel in the Defence Team*, Director General Military Personnel Research and Analysis Technical Memorandum 2013-025 (Ottawa, ON: Defence Research and Development Canada, 2013).

CHAPTER 5

THE IMPACT OF CANADIAN MILITARY CULTURE ON THE DEFENCE TEAM

Allan English

Culture, like the weather, is something everybody talks about but nobody does anything about – to paraphrase Mark Twain. Virtually every Canadian Armed Forces "transformation" in recent times has featured leaders who talked about the need for CAF cultural change. But few leaders have been able to effect lasting change,[1] because military culture and its connection to military effectiveness are not well understood, either inside or outside the CAF. One finds, for example, many stereotypes of Canadian military culture in the media and even scholarly works, ranging from an elite "caste of warriors" with the "status of permanent heroes" to "peacekeepers," who can also help out in natural disasters.[2] Effecting cultural change becomes more complicated when we factor in the civilian cultural dimension in the Defence Team. Civilians and military personnel work closely together in Canada's defence establishment, both in headquarters situations and even in the field, as our recent Afghanistan experience has shown, and these cultural differences have the potential to "cause misunderstandings and possible tensions between these two groups, which can affect the quality of working relations, and ultimately, organizational effectiveness."[3]

There are undoubtedly cultural differences between CAF personnel and civilians in the Department of National Defence, which will impact attempts at cultural change. But there are also important cultural similarities between CAF and DND personnel, which are often overlooked. And since both organizations are intended to work collaboratively to protect Canada and its interests, it is essential to examine these cultural similarities to understand cultural change inside National Defence.[4] Moreover, a look at the similarities between the military and civilian cultures may shed some light on the military culture itself. Accordingly, this chapter focuses on how those cultural similarities might lead to a better understanding of effective performance in the complex military-civilian cultural environment. I argue that an understanding of Canadian military culture in the post-Afghanistan era can provide civilian and military members of the Defence Team some insight into how to overcome cultural barriers and how to exploit cultural similarities to work more effectively together.

WHAT IS CULTURE?

Culture is complex, and approaches to it vary across disciplines and even within disciplines. For the purposes of this chapter, the term *culture* will be used as it often is in organizational behaviour literature, namely, as "the values, attitudes and beliefs which provide people with a common way of interpreting events." Based on this definition, the CAF and DND can be seen as social units where people "create systems of meanings that influence behaviour and develop routines and practices recognized as a distinct way of organizational life." An organizational culture in each unit then becomes "a learned way of coping with the challenges" faced by the organization, which also provides its members with "a common framework of reference and interpretation" enabling "them to deal with internal and external challenges." Since no organizational culture exists in isolation, but is always part of other cultures (e.g., national, regional, and functional), a culture is always in flux, responding to different and sometimes conflicting pressures. This dynamic can explain some of the seemingly irrational aspects of group and organizational behaviour.[5]

Early studies in organizational behaviour assumed that organizations were "rational agents for co-ordinating and controlling a group of people" and that culture served chiefly as a control mechanism. Since the mid-1980s, however, it has been recognized that organizations do not always act rationally and that culture often influences organizational behaviour in unpredictable ways. In this new model, organizational culture serves four basic functions: (1) it provides a sense of identity to members of the organization and, ideally, it increases their commitment to the organization; (2) it helps members interpret and make sense of organizational events; (3) it reinforces values in the organization; and (4) it serves as a control mechanism, providing norms that guide and shape behaviour.[6]

In order to fulfil these functions in new situations, organizations must be capable of modifying their cultures to adapt to new challenges. Changing an organization's culture can be difficult, however, because assumptions – the deepest level of culture – are unconscious, and it also means that they are frequently "nonconfrontable and nondebatable." Moreover, culture is often deeply ingrained, and the behavioural norms that manifest the culture are well learned; therefore, members must unlearn the old norms before they can learn new ones. As a result, cultures generally change slowly, with change usually measured over years and decades.[7]

The insights on culture articulated by Donna Winslow are also useful in analysing the impact of Canadian military culture on the Defence Team. Winslow describes three main approaches to culture in the organizational culture literature: integration, differentiation and fragmentation. The integrationist approach is the most common approach to military culture in the literature. With this approach, organizations like the CAF or DND can be understood as a single culture that can be defined and that includes identifiable values and norms generally shared by all members of the organization. This approach also assumes that change is a linear process and that effective leaders create strong cultures based on collectively shared visions. The CAF and DND have traditionally relied on the integrationist approach when looking at their cultures.

The differentiation approach depicts organizations as composed of many different groups, each with its own sub-culture. Cultural change, with this approach, can result from a struggle among groups as they try to place their representatives in key positions in an organization to influence the direction of change. However, the presence of multiple cultures in an organization means that strategies for planned change may have to consider multiple and interdependent changes within and between culturally heterogeneous groups. The fundamental principle here is that change in an organization is negotiated among groups, not directed by leaders from above.

The fragmentation approach describes organizations as loose structures of groups whose memberships overlap and whose members may coalesce in different ways with different interests, depending on the issue at hand. For example, on a professional judgement matter, all members of a single profession in the Defence Team may unite around one point of view; on a gender matter, Defence Team members may group by gender; and on matters specific to military versus civilian status, CAF and DND personnel may align with their respective groups. With this approach, therefore, organizational culture is a dynamic system permeated by ambiguity; thus leaders who implement change can invite unintended consequences because of the complicated, ad hoc way that interests coalesce within organizations. From the fragmentation perspective, culture is not a thing to be changed but a form of organizational learning.[8]

Based on Winslow's analysis, I assume that organizational cultures are amalgams of various cultures, sub-cultures and other group influences, which I will deal with here in a preliminary fashion. My focus, then, is on similarities between the CAF and DND sub-cultures and how these contribute to the effectiveness of the whole of the Defence Team – which brings us to the question of the relation between culture and performance.

CULTURE AND PERFORMANCE

The relationship between organizational culture and organizational performance has been the subject of a great deal of study and debate because most leaders assume that their organization's culture has a significant impact on its performance. We can look at this issue in three ways: the strong cultures perspective, the adaptation perspective, or the "fit" perspective. The advantages of a strong culture include predictability, orderliness and consistency, without the need for extensive written rules and regulations – all of which are desirable attributes in a military setting. However, the conformity often found in strong cultures can limit the range of values and styles of behaviour that are acceptable, which can limit the organization's ability to innovate to meet new challenges. Many military leaders believe that strong organizational cultures are the foundation of excellent performance, but research demonstrates only a moderate correlation between strong organizational culture and performance.

Advocates of the fit perspective argue that an organization's culture must complement its strategy, where the operating environment, work requirements and societal expectations are the factors that determine whether a culture fits an organization. The rigid hierarchy found in military headquarters, for example, may be appropriate for a static headquarters context, but may not be appropriate for field units that must react quickly to fluid situations. Either way, the fit perspective appears to explain short-term but not long-term performance in an organization.

A third approach to culture and performance is the adaptation perspective. Its advocates hold that excellent performance is found mainly in organizations whose cultures allow them to adapt easily to change. They argue that an adaptive culture encourages confidence and prudent risk-taking among members and focuses on the changing needs of stakeholders. In an adaptive culture, leaders pay close attention to all their constituencies and initiate change when required. In a non-adaptive culture, leaders are overly cautious and try to protect their interests by behaving insularly, politically and bureaucratically, while eschewing initiatives to deal with change.[9] These theoretical models about how culture is related to performance can help us understand the performance of armed forces in real situations, which will be discussed next.

WHAT IS MILITARY CULTURE?

Understanding military culture is essential to understanding armed forces as organizations, because we know that how armed forces fight is "more a function of their culture than their doctrine," their technology, or anything else for that matter.[10] Many factors shape military culture. One of the most important is the culture of the nation from which the military is drawn. The roles that armed services perform and the physical environment (e.g., land, sea, air) in which they operate also have a significant effect on their cultures. Another important factor is historical experience, or how an armed force has been employed and how its performance has been perceived both externally and internally.

The concept of military culture enables us to examine differences among services (i.e., army, navy, air force) and among units within the same service. These insights can help explain the distinctive approaches that the services, and units within the services, take to military operations, leadership and technology, and why the performance of similar units may be different in roughly the same circumstances. The ethos or "characteristic spirit" of a military is also shaped by culture and has an important influence on behaviour in military organizations.[11] Culture has been described as the "bedrock of military effectiveness" because the "motivations, aspirations, norms and rules of conduct" – what might be called the essence of an armed force – is thought to be intimately connected with its ability to perform.[12]

Culture also has a significant effect on how military organizations judge their own actions and those of others:

> Perceived irrationality is often the reflection of one's cultural values in evaluating the enemy's actions and reactions. An enemy commander is a product of a different society, traditions and culture. Hence, he may make decisions that are considered irrational although they are fully consonant with his own societal values and military culture.[13]

And, when viewed through the lens of a military culture, civilian bureaucrats have sometimes been characterized as an enemy that the CAF needs to "battle." Understanding the evolution of a military's self-conception or vision of itself is therefore essential in understanding its culture and how it will relate to society and to other institutions of government – especially when those institutions are as organizationally integrated with the military as the civilians in DND.[14]

CANADIAN MILITARY CULTURE

Canadian military culture is a complex blend of various sub-cultures, and no description can adequately capture all its nuances. It has undergone significant change since I last wrote in detail about it in 2004.[15] Therefore, this account will focus on some significant changes that have occurred since then, with particular attention to Canadian Army culture for three reasons: (1) it represents the dominant sub-culture in the CAF today, (2) more has been written about Army culture than about the other services' cultures, and (3) it is the one most Canadians conjure up when they envision Canadian military culture.[16]

Peter Kasurak has written extensively on the subject of Canadian Army culture, and his latest work presents a way of interpreting this culture in the long term. He argues that in the modern era two competing visions or self-conceptions of the Army have been used as models to depict its culture. The "traditionalist" model portrays the Army as an inward-looking institution, focused on the "warrior ethos" and on internal matters, such as training, acquiring new equipment, and developing a "fighting spirit." The "modernist" vision advocates an outward-looking Army, one more closely integrated with Canadian society, one based on professional norms formed by education, and one more engaged in developing national security policy.[17]

The traditionalists often draw on Samuel Huntington's model of a "heroic" professional identity, epitomized by a warrior elite living apart from society and imbued with its own sense of values and beliefs. This view has been reinforced in the Canadian Army by the idea – drawn from its British heritage – that character and personal qualities are more important than education in developing leaders, especially the officer corps. In this tradition, the preferred way to develop officers is to take young men with junior matriculation into the Army and "form their characters."[18] Huntington's model of the isolated warrior elite has been criticized for producing the excesses of the Somalia scandal, where members of elite CAF units had developed sub-cultures that did not reflect the norms of Canadian society and that impaired their ability to carry out their assigned mission.[19]

The modernists have relied on Morris Janowitz's theories to support their arguments. They depict armed forces in Western democracies as integral parts of the societies they defend, rather than as separated warrior elites. Modernists have used Janowitz's ideas about the convergence of military and civilian institutions as a way to help militaries cope with demographic, social, legal and political change. Although pointing to potential similarities in culture between the military and civilian worlds, this approach has been criticized for producing a "management culture" in the CAF that favours bureaucratic efficiency over military effectiveness and for encouraging a social engineering of the military that undermines the martial spirit.[20]

Since the Second World War, Kasurak says, there have been sporadic efforts to replace the "traditionalist" with the "modernist" culture in the CAF; however, he concludes that by the 1980s neither the Canadian Army nor the CAF had a "clear view of its own profession."[21] This situation led to a series of tragic events, which mainly involved the Army operating as part of a United Nations peacekeeping mission in Somalia (1992-93), including the murder of a Somali national in CAF custody and other deplorable incidents.[22] In response, the government established the Somalia commission to investigate these events. Its report, published in 1997, set in motion a whole series of reforms aimed at moving the CAF's culture towards a more "modernist" orientation. The Somalia commission's (and subsequent) reports concluded that there was a dearth of both strategic thinking and forward planning in the CAF, and that almost all Canadian military intellectual activity concentrated "either on the practicalities of doctrine, on tactical matters, or on administration."[23] One observer of senior officer education at the Canadian Forces College, Toronto, a centre of the CAF's intellectual activity, put it this way: "[students] operate on 'gut feeling' and past experience; they are not naturally innovative, resist change and prefer the status quo."[24] In light of this, the CAF launched a major effort to modify its culture using its Professional Military Education (PME) system as a key agent of change.[25]

Another outcome of the Somalia reports was the publication in 2003 of *Duty with Honour: The Profession of Arms in Canada*, declared by the Chief of the Defence Staff (CDS) to be "a defining document for Canada's profession of arms."[26] However, Kasurak criticizes it for failing to address adequately crucial issues confronting the profession. He describes it as "strongly modernist in orientation," but notes that it also endorses such "traditionalist" concepts as "warrior's honour," duty to obey lawful orders, and unlimited liability. Nevertheless, in 2011, Kasurak concluded that the "traditionalist, paternal, aristocratic model is finally dead" and that modernism had prevailed in the Canadian Army.[27]

His assertion finds some support in studies based on interviews with Canadian general and flag officers who led overseas operations between 2000 and 2005. One study, for example, found that the CAF may have certain advantages in conducting coalition operations, compared with the U.S. armed forces, because of the CAF's "modernist" culture. These advantages were described as the self-deprecating nature of Canadians; Canada's military culture, which includes bilingualism and multiculturalism; our history of alliance and UN operations; the CAF's focus on operational and command competence, enlightened leadership and management techniques; and the CAF's judicious exploitation of available technology.[28]

THE RISE OF OPERATIONS PRIMACY

However, the traditionalist model had not breathed its last, as the warrior culture re-asserted itself during the tenure of the charismatic General Rick Hillier (CDS from 2005 to 2008), and it appears to be alive and well today.[29] A key goal of Hillier's and his acolytes' transformation initiatives has been to replace the CAF's "management" culture with an "operations primacy" culture.[30] A number of factors converged to help them propel the CAF, and particularly the Army, towards this more "traditionalist" culture. Foremost among them was Canada's nine years of combat operations in Afghanistan (2002-2011), which made a close relationship with the U.S. Army and its strong warrior culture even closer.[31] In addition, massive new equipment purchases impacted on all CAF roles, with the Royal Canadian Air Force, for example, portrayed as a "taxi service" for the Army following the multi-billion dollar purchase of transport aircraft (i.e., C-17 Globemaster IIIs, CC-130 Hercules and CH-147 Chinooks) as opposed to purchasing aircraft with combat capability (e.g., fighters or maritime patrol aircraft).[32] These factors, combined with the increased visibility of the military at sports and other public events and government actions designed to extol the Canadian military and its warrior virtues, have contributed considerably to the culture change seen in many parts of the CAF since 2005.[33]

With the elevation of traditional warrior virtues over a modernist ethos, which was based on scholarly as well as martial skills for senior officers, operational experience was deemed to be more valuable than professional education, reflecting a similar trend in the U.S. military.[34] The effects of this trend were described by a leading U.S. defence commentator:

> Recently, one defense official defended a proposal to shut down temporarily parts of the Army's advanced professional military educational system with the remark, "Some of the experiences they are getting today are better than anything they will get in a classroom....It's not giving up something for nothing. We have a generation of leaders in the Army today that are battle-tested and are much more capable of leading the Army from the actual experience they have."

The stupidity of this last remark is...depressing....It implies that knowing how to maneuver a battalion through an urban fight is the same thing as crafting a strategy for winning a counterinsurgency... some of our most successful commanders ...declare that their master's and PhD degrees in history, or political science, or anthropology, provided some of the best preparation possible for the novel challenges of insurgent warfare.[35]

My own experience teaching senior officer Professional Military Education (PME) at the Canadian Forces College over the past decade reflects the U.S. situation. When the Advanced Military Studies course (for lieutenant-colonels and colonels and their naval equivalents) was discontinued in 2007 after running for almost ten years, I was told by a senior staff officer that its demise was due to the perception that operational experience in Afghanistan and elsewhere had made the course unnecessary. Similarly, in 2009, I was told by a number of students attending the National Security Program (for colonels and brigadier-generals and their naval equivalents) that they did not understand why they had to spend ten months on this advanced PME course when they already possessed valuable operational experience and that they would miss out on other important operational assignments while on course. At the time, I was surprised by how little the CAF's previous efforts to promote the importance of senior officer PME had appeared to accomplish. In retrospect, one can see that this shift in attitudes and beliefs was a direct result of the post-2005 rise of the traditionalist culture in the CAF, where operational experience was valued and rewarded more than educational accomplishments.

As a result of this shift in values, attitudes and beliefs, the term "operations primacy" has become the watchword for the CAF's current transformation agenda. The perception in some quarters is that the CAF's operational effectiveness has been constrained by "bureaucratic shackles."[36] The working assumption here is that operational effectiveness and efficient management are polar opposites and that, since the "bureaucratization" of the military is incompatible with its real role of "fighting," operational effectiveness must be put ahead of bureaucratic efficiency.[37]

POLAR OPPOSITES OR DIFFERENT SIDES OF THE SAME COIN? LEADERSHIP AND MANAGEMENT IN THE CAF AND DND

Another way of looking at operational effectiveness and efficient management is that they are different sides of the same coin of Canadian military culture. For example, CAF leadership doctrine, approved by General Hillier when he was CDS, tells us that because of the complexity of the inter-relationships among command, management, and leadership *functions*, it is often difficult "to disentangle the command, management, and leadership *effects* achieved by individuals in positions of authority." Nevertheless, in military organizations "favourable results tend to be attributed to extraordinary leadership even when they may, in fact, be the result of command or management skills, some combination of all three, or other factors – including luck."[38] Figure 5.1 shows us one way of visualizing the relationships among the concepts of military command, general management, leadership and resource management. In sum, the CAF recognizes that effective leaders must have the ability to command, lead *and* manage.[39]

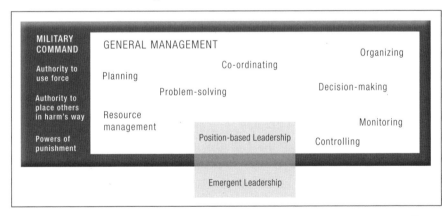

FIGURE 5.1: Inter-relationships of Command, Management and Leadership[40]

The defence management literature has emphasized that armed forces are large bureaucracies that ignore efficiency and managerial skill at their peril. Historians have documented many cases where successful resource management skills have been an essential part of success or failure in large-scale military operations. For example, in order for the Royal Air Force's Bomber Command to meet its expansion goals, its commander, Air Marshal Arthur "Bomber" Harris, decided to withdraw aircrews and aircraft from operations to build up his training organization, so that in 1943 more of his 5,300 medium and heavy bombers were being used for training than for operations against the enemy. Conversely, his opponents in the German Luftwaffe followed a rigorous but ruinous "operations primacy" policy, starving training units of resources. The result was that even though German fighter production reached an all time high in July 1944, there were not enough pilots to fly the new aircraft and, unable to replace its aircrew losses, the Luftwaffe disintegrated as a fighting force.[41] In the Canadian context today, commanding a large air base involves "managing a couple of thousand people, budgets of hundreds of millions of dollars, community relations, politics at the local level, equipment, maintenance, everything," according to a former Chief of the Air Staff.[42]

Furthermore, one of the leading experts on the "operational art," writing on what has become the epitome of CAF warrior culture among senior officers today, reminds us that "the mundane business" of logistics and other management-related activities lies at the heart of the operational art.[43] An American expert on the subject stated that "operational planning is about 90 percent logistics planning."[44] Thus, if we recognize that effective management skills are an essential component of the military profession, then civilian and military members of the Defence Team may have more in common than is usually acknowledged.

And yet defence management is different from civilian management for a number of reasons. David Detomasi tells us that most civilian management models depend on more "strategic clarity" than is normally present in the "persistent, incurable uncertainty" of the military strategic environment, where surprise may be the chief characteristic of defence management.[45] He suggests, therefore, that traditional civilian management techniques must be modified to be effective in a defence setting. He argues, for example, that efficiency should be re-defined as a "prudent reserve of resources and flexible management procedures in the hands of adroit professionals."[46] If this is the case, then an important role for civilian members of the Defence Team could be to act as a bridge between the CAF's military culture and civilian cultures in other parts of government and in society. Yet this may not seem likely in an era where the CAF is dominated by a warrior culture and where management skills are often disparaged. But CAF culture may already be changing.

CHAPTER 5

A NEW "DECADE OF DARKNESS" AND THE RESURGENCE OF MANAGEMENT?

Canadian Armed Forces culture will continue to be influenced by long-term factors that have had an impact on it since at least the beginning of the Cold War; for example, a Canadian national culture that – rightly or wrongly – still portrays members of the CAF as peacekeepers instead of warriors; a Canadian historical experience that calls into question costly foreign wars when no major threat to Canada exists; and government policies that recognize that the first priority of Canada's armed forces should be in helping ensure Canada's sovereignty, not only from potential enemies, but also from powerful neighbours (the so-called defence from help imperative in Canadian security and defence policy).[47]

However, the greatest impact on CAF culture in the short term may come from major changes to CAF roles and from economic circumstances. As an era of high-intensity overseas combat operations ends, new CAF domestic sovereignty roles and government deficits may cause DND culture to resemble one from its recent past – the so-called Decade of Darkness. This was a time in the 1990s when the CAF's reputation was at a historic low, as defence retrenchment and cuts to the CAF at the end of the Cold War were exacerbated by public perceptions of wrongdoing in the Somalia mission and by widespread distrust in the senior leadership of the CAF.[48] This decade has been described as a time when DND "focused on efficiency" not "effectiveness,"[49] based on a "management and bureaucratic way of thinking" that was "inherited from the changes that took place in the 1960s and 1970s."[50]

A new decade of darkness may be imminent, as ominous economic predictions have prompted reduced funding to all government programs, especially to defence – the government's largest discretionary expenditure.[51] Furthermore, recent procurement fiascos due to a hollowed out DND project management capability recall the era of the 1960s and 1970s when "massive cost overruns" in major defence capital projects made it "clear that the higher organization" of defence "in Canada was in disarray."[52] This view may be shared by the government today, because it has revealed plans to take away many of DND's major procurement responsibilities and give them to other government agencies if DND cannot get its project management and procurement house in order.[53] In this same vein, media reports have suggested that the Prime Minister recently appointed General Tom Lawson as CDS (from among other contenders) because he wanted a CDS who could manage major new procurements while cutting the defence budget, and that it was Lawson's "manager's skills – as an administrator and communicator – that won him the top job."[54] As we potentially enter a new decade of darkness, therefore, it may be that efficient management will regain its lustre in DND and the CAF.

IMPLICATIONS FOR THE DEFENCE TEAM

I have argued that military culture changes over time, and that these changes have important implications for the effectiveness of the Defence Team. Historically, we can see two major ways of conceptualizing the CAF's influential, and recently dominant, Canadian Army culture: the traditionalist model that depicts a more inward-looking culture emphasizing the warrior ethos and fighting spirit, and the modernist model that depicts a more outward-looking culture based on professional norms, including efficient management practices that are more congruent with those of Canadian civil society.

Instead of being polar opposites, as they are often presented, I see these outlooks as two essential aspects of Canadian military culture – as different sides of the same coin. The warrior spirit will always be a critical part of an organization whose primary purpose is "the ordered, lawful application of force," as directed by the Government of Canada.[55] If it is to be able to carry out this mission effectively, however, the CAF must rely on the Defence Team's skills to manage a large and complex bureaucracy that functions within a larger government bureaucracy and within Canadian society. The key to military effectiveness, therefore, is to strike a balance between these two essential aspects of CAF culture.

It has been suggested here that military and civilian members of the Defence Team may have more in common than is often acknowledged. Defence management is a unique discipline with its own imperatives, requirements, and, therefore, necessary skills. As the threat of a new decade of darkness looms for the CAF, these skills may become increasingly important for managing large equipment procurement programs during an era of diminishing resources. While there will always be differences between military and civilian cultures, with an understanding of Canadian military culture, all members of the Defence Team may find it easier to bridge existing cultural gaps and, thereby, make the CAF and DND a more effective defence organization.

ENDNOTES

1   Daniel Gosselin, "Navigating the Perfect Wave: The Canadian Military Facing its Most Significant Change in 50 Years," *Canadian Military Journal* 8, no. 4 (Winter 2007-2008): 83; Michael Rostek, "A Framework for Fundamental Change? The Management Command and Control Re-Engineering Initiative," *Canadian Military Journal* 5, no. 4 (Winter 2004-2005): 65-72; and Allan English, "Outside Canadian Forces Transformation Looking In," *Canadian Military Journal* 11, no. 2 (2011): 12-20.

2   See, for example, Ian McKay and Jamie Swift, *Warrior Nation* (Toronto: Between the Lines, 2012), 205; and Murray Brewster, "Troops Best as Peacekeepers, Canadians Say," *Globe and Mail*, September 5, 2008, retrieved from http://www.theglobeandmail.com/news/national/troops-best-as-peacekeepers-canadians-say/article1060912/

3   Prospectus for "The Defence Team: Military and Civilian Partnership in the Canadian Forces and Department of National Defence" sent to author June 18, 2012.

4   Department of National Defence, "What is the Relationship between DND and the Canadian Forces?" National Defence and the Canadian Forces, retrieved from http://www.forces.gc.ca/site/about-notresujet/index-eng.asp

5   Allan English, *Understanding Military Culture: A Canadian Perspective* (Montreal & Kingston: McGill-Queen's University Press, 2004), 15.

6   English, *Understanding Military Culture*, 16.

7   English, *Understanding Military Culture*, 23.

8   Winslow's concepts are described in detail in D. J. Winslow, "Canadian Society and its Army," in *Towards a Brave New World: Canada's Army in the 21st Century*, eds. Bernd Horn and Peter Gizewski (Kingston, ON: Directorate of Land Strategic Concepts, 2003), 1-22, and summarized in Winslow, "Canadian Society and its Army," *Canadian Military Journal* 4, no. 4 (Winter 2003-04): 11-24. This section is based on the two previous works and an application of Winslow's concepts to Canadian Air Force culture in Allan English and John Westrop, *Canadian Air Force Leadership and Command: The Human Dimension of Expeditionary Air Force Operations* (Trenton, ON: CF Aerospace Warfare Centre, 2007), 156-60.

9   English, *Understanding Military Culture*, 30.

10   Paul Johnston, "Doctrine is not Enough: The Effect of Doctrine on the Behavior of Armies," *Parameters* 30, no. 3 (Autumn 2000): 30, 35.

11   English, *Understanding Military Culture*, 5-6.

12   Walter F. Ulmer, Jr. et al., *American Military Culture in the Twenty-First Century* (Washington, DC: Center for Strategic and International Studies Press, 2000), xv.

13   Milan Vego, "Science vs. the Art of War," *Joint Force Quarterly* 66 (3rd Quarter 2012): 69.

14   Peter Worthington, "Canadian Military Needs a Battle on Bureaucracy," *Huffington Post* (October 10, 2011), retrieved from http://www.huffingtonpost.ca/peter-worthington/canadian-military_b_1003309.html

15   English, *Understanding Military Culture*, 87-151.

16   English, "Outside the Canadian Forces Transformation Looking In," 13-16. McKay and Swift, in their recent book *Warrior Nation* criticizing the new "warrior culture" in the CAF, use examples taken almost entirely from an Army context, and, when an Air Force officer was appointed CDS recently, he was referred to as "Canada's new top soldier," Janyce McGregor, "Five Issues Facing Canada's New Top Soldier," CBC News (August 28, 2012), retrieved from http://www.cbc.ca/news/canada/story/2012/08/27/pol-lawson-list-new-cds.html

17   Peter Kasurak, "Concepts of Professionalism in the Canadian Army, 1946-2000: Regimentalism, Reaction, and Reform," *Armed Forces & Society* 37, no. 1 (2011): 96.

18   Peter Kasurak, "Concepts of Professionalism in the Canadian Army," 98, 112-13.

19   See, for example, Donna Winslow, "Misplaced Loyalties: The Role of Military Culture in the Breakdown of Discipline in Peace Operations," *Canadian Review of Sociology and Anthropology* 35, no. 3 (August 1998): 346-65.

20   Kasurak, "Concepts of Professionalism in the Canadian Army," 97, 107-8, 110.

21   Ibid., 108.

22   See, for example, David Bercuson, *Significant Incident: Canada's Army, the Airborne, and the Murder in Somalia* (Toronto: McClelland and Stewart, 1996); and Peter Desbarats, *Somali Cover-up: A Commissioner's Journal* (Toronto: McClelland & Stewart, 1997).

23   Ronald G. Haycock, "The Labours of Athena and the Muses: Historical and Contemporary Aspects of Canadian Military Education," *Canadian Military Journal* 2, no. 2 (Summer 2001): 8.

24   Colonel Howie Marsh, cited in Haycock, "The Labours of Athena and the Muses," 21 n.63.

25   See Haycock, "The Labours of Athena and the Muses," 5-22 for a summary of the changes to CAF PME that occurred at this time.

26   Canadian Armed Forces, Chief of the Defence Staff, *Duty with Honour: The Profession of Arms in Canada* (Kingston, ON: Canadian Forces Leadership Institute, 2003), 1.

27   Kasurak, "Concepts of Professionalism in the Canadian Army," 112-4.

28   G. E. (Joe) Sharpe and Allan English, *Network Enabled Operations: The Experiences of Senior Canadian Commanders*, Defence Research and Development Canada Contract Report 2006-112 (Toronto, ON: Defence Research and Development Canada, 2006), available at http://cradpdf.drdc.gc.ca/PDFS/unc54/p526467.pdf. See also English, et al., *Networked Operations and Transformation* (Montreal & Kingston: McGill-Queen's University Press, 2007), 56.

29   Department of National Defence, "Report on Transformation 2011," 2, 47, 59, retrieved from   http://www.forces.gc.ca/site/reports-rapports/transfo2011/index-eng.asp. This document is often referred to as the "Leslie Report" after its primary author, Lieutenant-General Andrew Leslie.

30   Gosselin, "Navigating the Perfect Wave," 84.

31   Gosselin, "Navigating the Perfect Wave," 86, and Matthew Fisher, "After 9 Years, Canada Ends Combat Operations in Afghanistan," *Vancouver Sun* (July 7, 2011), retrieved from http://www.vancouversun.com/news/After+years+Canada+ends+combat+operations +Afghanistan/5067324/story.html

32   Scot Robertson, "What Direction? The Future of Aerospace Power and the Canadian Air Force – Part 1," *Canadian Military Journal* 8, no. 4 (Winter 2007-2008): 5-13.

33   Michael Valpy, "Canada's Military: Invisible no More," *Globe and Mail* (November 20, 2009), retrieved from http://www.theglobeandmail.com/news/politics/canadas-military-invisible-no-more/article4215847/?page=all; Joe Friesen, "Ottawa Pumps up Military Role in Citizenship Ceremonies," *Globe and Mail* (June 30, 2011), retrieved from http:// www.theglobeandmail.com/news/politics/ottawa-pumps-up-military-role-in-citizenship-ceremonies/article586789/; and McKay and Swift, *Warrior Nation*, 14-5.

34   Kasurak, "Concepts of Professionalism in the Canadian Army," 112.

35   Eliot A. Cohen, "Neither Fools nor Cowards," *The Wall Street Journal* (May 13, 2005), A12.

36   Gosselin, "Navigating the Perfect Wave," 86.

37   Michael K. Jeffery, *Inside Canadian Forces Transformation* (Kingston, ON: Canadian Defence Academy Press, 2009), 42, 46, 92, 113, 118, 125-6. Note also that a recent CAF recruiting campaign featured the slogan: "Fight Fear. Fight Distress. Fight Chaos. Fight with the Canadian Forces," mentioned in McKay and Swift, *Warrior Nation*, 249.

38   Department of National Defence, Canadian Forces Leadership Institute, *Leadership in the Canadian Forces: Conceptual Foundations*, National Defence ID number: A-PA-005-000/AP-004 (Kingston, ON: Canadian Defence Academy, 2005), 10 [emphasis in original].

39   Department of National Defence, *Leadership in the Canadian Forces*, 13.

40   Department of National Defence, *Leadership in the Canadian Forces*, 11, Figure 1-4.

41   Great Britain, Air Ministry, *Flying Training, Vol. 1 Policy and Planning – Air Publication 3233* (London: HMSO, 1952), 199; and Williamson Murray, *Strategy for Defeat: The Luftwaffe 1933-45* (Secaucus, NJ: Chartwell Books, 1986), 274-5, 277-8, 302, 312. For a detailed discussion of these issues in a Canadian context, see Allan English, *The Cream of the Crop: Canadian Aircrew 1939-1945* (McGill-Queen's University Press, 1996), chapters 1, 2, 3, 6, 7.

42   Campbell Clark, "Canada's New Top Soldier 'Somebody Who Knows How to Play Ball,'" *Globe and Mail* (August 27, 2012), retrieved from http://www.theglobeandmail.com/news/politics/canadas-new-top-soldier-somebody-who-knows-how-to-play-ball/article4504183/.

43   John English, "The Operational Art: Developments in the Theories of War," in *The Operational Art: Developments in the Theories of War*, eds. B. J. C. McKercher and Michael A. Hennessy (Westport, CT: Praeger, 1996), 19.

44   David Schrady cited in Allan English, "The Operational Art," in *The Operational Art – Canadian Perspectives: Context and Concepts*, eds. Allan English, et al. (Kingston, ON: Canadian Defence Academy Press, 2005), 48.

45   David Detomasi, "The New Public Management and Defense Departments: The Case of Canada," *Defense & Security Analysis* 18, no. 1 (2002): 51-73.

46   Detomasi, "The New Public Management and Defense Departments," 68-70.

47   See, for example, Douglas Bland, "The Afghan Mission has Taught our Politicians a Lesson," *Globe and Mail* (Nov 27, 2008), retrieved from http://www.theglobeandmail.com/commentary/the-afghan-mission-has-taught-our-politicians-a-lesson/article794675/. Douglas Bland, "Response to Colin Robertson," *3Ds Blog* (Oct 25, 2010), retrieved from http://www.cdfai.org/the3dsblog/?m=201010; Rob Huebert, "Canadian Arctic Maritime Security: The Return to Canada's Third Ocean," *Canadian Military Journal* 8, no. 2 (Summer 2007): 9-16; and Murray Brewster, "Federal Officials Fret over Army 'War Fighting' Training in Arctic," *Ottawa Citizen* (August 23, 2012), retrieved from http://www.ottawacitizen.com/story_print.html?id=7135735&sponsor=

48   G. E. (Joe) Sharpe and Allan English, "The Decade of Darkness – The Experience of the Senior Leadership of the Canadian Forces in the 1990s" (paper written for the Canadian Forces Leadership Institute, February 24, 2004). The expression "Decade of Darkness" was popularized by General Rick Hillier when he was CDS, but it was actually coined by Lieutenant-General (Retired) Al DeQuetteville in an interview in 2003 with Joe Sharpe.

49   Jeffery, *Inside Canadian Forces Transformation*, 7.

50   Gosselin, "Navigating the Perfect Wave," 84.

51   David Pugliese, "Defence Department Bureaucrats Have Gone 'Rogue' Says Opposition, Auditor General Fights Back Against DND Claims," *Ottawa Citizen* (May 15,

2012), retrieved from http://blogs.ottawacitizen.com/2012/05/15/defence-department-bureaucracts-have-gone-rogue-says-opposition-auditor-general-fights-back-against-dnd-claims/; and Murray Brewster, "DND Cuts Account for One-fifth of Federal Budget Cuts over Next Three Years," *Winnipeg Free Press* (March 29, 2012), retrieved from http://www.winnipegfreepress.com/fpnewstopstory/dnd-cuts-account-for-one-fifth-of-federal-budget-cuts-over-next-three-years-144956585.html

52   Quotation from Kasurak, "Concepts of Professionalism in the Canadian Army," 100; Jeffrey Simpson, "Defence Spending is a Blur of Mismanagement," *Globe and Mail* (July 21, 2012), retrieved from http://www.theglobeandmail.com/commentary/defence-spending-is-a-blur-of-mismanagement/article4431739/; and Janet Thorsteinson, "All Hands on Deck: So Who is Building New Ships?" *Canadian Naval Review* 5, no. 2 (Summer 2009): 28-9.

53   Steven Chase, "Ottawa Eyes Plan to Loosen DND's Grip on Military Procurement," *Globe and Mail* (July 19, 2012) at http://m.theglobeandmail.com/news/politics/ottawa-eyes-plan-to-loosen-dnds-grip-on-military-procurement/article4426707/?service=mobile

54   Clark, "Canada's New Top Soldier 'Somebody Who Knows How to Play Ball.'"

55   Department of National Defence, *Duty with Honour*, 4.

CHAPTER 6

CULTURAL INTELLIGENCE, LEADERSHIP AND PROFESSIONAL IDENTITY

Karen D. Davis

Military and defence analysts have come to recognize that operational success depends on developing military leaders' cultural competence – or, in other words, their cultural intelligence (CQ). Military leaders always operate in culturally complex environments, whether aiding domestic civilian operations, developing whole-of-government strategies for international missions, influencing local civilians to cooperate with security efforts, or conducting combat operations within joint, interagency, multi-national, and public peace support contexts. As a result, military leaders must be able to adapt to the complex multicultural dynamics of both belligerents and allies, who represent the interests of military and civilian organizations, networks, and communities. In achieving the defence mission, military and civilian members must also collaborate and work effectively within the defence establishment.

This chapter explains what CQ is, why it is an important part of leader development, and how CQ can be used to further mutual understanding and cooperation on the Defence Team. The first section of the chapter introduces CQ, with an emphasis on its multi-dimensional character and the relationships among its various dimensions. In the second part of this chapter, I argue that the dimensions and attributes of the Canadian Forces Leadership Institute's (CFLI) Leadership Development Framework (LDF) mirror many dimensions and attributes of CQ as a meta-competency; thus, CQ can be understood as an extension of the LDF. In the third section, I discuss how CQ can provide insight into the workings of the Defence Team. Professional identities, which are closely aligned with those values, beliefs, and taken-for-granted assumptions that reflect organizational cultures,[1] are an important aspect of this discussion. I argue that the values and ethics common to the professional identities of civilian Department of National Defence employees and Canadian Armed Forces members can bridge the collaborative gaps in the Defence Team and, ultimately, I suggest that the CQ model developed here can function as a guide for both military and civilian leaders as they develop strategies for working together effectively – and not only across the civilian-military divide on the Defence Team, but also across the ethnocultural and national communities that the Defence Team must navigate to fulfil the defence mandate.

WHAT IS CULTURAL INTELLIGENCE?

The study of cognitive processes and how they are shaped by the cultures of institutions is not new. In 1967, for example, sociologists Peter Berger and Thomas Luckmann called attention "to the processes by which individuals, in interaction, create definitions of social reality: first inventing distinctions or 'typifications,' then treating these productions as something objective and external to their own actions."[2] Sorting groups of people into categories, for example, is a natural way to make sense of their differences and similarities. But CQ goes beyond cognitive processes. It is rooted in theories of intelligence and cultural competence and grew out of the work of cultural psychologist Harry Triandis, who looked at relationships among environment, social environment, values, and psychological processes.[3] Thus CQ seeks to understand the ways in which all actors – including oneself and one's professional and cultural values and identity – operate dynamically with the culture and values of others. In other words, CQ is about self-awareness and understanding how both the perceiver and perceived are together shaping perceptions and thus the interactions between them.

In light of the dynamic nature of culture and cultural understanding, researchers have conceived of CQ[4] as a meta-competency: having it means possessing the competencies, attributes, and skills that enable an individual to interact, to adapt, and to make effective decisions in unfamiliar and complex cultural environments. As illustrated in Figure 6.1A, the CQ model is multi-dimensional, focusing on relationships among cognitive and meta-cognitive factors, behavioural and motivational dimensions,[5] attitudes, skills, and knowledge[6] (or knowledge, mindfulness, and skills).[7] The CFLI used the relationships illustrated in Figure 6.1A to expose the links between CQ competencies and to explore how CAF leaders could develop and apply them.[8] Figure 6.1B shows the five dimensions of CQ: Knowledge, Cognition, Motivation, Behaviour, and Mindfulness. The dimensions (and their attributes) presented in Figure 6.1B will form the basis for a comparison between the CQ dimensions and the dimensions of the CAF Leadership Development Framework later in the chapter. I note for the sake of clarity that the distinction between Knowledge and Cognition follows that of Christopher Early and Soon Ang:[9] Knowledge refers to *what* one knows about a particular culture and Cognition refers to *how* one thinks and learns about a culture.

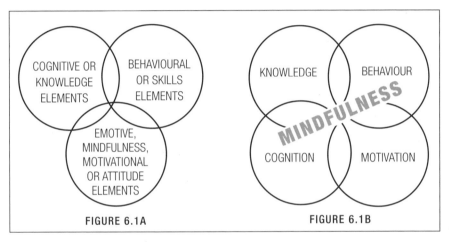

FIGURE 6.1A   FIGURE 6.1B

FIGURE 6.1: Cultural Intelligence, a Multi-Dimensional Meta-Competency[10]

The Motivation dimension of CQ comprises both intrinsic motivation – i.e., the extent to which an individual derives satisfaction from culturally diverse experiences – and extrinsic motivation – i.e., the tangible benefits that can be gained by becoming competent in culturally diverse situations.[11] Openness to learning and goal setting are important variables in this dimension. In general, a motivated individual would be someone who strives for self-awareness and self-development to enhance his or her effectiveness in different cultural situations. In a profile of an inter-culturally effective person developed for the Canadian Foreign Service Institute Centre for Intercultural Learning (CFSI CIL), Vulpe et al. identified personal and professional commitment as one of nine major competencies.[12] Motivation also encompasses, for example, the extent to which CAF members understand the significance of cultural influences and commit to a strategy to better understand the values, priorities, and roles of public servants in DND (and vice versa).

The Cognition dimension focuses on how one thinks about thinking and how one gains new cultural knowledge, recognizing that different strategies might be required to learn about and to adapt within different cultures.[13] Triandis points out, for example, that members of different cultures sample and weigh information from other cultures in different ways.[14] The cognitive scripts that guide our behaviour are informed by these cultural values, which are internalized from the surrounding culture. Our internalized cognitive scripts shape our social perception – that is, how we interpret events and their causes in the world around us. On this model, the different socialization experiences of military and civilian personnel – reinforced by their different functions within DND and the CAF – will shape how these two groups understand each other.

The Knowledge domain focuses on what one knows about culture, including the concept of culture and how it influences people and societies.[15] In an organizational context, both low and high visibility cultural aspects are important. In the military, for example, distinctions between army, navy and air force and those between ranks are very visible, though the meaning and significance of these visible indicators is not readily apparent. It is equally important for the interpreter of culture to understand his or her own basic assumptions and "givens," which influence how things get done and how things are interpreted within his or her organization. An organization's espoused and practised values, its status hierarchy (and how decisions are made), its history, and the demographic characteristics of its members are important sources of information about how an interpreter understands others and their motivations.[16] In the case of the Defence Team, increasing each side's knowledge of the other's culture (e.g., in recognizing stereotypes) can only be beneficial, given the degree of integration between military and civilian workforces. Such knowledge would include military professional ideology, the roles of civilians in the development of defence policy, and civil-military relations more generally.[17]

The Behaviour (or Skills) dimension of CQ represents the integration of Motivation, Cognition, Knowledge and Mindfulness. Each of these dimensions influences the ability to adapt one's behaviour to the cultural context. Behaviour includes everything said and done in an unfamiliar cultural environment. It can involve speaking another language, expressing interest in understanding another language by using a few key words, conveying respect for the concerns and perspectives of another organization or culture, and adjusting body language to the situation. The Behaviour dimension also encompasses the skills identified by Vulpe et al., such as relationship building, intercultural communication, and organizational skills.[18] Given that 64% of civilian personnel work within a military structure and 2,000 military personnel perform departmental functions, and given the regular interactions between military and civilian personnel, it is clear that military and civilian personnel need the behavioural skills to work effectively as a team and to build and maintain optimal relationships with one another.

Mindfulness, according to David Thomas, is a key component linking the cognitive activities in the Knowledge and Behaviour dimensions. Mindfulness has a number of facets: being aware of our own assumptions, ideas, and emotions; noticing what is apparent about others and trying to understand their assumptions; using all the senses to perceive situations; viewing situations from several perspectives (i.e., with an open mind); attending to context to help understand what is happening; creating and revising mental maps of others' personalities and cultural backgrounds in order to respond to them; seeking out fresh information to confirm or disconfirm our mental maps; and being empathetic toward the cultural backgrounds of others.[19] In short, Mindfulness means challenging assumptions, re-framing perspectives, and creating alternative interpretations and analyses of cultural phenomena to discover the unfamiliar and the unknown.

It is important not to lose sight of the whole when looking at the parts. Dividing CQ into its dimensions helps us see the cognitive processes and the knowledge, skills and abilities (KSA) that contribute to CQ. But CQ is a meta-competency that depends on the integration of its five domains. We can see why when we look at the conceptual overlap across the five dimensions of CQ discussed above. The cognitive activities that Thomas characterizes as Mindfulness, for example, are closely related to the Cognition dimension. Similarly, self-awareness contributes to Motivation, but also involves Cognition. Decision making is a cognitive process that is also a Behaviour, which is in turn impacted by Motivation, Cognition and Knowledge. While knowledge of a foreign language, for example, can contribute to cultural knowledge – placing it in the Knowledge dimension – the ability to effectively apply knowledge of a language overlaps with the Behaviour dimension. Because of the overlap between dimensions, the absence of one can considerably weaken CQ competency.

LEADERSHIP AND CULTURAL INTELLIGENCE

Researchers and analysts have recognized the need to develop leaders' cultural knowledge.[20] Various research initiatives have sought to measure cultural competence and cultural knowledge under various conceptions of CQ: global competency,[21] intercultural adjustment,[22] cross-cultural adaptability,[23] ethnocultural empathy,[24] intercultural effectiveness,[25] and intercultural sensitivity.[26] Initiatives such as the Global Leadership and Organizational Behaviour Effectiveness (GLOBE) research program, for example, explore different concepts and practices of leadership across national cultures[27] and across organizational cultures within societies.[28] Yet cultural competence and leadership are often still considered discrete attributes – in other words, CQ is often not seen as an essential attribute of a good leader. In this section, I look at the frameworks that guide the development of leadership in the CAF and the Public Service, and the intersection of the attributes of CQ and the CAF's LDF. I then propose a model of cultural competence that can function as a learning tool for understanding the relationship between leadership development and cultural competence.

In both the CAF and the Public Service, leadership development plays a key role in developing the core capacities of the professions. And in both cases, leadership models are values-based and guided by a core set of leadership competencies that will shape members from initial entry through senior leadership training and executive development. In the CAF, the LDF defines five capacities – expertise, cognitive capacities, social capacities, change capacities, and professional ideology – and sixteen attributes considered the necessary core competencies of effective CAF leadership.[29] As illustrated by the concentric circles in Figure 6.2, professional ideology permeates all aspects of professional development. The military ethos animates the professional ideology with a powerful cultural framework for shaping military professional identity.

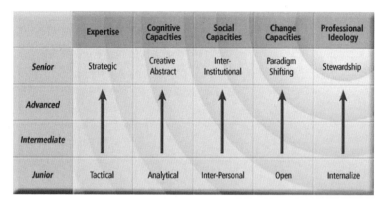

	Expertise	Cognitive Capacities	Social Capacities	Change Capacities	Professional Ideology
Senior	Strategic	Creative Abstract	Inter-Institutional	Paradigm Shifting	Stewardship
Advanced	↑	↑	↑	↑	↑
Intermediate					
Junior	Tactical	Analytical	Inter-Personal	Open	Internalize

FIGURE 6.2: The CAF Leadership Development Framework

The Public Service's Leadership Competencies Profile (Figure 6.3) shares some similarity with the CAF's LDF. The four key leadership competencies in the Public Service model – management excellence, engagement, strategic thinking and values and ethics – encompass effective behaviours applicable to six levels of the leadership-management continuum, from workplace supervisors to deputy ministers of federal departments.[30] For example, all are expected to exemplify professional values and ethics, and to teach and learn from others. Supervisors are expected to manage their work activities with transparency and fairness, while deputy ministers are expected to exert broad influence to develop cultures of respect and fairness across the Public Service.[31] Leadership development across federal government departments is supported by the Canada School of Public Service (CSPS), which provides standardized leadership courses for leaders at all points along the seniority continuum, from the entry level through to the most senior leadership levels.[32] Because this program is applicable to all public servants across government departments, it does not address the defence mission specifically.[33] Nonetheless, some senior public servants from DND and other departments do attend courses with senior military leaders at the Canadian Forces College.

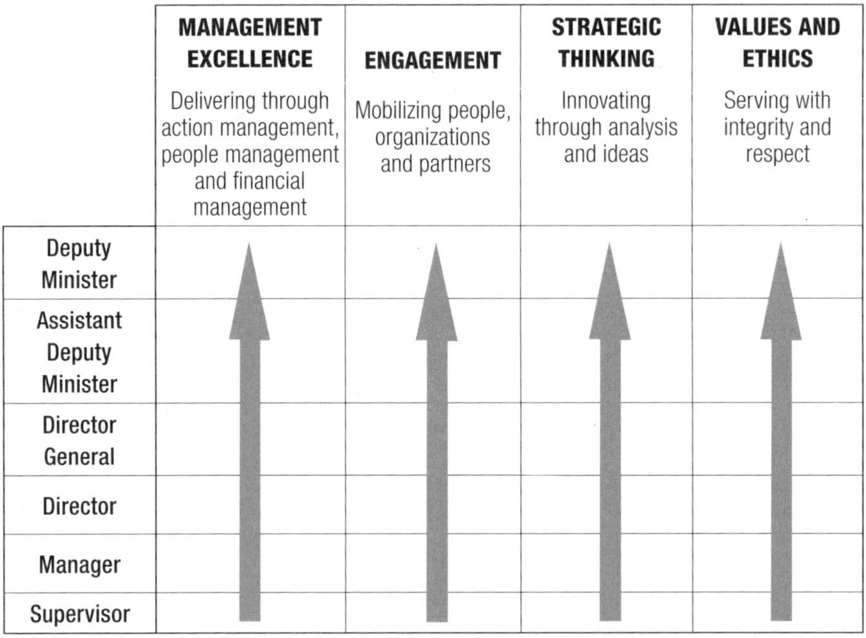

MANAGEMENT EXCELLENCE	ENGAGEMENT	STRATEGIC THINKING	VALUES AND ETHICS
Delivering through action management, people management and financial management	Mobilizing people, organizations and partners	Innovating through analysis and ideas	Serving with integrity and respect
Deputy Minister			
Assistant Deputy Minister			
Director General			
Director			
Manager			
Supervisor			

FIGURE 6.3: Public Service Commission of Canada, Key Leadership Competencies Profile (Adapted from Treasury Board's Key Leadership Competencies).

The defence civilian leadership curriculum, which is organized around the domains in the Public Service's competency profile, is taught through a network of learning and career centres, including the Canadian Forces College.[34] Most of the CSPS's defence-specific content is presented in the management excellence and engagement domains (e.g., Canadian Forces 101 for Civilians, National Defence Manager's Network). The engagement domain also includes two mandatory courses for senior civilian leaders in DND, Executive Orientation to DND and the Executive Leaders Programme. Courses within the strategic thinking domain include two defence-unique courses, one on risk management and the other being the Canadian Security Studies Programme. The Canadian Security Studies course and the Executive Leaders Programme are mandatory for senior leaders in DND. The courses are taught at the Canadian Forces College, and they are attended by both senior civilian managers and senior military personnel (officers and non-commissioned members).

When considering the key dimensions and attributes of leadership, the first major point of contact is the extent to which the competencies and attributes that constitute CQ are reflected within the five capacities and sixteen attributes in the CAF's LDF (and to a significant degree within the Public Service's leadership framework). In simpler terms, the leader attributes in the LDF (see CAF Leadership in Table 6.1) can be understood in the dimensions of the CQ model presented here. Consider, first, that the cognitive capacities required to lead people are much the same as those required for cultural adaptability and effective inter-cultural relations. One needs both analytical abilities to prepare for intercultural encounters and creative abilities to challenge conventional ways of thinking and to create new mental maps of the culture and personalities of cultural outsiders. The social capacities needed for leadership – flexibility, communication, teambuilding, and interpersonal proficiency – are all imperative to CQ and relate to its cognitive and motivational elements.[35] The military ethos and social identity also influence the cognitive domain of CQ.

The second thing to notice is that several attributes have a particular influence on the development of CQ (see the italicized terms in Table 6.1) and position and enhance national defence as a learning organization. These influential attributes include the development of self-awareness through reflection, dialogue and feedback over a lifetime, awareness of the relationship between professional ideology (and the military ethos) and social identity, as well as knowledge and understanding of the influence of culture. Mindfulness is especially important, because one must become aware of the assumptions, emotions and values that shape one's worldview – i.e., awareness of the belief system that informs how members of particular societies and communities make sense of their day-to-day world.[36] This includes an understanding of how one's own worldview contributes to one's perceptions of others and their motivations, and how others perceive oneself and one's organization. These attributes are essential for leaders immersed in diverse groups of personnel with distinct cultures and identities – as is the case on the Defence Team.

	CAF LEADERSHIP	CQ
MOTIVATION (LDF professional ideology and change capacities)	change capacities - self change capacities - group professional ideology - credibility & impact change capacities *learning organization*	*self-awareness* openness goal setting open to learning commitment
COGNITION (LDF professional ideology and cognitive capacities)	professional ideology - moral reasoning cognitive capacities - analytic cognitive capacities - creative professional ideology *internalized military ethos*	*social and professional identity* perceptual acuity flexibility empathy self-actualization sensory perception decision making
KNOWLEDGE (LDF expertise)	specialist/technical military/organizational strategic/institutional	*cultural complexity & influences* culture-specific knowledge culture-specific language
BEHAVIOUR (LDF social capacities)	team building / collaboration communication skills partnering inter-personal flexibility	communication skills culturally appropriate actions relationship building
MINDFULNESS (Relationship to LDF change and cognitive capacities)		*awareness of own assumptions, ideas, emotions* awareness of others using all senses to perceive open mind, viewing from all perspectives create new mental maps; challenge own thinking attentive to context, activity and change within

TABLE 6.1: CAF Leadership and CQ Attributes by Dimensions of CQ[37]

It is also important to note that the attributes and skills highlighted in the Behaviour dimension of CQ are well covered in the CAF LDF. However, the other dimensions of CQ are important for effective cross-cultural adaptability. Culturally appropriate behaviours can be well rehearsed and perfected, but one's CQ ability will determine the extent to which behaviours can be effectively adapted to new situations and unexpected scenarios. Furthermore, Figure 6.4 illustrates that professional identity has an important influence within the cognitive dimension of CQ, which influences and is influenced by the other domains of CQ.

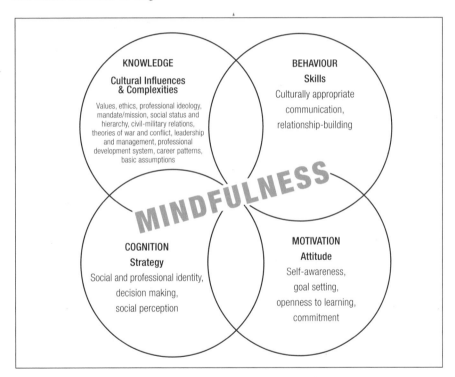

FIGURE 6.4: Cultural Intelligence: Concepts and Relationships[38]

Within the five-dimension CQ meta-competency model, there are numerous relationships among the attributes within each dimension. Many of these attributes (e.g., engagement and building relationships) are essential to leadership and, as such, are embedded within the LDF. However, this discussion suggests that the effectiveness of military leaders can be enhanced by adopting individual and institutional learning and development strategies to integrate cultural competence into leader development. As summarized within the knowledge domain of Figure 6.4, this includes the development of awareness regarding military, Public Service and defence cultures and their relationship to defence policy and implementation on behalf of Canadians. This discussion suggests that CQ is an important tool to guide both military and civilian leaders as they develop strategies for working effectively, not only across ethnocultural, national and inter-organizational communities, but also across the civilian and military domains that contribute to the defence and security of Canada. The following section expands upon the important influence of professional identity within the CQ model and professional ideology within the CAF LDF, as they influence relationships among military and civilian members of the Defence Team.

MILITARY AND CIVILIAN PROFESSIONAL IDENTITIES – CQ FOR THE DEFENCE TEAM

Professional identity develops as an individual appropriates a common body of knowledge, as well as the shared history, social practices, skills and discourses of his or her chosen profession.[39] According to CAF leadership doctrine, the profession of arms involves four professional attributes – i.e., responsibility, expertise, identity and professional ideology[40] – and four core military values – i.e., duty, loyalty, integrity and courage.[41] Even though CAF members are trained and employed in different occupational and professional capacities, all share these values and professional attributes. Military history and doctrine further reinforce the fundamental beliefs and expectations that shape the unique responsibilities of the military and its members, including physical fitness, teamwork, unlimited liability (mission before self), fighting spirit, and a high standard of discipline "generated from an understanding of the demands of combat, a knowledge of comrades and trust in leaders."[42] Training and development shape and reinforce these qualities in CAF members, while a vertical chain of command (made highly visible through uniforms with rank insignia) enforces them. At the top of the chain of command is the Chief of the Defence Staff, who is the head of the profession of arms in Canada.

Professional identity is also influenced by one's national culture or national identity.[43] In this sense, similar cultural values, complemented by motivation to serve Canadians, influence the professional identities of CAF and civilian members of DND. Civilian public servants represent a broad range of occupational and professional expertise; however, as members of the Public Service Commission of Canada, they are expected to adhere to the values and behaviours set out in the *Values and Ethics Code for the Public Service* – including respect for democracy, respect for people, integrity in upholding honesty, fairness and impartiality, stewardship in the use of public resources, and excellence in the design and delivery of public sector policies, programs and services.[44] As noted in *A Strong Foundation: Report of the Task Force on Public Service Values and Ethics*, moreover, the Public Service recognizes that professionalism requires investing in education and experience:

> Some length of time is normally required to gain the knowledge, skills, sensitivities and outlook the profession requires. Some significant portion of life is usually devoted to acquiring the intellectual and moral capital to perform at a high level of professional competence.[45]

Like their counterparts in the CAF, many public servants will spend most of their careers in the Public Service and some will spend most of their careers in DND. At the top of the civilian chains of command are deputy ministers, who are responsible to the professional head of the Public Service, the Clerk of the Privy Council.[46]

Taken together, the professional identities of military leaders in the CAF and those of civilian leaders in DND overlap in many domains. Professional and leadership development in both organizations shapes the organizational cultures and the identities of members to ensure effective behaviours and outcomes.[47] At the same time, however, we cannot ignore the differences between the two cultures and two professional identities. For all the overlap, public servants and CAF members do not share the same professional experience or the same development model, because the Public Service focuses on *management* and the CAF focuses on *leadership*. This key difference in orientation demands that military and public service professionals understand each other's efforts and potential roles,[48] and it requires greater awareness of how the assumptions, beliefs, and behaviours of each component of the Defence Team will impact integrated defence efforts.

This brief overview of identity formation in the Defence Team's military and civilian cultures represents an application of CQ. Given the role of identity in shaping cognitive processes and the central role of values and ethics in the Public Service's and CAF's professional identities, I suggest that professional identity and those attributes that shape it are important for bridging collaborative gaps. Ultimately, I suggest that fostering the cultural competence of CAF and DND leaders is conducive to optimizing relations between military and civilian personnel in a way that appreciates and respects the different cultures and professional identities of these two different groups.

CONCLUSION

Developing leaders who understand how culture influences both themselves and others is important for the CAF and the defence organization as a whole. The cultural values systems we internalize during identity development inform the cognitive processes that underlie our decision making and our moral reasoning. For CAF leaders, the military ethos and the professional military ideology are essential components of their professional development; thus these factors are important contributors to how CAF members perceive and make sense of their world. Similarly, the *Values and Ethics Code for the Public Service* informs the professional orientation and identity of public servants. No doubt, there are important differences between military and civilian professional identities – principally, civilian professionals' management orientation and military professionals' leadership orientation. But my CQ analysis showed that there are also important similarities between the two cultures that can be leveraged by culturally sensitive leaders to optimize working relations on the Defence Team.

ENDNOTES

1   Mats Alvesson, "Organizational Culture: Meaning, Discourse and Identity," in *Handbook of Organizational Culture and Climate*, eds. Neal M. Ashkanasy, Celeste P. M. Wilderom, and Mark F. Petersen (Thousand Oaks, California: Sage, 2011), 11-28.

2   See Peter L. Berger and Thomas Luckmann, Social Construction of Reality (New York: Doubleday, 1967), cited in W. Richard Scott, *Organizations: Rational, Natural, and Open Systems* (Englewood Cliffs, NJ: Prentice Hall, 1992), 136.

3   P. Christopher Earley and Soon Ang, *Cultural Intelligence: Individual Interactions across Cultures* (Stanford, CA: Stanford U. P., 2003).

4   Although CQ does not represent a mathematical relationship of capabilities in the same way as an intelligence quotient (IQ), it is a unique construct of intelligence that reflects adaptation to varying cultural contexts (Earley and Ang, *Cultural Intelligence*, 4).

5   Earley and Ang, *Cultural Intelligence*.

6   James P. Johnson, T. Lenartowicz, and Salvador Apud, "Cross-Cultural Competence in International Business: Toward a Definition and a Model," *Journal of International Business Studies* 37, no. 4 (2006): 525-43.

7   David C. Thomas and Kerr Inkson, *Cultural Intelligence: People Skills for Global Business* (San Francisco: Berrett-Koehler, 2003).

8   Karen D. Davis and J. C. Wright, "Culture and Cultural Intelligence," in *Cultural Intelligence & Leadership: An Introduction for Canadian Forces Leaders*, ed. Karen D. Davis (Kingston, ON: Canadian Defence Academy Press, 2009).

9   Ibid.

10   Kimberley Ann Ford and Karen D. Davis, *Cultural Intelligence, Emotional Intelligence and Canadian Forces Leader Development*, Canadian Forces Leadership Institute Technical Report 2007-01 (Kingston, ON: Canadian Forces Leadership Institute and Defence Research and Development Canada, Centre for Operational Research and Analysis, 2007).

11   David Livermore, *Leading with Cultural Intelligence* (New York: AMACOM, 2010), 26.

12   T. Vulpe, D. Kealey, D. Protheroe, and Doug MacDonald, *A Profile of the Interculturally Effective Person* (Ottawa, ON: Foreign Affairs Canada, Canadian Foreign Service Institute, Centre for Intercultural Learning, 2000). Other competencies described in this volume include adaptation skills; an attitude of modesty and respect; understanding of concept of culture; knowledge of host country and culture; relationship building; self-knowledge; intercultural communication; and organizational skills.

13   As Earley and Ang note: "The importance of role identity for the cognitive facet of CQ cannot be understated. A person's role identities, social hierarchy, and face are strong determinants of how people process the cues relevant for cross-cultural interaction." (*Cultural Intelligence*, 69).

14   Harry Triandis, "Cultural Intelligence in Organisations," *Group & Organization Management* 31, no. 1 (2006): 23.

15   In their CFSI CIL profile, Vulpe et al. also emphasize the importance of understanding the concept of culture as a universal concept, as well as knowledge specific to a "host" country and culture (*A Profile of the Interculturally Effective Person*).

16   See the adaptation of Edgar H. Schein, *Organizational Culture in Leadership* (San Francisco: Jossey-Bass, 1985), 15, in Karen D. Davis and Brian McKee, "Culture in the

Canadian Forces: Issues and Challenges for Institutional Leaders," in *Institutional Leadership in the Canadian Forces: Contemporary Issues*, ed. Robert W. Walker (Kingston, ON: Canadian Defence Academy Press, 2007), 35.

17   Lorne W. Bentley, *Canadian Forces Transformation and the Civilian Public Service Defence Professional*, Canadian Forces Leadership Institute Technical Report 2007-01 (Kingston, ON: Canadian Forces Leadership Institute, 2007), 50.

18   Vulpe et al., *A Profile of the Interculturally Effective Person*.

19   David C. Thomas, "Domain and Development of Cultural Intelligence: The Importance of Mindfulness." *Group and Organisation Management* (2006): 78-99.

20   Kok Yee Ng, R. Ramava, Tony M. S. Teo, and Siok Fun Wong, "Cultural Intelligence: Its Potential for Military Leadership Development" (paper presented at the International Military Testing Association Conference, Singapore, October 2005).

21   R. T. Moran and J. R. Riesenberger, *The Global Challenge: Building the New Worldwide Enterprise* (London: McGraw-Hill, 1994).

22   D. Matsumoto, J. LeRoux, C. Ratzlaff, H. Tatani, C. Kim, and S. Araki, "Development and Validation of a Measure of Intercultural Adjustment Potential in Japanese Sojourners: The Intercultural Adjustment Potential Scale (ICAPS)," *International Journal of Intercultural Relations* 25 (2001): 483-510.

23   C. Kelley and J. E. Meyers, "Cross-Cultural Adaptability Inventory," in *Intercultural Sourcebook: Cross-Cultural Training Methods*, Vol. 2, eds. S. M. Fowler and M. G. Mumford (Yarmouth, ME: Intercultural Press, 1999); and M. Vanderpool, *The Cross Cultural Adaptability Scale: A Comparison of the Psychometric Properties Observed in a Canadian and an Australian Administration* (Ottawa, ON: Director Human Resources Research and Evaluation, National Defence Headquarters, 2002).

24   Y. W. Wang, M. F. Davidson, O. F. Yakushko, H. B. Savoy, J. A. Tan, and J. K. Bleier, "The Scale of Ethnocultural Empathy: Development, Validation, and Reliability," *Journal of Counselling Psychology* 50 (2003): 221-34.

25   M. Walter, N. Bartosh, K. Choonjaroen, and C. H. Dodd, "Scale With E-Model for Intercultural Effectiveness," in *Dynamics of Intercultural Communications*, 5th ed., ed. C. H. Dodd (New York: McGraw-Hill, 1998).

26   D. P. S. Bhawuk and R. Brislin, "The Measurement of Intercultural Sensitivity Using the Concepts of Individualism and Collectivism," *International Journal of Intercultural Relations* 16, no. 4 (1992): 413-6.

27   Robert J. House, "Illustrative Examples of GLOBE Findings," in *Culture, Leadership and Organizations: The GLOBE Study of 62 Societies*, eds. Robert J. House, Paul J. Hanges, Mansour Javidan, Peter W. Dorfman, and Vipin Gupta (Thousand Oaks, CA: Sage, 2004).

28   Marcus W. Dickson, Renee S. BeShears, and Vipin Gupta. "The Impact of Societal Culture and Industry on Organizational Culture," in *Culture, Leadership and Organizations: The GLOBE Study of 62 Societies*, eds. Robert J. House, Paul J. Hanges, Mansour Javidan, Peter W. Dorfman, and Vipin Gupta (Thousand Oaks, CA: Sage, 2004).

29   Robert W. Walker, *The Professional Development Framework: Generating Effectiveness in Canadian Forces Leadership*, Canadian Forces Leadership Institute Technical Report 2006-01 (Kingston, ON: Canadian Forces Leadership Institute, 2006).

30   Treasury Board Secretariat, *Key Leadership Competencies*, Publication No. CP54-10/2006, Canadian Public Service Agency and the Public Service Commission, 2006, rev., 2007.

31   Ibid.

32   These courses include leadership for supervisors and managers; Executive Level (EX) minus 1 and EX minus 2 who aspire to be executives (Direxion); new EX-01s (Management Suite for New EX-01s); experienced EX-01s and equivalent (Living Leadership: The Executive Excellence Program); and EX-02 and EX-03 (ConnEXion: Senior Leaders for Tomorrow); see Canada School of the Public Service, Courses and Programs, retrieved from http://www.csps-efpc.gc.ca/forlearners/coursesandprograms

33   Bentley, *Canadian Forces Transformation*, 46.

34   Department of National Defence, Human Resources–Civilian, Defence Leadership Curriculum, retrieved from http://hrciv-rhciv.mil.ca/en/p-dlc-default.page.

35   Ford and Davis, *Cultural Intelligence, Emotional Intelligence and Canadian Forces Leader Development*.

36   David Jary and Julia Jary, *Collins Dictionary of Sociology* (London, UK: HarperCollins, 2000).

37   Karen D. Davis, *Cultural Intelligence and Military Identity: Implications for Canadian Force Leader Development*, Canadian Forces Leadership Institute Technical Note 2012-01 (Kingston, ON: Canadian Forces Leadership Institute, 2012), 8.

38   Adapted from Davis, *Cultural Intelligence and Military Identity*, 4.

39   Anna Reid, Lars Owe Dahlgren, Peter Petocz, and Madeleinge Abrandt Dahlgreen, "Identity and Engagement for Professional Formation," *Studies in Higher Education* 33, no. 6 (2008): 729–42.

40   Canadian Armed Forces, Chief of the Defence Staff, *Duty with Honour: The Profession of Arms in Canada* (Kingston, ON: Canadian Defence Academy-Canadian Forces Leadership Institute, 2003; rev., 2009).

41   Ibid., 32-3.

42   Ibid., 28.

43   See, for example, discussion of social, professional, and national identity in Siddharth Bannerjee, Jack Jedwab, Tieja Thomas, and Stuart Soroka, *Cultural Intelligence and Identity Development: Concepts, Measures and Relationship to Canadian Forces Professional Development* (Kingston, ON: Canadian Forces Leadership Institute and Defence Research and Development Canada, 2011).

44   Treasury Board Secretariat, *Values and Ethics Code for the Public Service*, retrieved from http://www.tbs-sct.gc.ca/pol/doc-eng.aspx?id=25049&section=text#cha4.

45   Government of Canada, Canadian Centre for Management Development, Task Force on Public Service Values and Ethics, *A Strong Foundation: Report of the Task Force on Public Service Values and Ethics*, Publication no. SC94-72/1996 (Canadian Centre for Management Development, 1996, rev. 2000).

46   Bentley, *Canadian Forces Transformation*, 39.

47   The relationship between military members and civilians in defence has become increasingly integrated since the 1960 Royal Commission on Government Organization (the Glassco commission) – a subject discussed in detail in the Chapter 1 by Gosselin (this volume). For more information regarding the evolution of civil–military relations, see Bentley, *Canadian Forces Transformation*, 7-13.

48   Bentley, *Canadian Forces Transformation*, 51.

CHAPTER 7

TRUST AND INTERAGENCY COLLABORATION: INSIGHTS FOR THE DEFENCE TEAM

Ritu Gill and Megan M. Thompson

If you cannot create harmony based on trust, across service lines,
across coalition-national lines, and across civilian-military lines…
you really need to go home because your leadership in today's age is obsolete.

– General Mattis[1]

The success of military operations has often depended on the supporting role played by civilian organizations. But lessons learned from the complex missions in Somalia, Kosovo, Bosnia, Afghanistan and Iraq[2] have demonstrated the increased complexity of contemporary missions. More and more, effective responses require "a multiagency, interdisciplinary approach that brings the many diverse skills and resources of the federal government and other public and private organizations to bear."[3] In light of this, collaboration between civilian personnel in the Department of National Defence (DND) and military personnel in the Canadian Armed Forces (CAF) is critical.[4]

A synchronized military–civilian approach to complex operations has been variously called the "joined-up" approach, the "3-D" approach (i.e., Defence, Development, and Diplomacy), the "whole-of-government" (WoG) approach, the "comprehensive" approach,[5] and, most recently, the "integrated" approach.[6] In theory (if not always in practice) such a synchronized approach[7] involves creating a tailored, mission-specific and multi-agency team composed of military and a variety of other domestic and foreign government departments and agencies.[8] Key organizational factors that facilitate synchronization include a plan for organizational interoperability and a common communication system.[9] Key social factors include the adoption of a team attitude, the recognition of differences in organizational culture, the sharing of knowledge or information, and the building of trust between partners. Many countries, including Canada, the United States, the United Kingdom, Australia and the Netherlands, have adopted this approach. Indeed, the "comprehensive approach" is also a part of NATO and United Nations doctrine, notably used in humanitarian missions, disaster relief and international operations in failed and failing states. Needless to say, the same factors and processes that have proven successful in multi-agency and inter-governmental collaboration will also be important for successful collaboration between teams composed of military and civilian personnel from DND and the CAF.

This chapter focuses on trust and its importance in establishing and maintaining effective collaboration among interagency partners. We first review the organizational trust literature, examining trust as an enabler of collaboration. We then explore lessons learned from past interagency collaborations: how trust fosters successful interagency collaboration and the strategies organizations can use to develop and to maintain trust. Our aim here is to uncover insights from the research on interagency trust that could be adopted by the civilian-military Defence Team.

TRUST AND TRUST DEVELOPMENT

Trust can be defined as the willingness to be vulnerable to another party on the expectation that the other party will perform actions important to oneself, irrespective of one's ability to monitor or control the other party.[10] Trust involves three foundational features – interdependence, vulnerability and risk – and the decision to trust someone typically involves assessments of that person along four dimensions: competence (e.g., abilities, skills and knowledge), benevolence (e.g., positive, unselfish motives with respect to another), integrity (e.g., adherence to a mutually acceptable set of principles), and predictability (e.g., future reliability), with the most common sources of trust encompassing the first three dimensions.[11] These dimensions are often positively correlated in our individual trust assessments. Yet researchers consider the dimensions distinct because, for example, one individual may be highly skilled (high competence), but self-centred (low benevolence), while another might be strict and stern (low benevolence), but highly principled and fair (high integrity). In short, then, the three salient features of trusting relationships are interdependence, vulnerability and risk, and trust between individuals depends on mutual perceptions of competence, benevolence, integrity and predictability. Based on this model of trust, one would expect that trust between military and civilian personnel on the Defence Team would be shaped by inter-group perceptions of competence, benevolence, integrity and predictability, within contexts of interdependence, vulnerability and risk. The next question, accordingly, is how trust develops and matures.

Both organizational and interpersonal trust literatures depict trust as generally developing over time, a result of repeated successful meetings of important needs in situations of increasing risk or vulnerability.[12] Once a pattern of trustworthy behaviour is established, it becomes easier to trust the other individual; hence, trust becomes more automatic, even as the risks associated with doing so increase. While trust is built on a history of reliable and credible interactions, trust relationships have been classified by researchers into four types – calculus based, knowledge based, relational based and identification based[13] – where each type is located along a spectrum of shallow to deep emotional depth and along a continuum from external, economic exchange or rewards to intrinsic and personal rewards and social or communal exchange.[14]

Calculus-based trust is considered the most impersonal and shallow type of trust. Centred on a comparison of the benefits and risks of trusting, it operates on a reward–punishment system, where failing to provide needed support has material consequences.[15] Not surprisingly, calculus-based trust is most focused on the costs of one's trust being betrayed in a specific situation. Over time, regular interaction allows people to "cultivate their knowledge of each other by gathering data, seeing the other in different contexts and noticing reactions to different behavior."[16] This is termed knowledge-based trust, and the focus here is on predicting the behaviour of others. In cases where interaction leads to a mutual understanding and appreciation of the other's goals, attitudes, beliefs, and values, and where an intrinsic interest in the well-being and concerns of the other develops, relational-based trust is said to exist. This is where the affective and social bases of trust become more apparent and influential, rather than the more self-centred and extrinsic bases of calculus- and knowledge-based trust. Identification-based trust is the deepest level of trust, and it occurs in cases where mutual understanding and appreciation is expressed as a collective mentality and *shared* group membership.[17] In the case of identification-based trust, people are comfortable with other group members acting for them, confident that their priorities and interests will be addressed and that their best interests will be protected.[18]

Organizational policies, such as joint goals or objectives, and shared values can support the development and maintenance of identification-based trust.[19] Indeed, within the DND and CAF institutional context, having shared or super-ordinate goals and values will all contribute to the development of identification-based trust. The development of this level of trust can be facilitated by working within a shared physical space and having a shared name (i.e., the "Defence Team").

TRUST VIOLATIONS AND TRUST REPAIR

A trust violation occurs when one party fails to perform in line with the expectations of the other.[20] Violations can affect any of the trust dimensions (competence, integrity, predictability, benevolence) and may occur with any type of trust (e.g., calculus-, knowledge-, relational-, or identification-based trust). Trust violations may lead to an "unwilling[ness] to take risks and demand[s for] greater protection against betrayal"[21] and, indeed, may even cause the level of trust between parties to plunge below the initial level. The extent of the damage caused by a trust violation depends on the nature of the violation and the stage of the relationship. For instance, when calculus-based trust is in its initial stages, it is quite fragile; thus parties may be more likely to deal with such trust violations by severing the relationship because a significant investment has not yet been placed in the relationship. A violation of knowledge-based trust is more disruptive, however, because it undermines feelings of predictability concerning the other and their motives.

Trust violations can be particularly challenging to repair, often requiring strategies different from those required to build trust in the first place.[22] Trust can also take a long time to rebuild and, as noted above, may never be restored to original levels.[23] Breaches of identification-based trust are considered to be the most profound because they disrupt beliefs about the shared values and the mutual identity that was thought to underlie the relationship.[24] The repair of knowledge- and relational-based trust are also seen to be more challenging to repair because the violations can call into question the violated party's perceptions of the relationship. Thus, the psychological costs are assumed to be greater for the trustor when knowledge-, relational-, or identification-based violations occur. Consequently, repairing these types of trust may take time.

Although some research[25] has demonstrated that specific repair strategies are best used in response to violations of different trust dimensions,[26] most researchers suggest that there are universal trust repair mechanisms applicable to all trust violations.[27] Specifically, the violator should recognize and acknowledge that a violation has occurred, determine the cause of the violation, admit that the act was destructive, accept responsibility for his or her part in the violation, and offer atonement or action to undo the violation.[28] Other researchers have noted, moreover, that apologies alone may not repair trust. Instead, they advocate outlining exactly how the violation will be avoided in the future. Others have argued that there must be active demonstrations of the behaviours that are intended to address the trust violation.[29] As the relationship is renegotiated, the injured party may also insist on instituting safeguards (e.g., contracts, agreements) to ensure violations are not repeated. However, an injured party's insistence on such safeguards means that trust is still vulnerable.

TRUST AND ORGANIZATIONAL EFFECTIVENESS

Research in communication, leadership, negotiation and self-managed work teams has found that trust is a key factor in successful cooperative and collaborative behaviour among individuals, groups and organizations.[30] For instance, high trust has been found to improve organizational effectiveness: it promotes the establishment of new associations and maintains existing ones,[31] improves job attitudes, increases organizational commitment and performance,[32] and reduces the likelihood of exploiting another's vulnerabilities.[33]

Of importance for the Defence Team, higher levels of trust are also associated with greater feelings of shared identity and increased efforts to promote the welfare of the group.[34] In fact, trust has consistently been recognized as important in nurturing collaborative processes,[35] as well as being a necessary precondition for successful collaboration[36] and an essential ingredient in successful inter-firm associations.[37] Trust has even been called the "single most important element of a good working relationship,"[38] and high-trust organizations are more likely to flatten their structures into decentralized, self-managed, team-based forms that foster a sense of empowerment among lower-level employees.[39]

Indeed, a recent study of corporate culture in Canadian defence spoke to the importance of trust on the Defence Team. Forty-five senior military and civilian decision makers indicated that enhancing trust is the main mechanism for bridging the gap between military and civilian cultures.[40] Yet those same interviews with high-ranking military and civilian Defence Team personnel revealed a lack of trust between the two sides in several capacities, a perceived suspicion between the two with respect to competence and commitment to the defence mandate, and a lack of resources and collective focus, an environment of competition, and a failure to evaluate the advantages of shared solutions to common challenges.[41] In the next part of the chapter, we explore further some of these challenges in a WoG context.

LESSONS LEARNED FROM WHOLE-OF-GOVERNMENT MISSIONS

A large number of organizations can be involved in WoG missions, each bringing different organizational agendas, objectives, doctrines and operating styles, not to mention the frequent turnover of personnel.[42] Hence, collaborating in WoG operations – especially in international peace and security missions – can make trust-building difficult. Building interagency trust means transcending differences in organizational structures and processes (including differences regarding flexibility, transparency and accountability), differences in organizational cultures (e.g., different planning and operational terminology used to describe similar processes), and differences in organizational independence (e.g., differences in the priority placed on coordination with other organizations).[43] A review of past interagency collaborations suggests that a variety of factors can affect interagency trust: (1) lack of common purpose (e.g., differing goals and objectives), (2) lack of a level playing field in consultative processes (e.g., non-government organizations emphasize power differences, whereas militaries treat international coordination efforts more like exercises), and (3) different guiding principles (e.g., civilian and military organizations having different values regarding what constitutes the greater good).[44]

Since similar challenges affect the Defence Team, lessons learned about trust building in multinational and interagency operations and exercises may be transferrable to the Defence Team. In response to some of the challenges outlined above, for example, some U.S. military personnel reported that consistent interaction with their civilian counterparts taught them to be more cognizant of their terminology and language.[45] In addition, the more each group worked with the other, the greater the cohesion between them. Similarly, a group of military commanders working within an interagency context cited the importance of bringing civilian and military staff physically together to align priorities and to ensure that all were working toward the same goal. The commanders held regular meetings to ensure that all parties shared information, aligned priorities and maintained communication.[46] In Haiti, moreover, a Joint Information and Interagency Center was established to synchronize communication efforts from the strategic to the tactical level for all interagency partners. All these trust-building activities echo the strategies cited in the organizational trust literature. Their effectiveness in a WoG context is a *prima facie* case for their effectiveness for the Defence Team.

In previous work,[47] we also proposed a variety of organizational strategies to enhance interagency trust, including learning the policies and cultures of collaborators' organizations: how they function and their roles, responsibilities and priorities. Similarly, several participants in the Canadian study with senior decision makers (mentioned earlier)[48] suggested the same sorts of activities to promote trust and cooperation in the Canadian defence context; for instance, opportunities for military and civilian personnel to work, train and learn together and directly observe each other were cited as potential trust-building activities.[49] Other research led by the second author of this chapter corroborates the usefulness of these strategies. In several studies exploring Canadian interagency education and training events, participants' assessments consistently indicated that such strategies work: they meet the training needs of the contributing agencies, and they are received very positively by military and civilian participants, leading to increased awareness of the other organization's mandates, policies and terminologies, as well as to higher evaluations of teamwork.

AN EXPERIMENT IN INTERAGENCY TRUST DEVELOPMENT, VIOLATION, AND REPAIR

The trust literatures show the importance of trust, the problems that can occur when trust is violated, and steps that may help repair trust. This literature also shows that it is critical that members of different organizations, such as CAF personnel and civilians in DND, be made familiar with each other in order to build the trust necessary for successful collaboration. To better understand and quantify the effects of these factors, we conducted what is to our knowledge the first experiment in which knowledge, trust violation and trust restoration were embedded and systematically varied in an interagency scenario.

In our experiment, 150 CAF participants read a fictional scenario based on subject matter expert accounts of working in various WoG environments and were instructed to imagine themselves as members of a fictional military collaborating with a fictional "other government department". The written scenario was presented in sections, beginning with a *baseline* provided to all participants, which described the background of an interagency mission in a war-torn country. The subsequent scenario sections (see Figure 7.1) contained the experimental manipulations: (1) *knowledge*: half the participants were given a one-page summary of the mission and mandate of the OGD vs. the control condition group who received no such background knowledge; (2) *trust violation*: one group of participants read that the OGD partner had not delivered on previously agreed-upon resources for the military vs. another group who were not exposed to this trust violation; (3) *trust repair*: one group of participants read about an apology the OGD partner issued to the military acknowledging limitations vs. another group who were not exposed to a trust repair strategy; and (4) *redress strategy*: one group of participants read about how the OGD partner would address the infraction moving forward vs. another group in which no redress strategy was provided. Trust measures were administered at the end of each scenario segment (i.e., baseline, post-knowledge, post-violation, post-repair and post-redress), allowing us to track the variations in levels of trust after each of the experimental manipulations.

		1. OGD Knowledge			
		Yes		No	
		2. Trust Violation			
		Yes	No	Yes	No
3. Trust Repair	No	(*n* = 25)	(*n* = 25)	(*n* = 25)	(*n* = 25)
Strategy (Apology & Redress Plan)	Yes	(*n* = 25)		(*n* = 25)	

FIGURE 7.1: Overview of Trust Study Conditions (*N* = 150)

Consistent with previous survey and interview studies,[50] our results showed that having some knowledge about an OGD prior to collaboration significantly increased the military respondents' initial levels of trust in the OGD partner, suggesting that incorporating information on partners into pre-deployment training could increase trust. Also consistent with previous research, we found that trust significantly dropped after the trust violation occurred. However, two of our findings were not consistent with the trust literature. First, prior knowledge – at least, as operationalized in our experiment – did not protect against significant drops in trust, relative to having no initial information. Second, although trust did subsequently rebound, it did so whether an OGD apology was read or not. Trust continued to significantly increase after the specific redress plan was outlined. Importantly, however, trust never recovered to initial levels after the trust violation – a finding also consistent with the organizational trust literature.

Our results therefore provide support for the importance of trust in interagency settings, the damaging effects of trust violations, and the potential for at least some amount of recovery, although not back to initial levels. It also provided some support for the importance of knowledge of the other organization in increasing at least initial trust levels, although the knowledge manipulation did not appear to buffer the impact of a trust violation. At the same time, however, we hasten to point out that our knowledge manipulation was a quite brief (one-page) summary of the general roles and mandate of the fictional OGD. That we found an initial effect of knowledge with such a limited manipulation is revealing. We would argue that more detailed knowledge of a partner organization's standard working procedures, identity, traditions, operational terminologies, security concerns, cultures and goals would better ensure successful trust building and collaboration, and might well buffer the effects of at least some violated expectations.

We also contend that the appropriate amount and type of interagency knowledge will help build trust between the members of the Defence Team. Embedding such knowledge in training and education opportunities may minimize stereotypes and misconceptions, while fostering the development of trust prior to entering the mission space. Similarly, implementing common terminologies or synchronizing deployment cycles may also be mutually beneficial.[51] A further finding from our experiment reinforced the findings about trust violations mentioned earlier, and it provides another important lesson for the Defence Team. Should a trust violation occur, our experimental results indicate that apologies alone do not improve trust, relative to the no apology condition (i.e., trust increased equally in both conditions post-repair). However, we did see that trust continued to increase significantly after the provision of a specific redress plan.

CONCLUSION

We examined the critical role of trust in building the relationships that foster successful interagency collaboration and how trust building must begin at the inception of collaborative partnerships.[52] We argued that understanding and meeting important needs develops trust. Trust violations need to be addressed as they can significantly impair the trusting relationship; and, once violated, trust may never fully return to pre-violation levels. The most severe violations will lead to a severing of the relationship altogether.

However, the highest levels of trust occur when parties perceive and embrace shared group membership and a collective identity, shared or joint goals and shared values.[53] Perhaps most important, trust based in shared values and the development of a shared identity will be the most robust in the face of challenges.

The organizational trust literature provides a good foundation for understanding these dynamics. And together with lessons learned from WoG missions, this chapter provided an essential understanding of how to build, maintain and repair trust that is applicable to military and civilian personnel on the Defence Team. Many of the important strategies for building trust discussed in the organizational literature – clear objectives, shared workload, equal ownership, effective communication, and the sharing of information and shared workspaces or co-location[54] – have been reinforced by lessons learned from past interagency collaborations. A number of other practices have also been shown to facilitate trust: consistent interaction with civilian and military counterparts; congruent terminologies; regular meetings to ensure that all parties share information; aligned priorities; the maintenance of communication; the establishment of a central hub for synchronizing communication efforts from the strategic to tactical level for all interagency partners; the creation of opportunities for military and civilian personnel to work, train, and learn together; and activities to facilitate the learning of others' organizational policies and cultures.

Pre-deployment training seems like an ideal time to optimize collaboration in the field, although the inclusion of knowledge at other training and educational opportunities is also encouraged. Whenever it occurs in a career, however, this knowledge will serve to minimize misconceptions and stereotypes, reducing the likelihood of many of the threats to trust that can occur in a complex and challenging mission space. Accordingly, future research could look to identify the specific knowledge dimensions (mission, procedures, constraints, etc.) that will most quickly and most efficiently establish trust in civil–military settings.

We conclude by noting that future international missions are expected to be complex, ambiguous and rapidly changing, a set of characteristics that entail a great deal of interaction between deployed militaries and civilian organizations.[55] This environment makes trust one of the key psychosocial enablers of effective interactions in operational environments.[56] Adopting lessons learned from WoG contexts characterized by similar conditions, therefore, could benefit the Defence Team. We anticipate that the resultant increase in trust between military and civilian personnel within DND and the CAF will be evidenced by intergroup perceptions of competence, benevolence, integrity, and predictability – all of which are expected to greatly enhance the quality of the collaboration, leading to mission success within Canada and abroad.

ENDNOTES

1   Quoted in Stephane Abrial, "Future of Warfighting," *The Three Swords, The Magazine of the Joint Warfare Center* (Stavanger: NATO, 2010): 6.

2   Lara Olson and Hrach Gregorian, "Interagency and Civil-Military Coordination: Lessons from a Survey of Afghanistan and Liberia," *Journal of Military and Strategic Studies* 10, no. 1 (2007): 1-48. Andrew Leslie, Peter Gizewski, and Mike Rostek, "Developing a Comprehensive Approach to Canadian Forces Operations," *Canadian Military Journal* 9, no. 1 (2008): 11-20; Olson and Gregorian, "Interagency and Civil-Military Coordination," 1-48; Stewart Patrick and Kaysi Brown, *Greater than the Sum of its Parts? Assessing "Whole of Government" Approaches to Fragile States* (New York: International Peace Academy, 2007); J. Simms, "The Joint, Interagency, Multi-National and Public (JIMP) Environment: Military Operations in a Crowded Battle-Space," in *Security Operations in the 21st Century: Canadian Perspectives on the Comprehensive Approach*, eds. M. Rostek and P. Gizewski, Queen's Policy Studies Series (Montreal and Kingston: McGill-Queen's U. P., 2011), 75-86.

3   Reinaldo Rivera, *The Joint Interagency Task Force Conundrum: Cooperation among Competitors, is Harmony Achievable Through Trust and Understanding?* Joint Military Operations Department Final Technical Report (Newport, RI: Naval War College, 2003), 1.

4   Although DND and the CAF are highly integrated workforces, they are still independent organizations under the authority of the Minister of National Defence. It is fair to say, therefore, that an "interagency" relationship exists between them.

5   Peter Gizewski and Mike Rostek, "Toward a JIMP-Capable Land Force," *Canadian Army Journal* 10, no. 1 (2007): 55-72; Olson and Gregorian, "Interagency and Civil-Military Coordination," 1-48.

6   Asia Pacific Civil-Military Centre of Excellence, *Strengthening Australia's Conflict and Disaster Management Overseas* (Queanbeyan: Asia Pacific Civil–Military Centre of Excellence, 2010), retrieved from http://acmc.gov.au/publications/strengthening-australia's-conflict-and-disaster-management-overseas/); Her Majesty's Government, A *Strong Britain in an Age of Uncertainty: The National Security Strategy*, 2010, retrieved from http://www.direct.gov.uk/prod_consum_dg/groups/dg_digitalassets/@dg/@en/documents/digitalasset/dg_191639.pdf?CID=PDF&PLA=furl&CRE=nationalsecuritystrategy

7   The commonly accepted term is "comprehensive approach." See Leslie, Gizewski, and Rostek, "Developing a Comprehensive Approach," 11-20.

8   For a full review see Leslie, Gizewski, and Rostek, "Developing a Comprehensive Approach," 11-20.

9   Ibid.

10   See Roger C. Mayer, James Davis, and F. David Schoorman, "An Integrative Model of Organizational Trust," *Academy of Management Review* 20, no. 3 (1995): 709-34.

11   Mayer, Davis, and Schoorman, "An Integrative Model of Organizational Trust," 70934. See also Denise M. Rousseau, Sim B. Sitkin, Ronald S. Burt, and Colin Camerer,

"Not so Different After All: A Cross-Discipline View of Trust," *Academy of Management Review* 23, no. 3 (1998): 393-404.

12   For example, Lewicki and Bunker, "Developing and Maintaining Trust," 114-39; Roy J. Lewicki and Carolyn Wiethoff, "Trust, Trust Development and Trust Repair," in *Handbook of Conflict Resolution: Theory and Practice*, eds. M. Deutsch and P. T. Coleman (Jossey-Bass: San Francisco, 2000), 86-107; Rousseau, et al., "Not so Different After All," 393-404.

13   Lewicki and Wiethoff, "Trust, Trust Development and Trust Repair," 86-107; Rousseau et al., "Not so Different After All," 393-404.

14   R. Serle, A. Weibel, and D. N. Den Hartog, "Employee Trust in Organizational Contexts," in *International Review of Industrial and Organizational Psychology*, vol. 23, eds. G. P. Hodgkinson and J. K. Ford (New York: Wiley, 2011), 143-91.

15   Lewicki and Wiethoff, "Trust, Trust Development and Trust Repair," 86-107; Rousseau et al., "Not so Different After All," 393-404.

16   Lewicki and Bunker, "Developing and Maintaining Trust," 122.

17   For example, J. Holmes, "Trust and the Appraisal Process in Close Relationships," in *Advances in Personal Relationships: A Research Annual*, vol. 2, eds. W. Jones and D. Perlman (London: Jessica Kingsley, 1991), 57-104; Lewicki and Bunker, "Developing and Maintaining Trust," 114–39.

18   Searle, Weibel, and Den Hartog, "Employee Trust in Organizational Contexts," 143-91.

19   Das and Teng, "Between Trust and Control," 491-512; Vangen and Huxham, "Enacting Leadership for Collaborative Advantage," 61-76.

20   Peter H. Kim, Cecily D. Cooper, Donald. L. Ferrin, and Kurt T. Dirks, "Removing the Shadow of Suspicion: The Effects of Apology Versus Denial for Repairing Competence-Versus Integrity-Based Trust Violations," *Journal of Applied Psychology* 89, no. 1 (2004): 104-18; Sim B. Sitkin and Nancy L. Roth, "Explaining the Limited Effectiveness of Legalistic Remedies for Trust/Distrust," *Organization Science* 4, no. 3 (1993): 367-92.

21   Tom R. Tyler and Roderick M. Kramer, "Wither Trust?" in Trust in Organizations: Frontiers of Theory and Research, eds. R. M. Kramer and T. R. Tyler (Thousand Oaks, CA: Sage, 1996), 4.

22   Kim et al., "Removing the Shadow of Suspicion," 104-18.

23   Paul Slovic, "Perceived Risk, Trust, and Democracy," *Risk Analysis* 13, no. 6 (1993): 675-82; Lewicki and Bunker, "Developing and Maintaining Trust," 114-39.

24   Lewicki and Bunker, "Developing and Maintaining Trust," 114-39.

25   Kim et al., "Removing the Shadow of Suspicion," 104-18.

26   Interestingly, Kim et al., "Removing the Shadow of Suspicion," 104-18, found that the extent to which trust was reparable and how effective different reparatory mechanisms

were depended upon which trustworthiness dimensions were negatively affected or violated. Specifically, competence violations were more successfully repaired with admissions of guilt, whereas integrity violations were better repaired with denials.

27   Lewicki and Bunker, "Developing and Maintaining Trust," 114-39.

28   Kim et al., "Removing the Shadow of Suspicion," 104-18; E. C. Tomlinson, B. R. Dineen, and R. J. Lewicki, "The Road to Reconciliation: Antecedents of Victim Willingness to Reconcile Following a Broken Promise," *Journal of Management* 30 (2004): 165-188.

29   N. Gillespie and G. Dietz, "Trust Repair After an Organization-level Failure," *Academy of Management Review* 34, no. 1 (2009): 127-45; Lewicki and Bunker, Developing and Maintaining Trust," 114-39

30   Leanne. E. Atwater, "The Relative Importance of Situational and Individual Variables in Predicting Leader Behavior," *Group and Organization Studies* 13, no. 3 (1988): 290-310; Robert Axelrod, *The Evolution of Cooperation* (New York: Basic Books, 1984); Max, H. Bazerman, *Judgement in Managerial Decision Making* (New York: Wiley, 1994); Robert L. Caslen and Bradley S. Loudon, "Forging a Comprehensive Approach to Counterinsurgency Operations," *Prism* 2, no. 3 (2011): 3-14; T. K. Das and Bing-Sheng Teng, "Between Trust and Control: Developing Confidence in Partner Cooperation in Alliances," *Academy of Management Review* 23, no. 3 (1998): 491-512; Kurt T. Dirks and Donald L. Ferrin, "Trust in Leadership: Meta-Analytic Findings and Implications for Organizational Research," *Journal of Applied Psychology* 87, no. 4 (2002): 611-28; Diego G. Gambetta, "Can We Trust Trust?" in *Trust*, ed. D. G. Gambetta (New York: Basil Blackwell, 1988), 212-37; David Good, "Individuals, Interpersonal Relations, and Trust," in *Trust*, ed. D. G. Gambetta (New York: Basil Blackwell, 1988), 131-85; Sarah A. Hill, *Corporate Culture in the Canadian Forces and Department of National Defence*, Defence Research and Development Technical Report 2007-19 (Toronto: Defence Research and Development Canada, 2007); P. Ken Keen, Matthew G. Elledge, Charles W. Nolan, and Jennifer L. Kimmey, "Foreign Disaster Response: Joint Task Force–Haiti Observations," *Military Review* 90, no. 6 (2010): 85-96; Edward E. Lawler, *The Ultimate Advantage: Creating the High-Involvement Organization* (San Francisco: Jossey-Bass, 1992); Brooke Schaab, Arwen DeConstanza, and Chadwick Hixson, *Behavioral, Attitudinal, and Cultural Factors Influencing Interagency Information Sharing* (Arlington, VA: U.S. Army Research Institute for the Behavioral and Social Sciences, 2011); Chris Thatcher, "Multinational Experiment Offers Holistic Picture of Afghan Operations," *Vanguard* (December 2005-January 2006), retrieved from http://www.vanguardcanada.com

31   Lewicki and Bunker, "Developing and Maintaining Trust," 114-39; Mayer, Davis, and Schoorman, "An Integrative Model of Organizational Trust," 709-34.

32   Dirks and Ferrin, "Trust in Leadership," 611-28.

33   Mayer, Davis, and Schoorman, "An Integrative Model of Organizational Trust," 709-34.

34   Marilyn B. Brewer and Norman Miller, *Intergroup Relations* (Pacific Grove, CA: Brooks/Cole, 1996).

35   Siv Vangen and Chris Huxham, "Enacting Leadership for Collaborative Advantage: Dilemmas of Ideology and Pragmatism in the Activities of Partnership Managers," *British Journal of Management* 14 (2003): 61-76.

36   Das and Teng, "Between Trust and Control," 491-512; Nirmalya Kumar, "The Power of Trust in Manufacturer-Retailer Relationships," *Harvard Business Review* 74, no. 6 (1996): 92-106.

37   John Child, "Trust: The Fundamental Bond in Global Collaboration," *Organizational Dynamics* 29, no. 4 (2001): 274-88; Das and Teng, "Between Trust and Control," 491-512.

38   Roger Fisher and Scott Brown, *Getting Together: Building Relationships as We Negotiate* (London: Penguin, 1988), 107.

39   Susan G. Cohen, Gerald E. Ledford, and Gretchen M. Spreitzer, "A Predictive Model of Self-Managing Work Team Effectiveness," *Human Relations* 49, no. 5 (1996): 643-76; Dexter Dunphy and Ben Bryant, "Teams: Panaceas or Prescriptions for Improved Performance?" *Human Relations* 49, no. 5 (1996): 677–99.

40   Hill, *Corporate Culture in the Canadian Forces.*

41   Ibid.

42   Olson and Gregorian, "Interagency and Civil-Military Coordination," 1-48.

43   Ibid.; see also Michael H. Thomson, Courtney D. T. Hall, and Barbara D. Adams, *Canadian Forces Education and Training for Interagency Operational Contexts*, Defence Research and Development Canada, Contract Report 2010-013 (Toronto: Defence Research and Development Canada, 2009).

44   Olson and Gregorian, "Interagency and Civil-Military Coordination," 1-48.

45   Thatcher, "Multinational Experiment." Notably, differences in language and terminology have also been an issue within the Canadian Defence Team.

46   Keen et al., "Foreign Disaster Response," 85-96.

47   Megan M. Thompson and Ritu Gill, "The Role of Trust in Whole of Government Missions," in *Mission Critical: Smaller Democracies' Role in Global Stability Operations*, eds. C. Leuprecht, J. Troy, and D. Last (Montreal: McGill-Queen's U. P., 2009), 225-44.

48   Hill, *Corporate Culture in the Canadian Forces.*

49   Ibid.

50   For example, Kristin M. Haugevik and Benjamin de Carvalho, "Civil-Military Cooperation in Multinational and Interagency Operations," NUPI Discussion Paper on Operational Terminologies and Assessment for Multinational Experiment 5, Security in Practice no. 2 (Oslo: Norwegian Institute of International Affairs, 2007).

51   Caslen and Loudon, "Forging a Comprehensive Approach," 3-14.

52   Fisher and Brown, *Getting Together.*

53   Caslen and Loudon, "Forging a Comprehensive Approach," 3-14; Ritu Gill, Megan M. Thompson, and Tara Holton, "Exploring Interagency Trust in Whole of Government Missions" (paper presented at the Annual American Psychological Association Convention, Honolulu, Hawaii, 2013); Keen et al., "Foreign Disaster Response," 85-96; Rivera, *Joint Interagency Task Force Conundrum*; Timothy A. Vuono, *Challenges for Civil-Military Integration During Stability Operations*, Senior Service College Fellowship Project (Carlisle Barracks, PA: U.S. Army War College, 2008).

54   Das and Teng, "Between Trust and Control," 491-512; Vangen and Huxham, "Enacting Leadership for Collaborative Advantage," 61-76.

55   Olson and Gregorian, "Interagency and Civil-Military Coordination," 1-48.

56   Rivera, *Joint Interagency Task Force Conundrum*.

CHAPTER 8

SOCIAL IDENTITY AND THE DEFENCE TEAM

Irina Goldenberg, Waylon H. Dean and Barbara D. Adams

There has always been a "Defence Team" in the figurative sense that both the Canadian Armed Forces and the Department of National Defence share the same mandate (national defence), under the same act of government (the *National Defence Act*), and fall under the purview of the same federal government minister (the Minister of National Defence). But two recent trends have given the concept of a Defence Team a more substantive meaning. The first is the federal government's move toward interagency or whole-of-government approaches to its responsibilities. This trend is reflected in the government's recent 20-year plan for national defence, the *Canada First Defence Strategy*, where the Defence Team is characterized as the "core element of a whole-of-government approach" to domestic and international security.[1] The second trend is the growing recognition of the importance of a long-standing reality: that much of the defence establishment consists of teams of DND civilians and CAF military personnel working side by side. And as many of the chapters in this volume show, the success of both interagency teams and whole-of-government approaches depends on the successful integration of the different cultures involved, and on building trust between the collaborators through a common identity.

Creating a shared identity to foster successful collaboration, however, is a special challenge for the Defence Team. On the one hand, the CAF and DND share a super-ordinate mandate as part of "the Defence Team" in the figurative sense of the expression mentioned above. On the other hand, the two institutions and their workforces have very different cultures. The military partner – the CAF – actively promotes among its membership a "common identity as military professionals and a shared military ethos," and its members' common identity is understood to be distinct from its members' civilian identity.[2] In addition, the military is more communal, more hierarchical, and places greater emphasis on discipline and control over its membership than civilian organizations like DND. Thus the military side of the Defence Team promotes a strong collective identity among its members that is both exclusive and qualitatively different from that of the civilian side of the team. A second issue is the inherent tension between a super-ordinate identity and the various management and "challenge" functions that civilians are meant to perform inside National Defence – as Daniel Gosselin, Alan Okros and Allan English have explained in their chapters in this volume. In other words, the benefits to be had from becoming a fully integrated member of the Defence Team cannot come at the cost of membership on the civilian Public Service team that answers to the government and its central agencies, or at the expense of a strong military identity imbued with a strong military ethos, military professionalism and unique allegiance to the Canadian Armed Forces.

The main question in this chapter, then, concerns the prospects for a super-ordinate Defence Team identity that mirrors and thus fosters the Defence Team's collaboration in achieving its common super-ordinate mandate while respecting the unique functions of both members of the Defence Team. We examine this question through social identity theory in the hope that understanding the identity dynamics between these two groups of personnel will shed light on how to overcome the inherent differences between the two sides of the Defence Team and thus build a super-ordinate identity. After all, social identity is the nexus of collaborative trusting relationships because our social identities inform our attitudes and behaviours and thus inform our interactions with members of other social groups. Accordingly, we begin by explaining the essentials of social identity theory and its organizational aspects. We then examine each side of the Defence Team through identity theory. In the third part, we look at strategies for enhancing military-civilian cooperation within the Defence Team that are consistent with the mandates of military and civilian personnel and that may promote the achievement of a super-ordinate identity.

SOCIAL AND ORGANIZATIONAL IDENTITY

An individual's social identity is part of his or her self-concept: it is one's knowledge of one's membership in one or more social groups "together with the emotional significance attached to that membership."[3] In other words, social identity is "part of a person's sense of 'who they are' associated with any internalized group membership."[4] Identifying with a given group involves cognition (e.g., knowledge and beliefs about the group), affect (e.g., emotive evaluations of the group), and behaviour (e.g., beliefs or ideologies about how group members should behave).[5]

A key assumption in social identity theory is that people are generally motivated to maintain a positive self-concept and, in the group domain, distinctive and positive social identities.[6] Forming and maintaining a positive social identity depends on favourable comparisons showing the positive distinctiveness of one's in-group relative to the out-group on some relevant dimension.[7] Through social comparison, then, group members may perceive themselves as having an advantaged status on a specific dimension in relation to an outside group. If an inter-group comparison yields an unfavourable result (i.e., a group sees itself as inferior to another group), social identity theory predicts that group members will take steps to improve their negative group identity.

Of course, social identity operates in human interactions on a continuum ranging from interpersonal to intergroup (with gradations and combinations within). On the interpersonal end of the continuum, people interact with one another primarily as individuals. At this end of the continuum, one's self-concept or personal identity manifests as one's unique or idiosyncratic attributes. On the intergroup end, identity is defined in terms of the social groups to which one belongs, and people interact as representatives of the different social groups that are salient and meaningful at that moment. Within this context, the focus is belonging and integration within one's in-group.

Because both ends of the continuum operate simultaneously, both interpersonal and intergroup motives are often at play in any given social context. As a result, researchers have developed a multi-level model of social identity:

- Personal identity: traits or characteristics that differentiate oneself as a unique individual.

- Relational identity: how one sees oneself in relation to specific others.

- Collective identity: how one sees oneself as a member of a social group in which one shares particular characteristics with others.[8]

The different forms of identity active at a given moment naturally shift, depending on the context; thus, the salience of the many identities available to us as individuals can vary. At home, for example, one may take on the role of being a parent as an important part of one's personal identity. In the work context, however, one's role as a parent is likely to be temporarily less salient, and one's sense of belonging to a particular team, workgroup or organization may dominate. Since our focus here is the organizational identity of civilians and military personnel in DND and the CAF, we will look at organizational aspects of social identity in more detail.

Organizational Identity and Social Comparisons

Organizational identity is the degree to which people define themselves as members of a particular type of social group – namely, an organization.[9] An organizational social group can be an organization in the formal sense of an employer or department, but it may also include less formal types of organizational groups, such as one's work group, club membership or union. Individuals can also identify with both a super-ordinate organization and with subgroups within an organization. Social identity theorists posit that people establish their identities within these social contexts.[10] As group members, people make social comparisons with other groups, and their perceptions of other groups – and their perceived position relative to these groups – are influenced by three variables:[11]

- Stability of status: the extent to which people believe that their group is likely to shift to a different status position.

- Legitimacy of status: the extent to which low and high status groups accept the status structure.

- Permeability of group boundaries: the extent to which group members can leave a group and become part of another group.

These variables have been hypothesized to work separately or in combination with one another to influence how group members work to manage their identities (i.e., their need to belong to their own group as well as to be positively distinctive from other groups).

Social identity theorists also posit that the three variables in organizational identity formation are managed using several strategies. The three most common (and best researched) are *individual mobility, social creativity* and *social competition*. When group boundaries are seen to be permeable, low-status group members have been shown to exploit individual mobility as an identity management strategy. They distance themselves – either physically or psychologically – from group goals in order to pursue their individual goals. Social creativity tends to be used when group boundaries are seen to be impermeable, and one's group status is seen to be relatively stable. Even though in-group members are unable to move outside the group, and their group status is stable, they are able to increase their own distinctiveness by making creative comparisons between their group and out-groups. One example cited in the literature is the use by African Americans (a typically low-status group) of the slogan "Black is beautiful" as a creative strategy to distinguish their group.[12] Social competition typically occurs when group boundaries are perceived as impermeable and group status is threatened or unstable. In these cases, individuals may preserve their identities by making comparisons on a value dimension that is shared by both in-groups and out-groups. Social competition strategies are reflected in collective action on the part of disadvantaged group members.[13]

In short, the drivers of identity management are the perceived status of one's group (i.e., its stability and legitimacy) and the perceived permeability of boundaries around one's group.[14] Which of the three strategies individuals use to manage their social status – individual mobility, social creativity and social competition – depends on how they see themselves in relation to other groups.

Identity and Bias

Social identity theory suggests that who we *are not* is an important part of who we are. The desire to categorize ourselves into groups is a common human propensity. Categories can be related to age, gender, religious affiliation or membership in a team or organization.[15] It is often hypothesized that categorization simplifies and constrains the social environment, allowing individuals to locate themselves in relation to others within the social space.[16] Henri Tajfel argues that belonging to a group enhances the degree to which people see themselves as similar to other members of the group.[17] The more we identify with our in-group, however, the more we can feel aligned with in-group members and distinct from out-group members.[18] As a consequence, we can fall into extending preferential treatment to people belonging to our group, a tendency called *in-group bias*. Similarly, our desire to maintain a positive social identity can lead us to denigrate outsiders, a tendency called *out-group bias*. And history suggests that in- and out-group biases can spiral out of control and lead to intergroup conflict,[19] prejudice and discrimination.[20]

Research has shown that in-group biases can occur in response to both real distinctions and to arbitrary distinctions. For example, social psychology research has shown that even dividing groups on the basis of an arbitrary distinction (e.g., eye colour; minimal group paradigm) can give rise to in- and out-group distinctions.[21] Definitions of oneself versus others are intended to be "relational and comparative,"[22] because they are most meaningful in comparison to other categories (e.g., the category young receives much of its meaning in opposition to the category old). In-group bias is not necessarily an inevitable outcome of categorization, however; and some have argued that it relies on three conditions:[23]

- the degree to which identification with the in-group defines one's self-concept;

- the extent to which the context allows for comparison and competition between groups; and

- perceived relevance of the compared out-group in both relative and absolute status.

If these three conditions are met, categorization or comparison processes may lead to in-group bias. If these three conditions are not met, people may use other means to invoke positive social identity. All the same, there is strong empirical evidence that seeing oneself as a member of an in-group and different from an out-group is sufficient to elicit discriminatory behaviour and attitudes in favour of the in-group and at the expense of the out-group.[24] These biases can lead to stereotypes, which are beliefs regarding the characteristics, attributes and behaviours of specific others, and they are based on the knowledge, beliefs, and expectations we hold about a group.[25] Stereotypes are generalizations about groups that are accurate or inaccurate and either positively or negatively valenced. Stereotypes guide our expectations about group membership and can colour how we interpret group members' behaviours and traits.[26]

Events or occurrences that increase the salience of social categorization processes can also enhance in-group biases and produce stereotypes.[27] For instance, conflict with out-group members tends to enhance positive views of one's own in-group. Conversely, events that reduce the salience of social categories (e.g., focusing on individual factors rather than group factors) will reduce in-group bias. While in- and out-group bias is undoubtedly the "dark side" of social identification, social identity theory also exerts a positive influence at the personal, social and organizational level.

Organizational Identity, Organizational Performance, and Personal Well-Being

Recent research has found that organizational identity is important for organizational performance and personal well-being. At the personal level, social identity helps people manage the uncertainty in their lives and their self-perceptions;[28] it has been closely linked to social support;[29] and it can serve as a buffer against adversity.[30] The salience of organizational identity also has implications for personal motivation and, thus, for organizational performance.[31] Left on one's own with a difficult work task, for example, one's sense of motivation and engagement may wane. Being joined by other members of one's team, and identifying oneself as a valued team member who needs to make a contribution to the team can shift one's motivation from low to high. The fact that identity serves a motivational function is argued to be one of the key reasons that social identity theory has received prominent attention in recent years.[32]

At the intergroup level, moreover, shared identity among team members is recognized as a key feature of high-performance teams. Evidence suggests, for example, that strong workgroup identities can diminish the dangers of diverse teams where conflict can arise from unhealthy coalitions within the workgroup.[33] Similarly, team identity has been linked to more positive attitudes and perceptions of other team members, even at the end of stressful team projects.[34] Taken together, this research suggests that social and group identity can buffer conflict within teams or workgroups.

Organizational identification has been linked to both individual well-being and improved organization performance in other ways as well.[35] Blake Ashforth and Fred Mael argue that identifying with an organization fills a range of existential needs related to organizational behaviour, including connectedness, searching for meaning and empowerment.[36] S. Alexander Haslam, Tom Postmes and Naomi Ellemers argue that there is conclusive evidence that organizational identity positively influences key organizational outcomes, including "loyalty, productivity, organizational citizenship, desire to comply with organizational rules, reactions to organizational change and willingness to communicate."[37] Research by Michael Riketta has shown significant positive associations between organizational identity, job challenge and extra-role performance, and a negative correlation between organizational identification and intentions to leave the organization.[38] Overall, then, organizational identification is strongly linked with key aspects of organizational performance and personal well-being.

Regardless of the type of group one perceives oneself to belong to – whether a family, a small work group or team, or an organization – identifying with a group seems to provide a wide range of benefits, including personal well-being, better conflict management, and improved organizational commitment and performance.[39] It stands to reason that we should examine the social and organizational identities of civilian and military personnel and the salience of these identities in the context of a Defence Team, where both work together toward a common mandate.

SOCIAL IDENTITIES WITHIN THE DEFENCE TEAM

From a social identity standpoint, the two groups composing the Defence Team and their relationship with each other are unique in two important ways. The first major difference is that CAF members have a strong and exclusive collective identity as military members, while the identity of DND civilians as defence civilians is comparatively weak. The second major difference is the organizational arrangement underlying the Defence Team. Although both DND and the CAF work in tandem, the mandate of DND is to provide "advice and support to the Minister of National Defence and in implementing the decisions of the Government on the defence of Canada and of Canadian interests at home and abroad."[40] Meanwhile, the CAF provides the "defence of Canada and of Canadian interests" function that receives the "advice and support" from its civilian counterpart. In a manner of speaking, then, the primary role of civilians on the Defence Team is to play a supportive and supplemental role to the military part of the team. We will look at each of these factors and how they affect the Defence Team in more detail.

Military and Civilian Organizational Identities

Because military effectiveness depends on social cohesion, the CAF inculcates a strong collective social identity in its membership. As Justin Wright observes in the next chapter, the CAF's formal socialization process "assumes that the new recruit should be treated as a 'blank slate' whose identity must be shaped and moulded according to organizational values, attitudes and behavioural norms."[41] One of the CAF's foundational documents on military identity, *Duty with Honour*, shows that each of the cognitive, affective and behavioural aspects of identity is determined for CAF members: they are to think of themselves as sharing a collective identity in virtue of the "unique function they perform"[42] and that the core of this unique and collective identity is their common commitment to "voluntary military service, unlimited liability and service before self." Moreover, CAF members are to internalize the military ethos, which "embodies the spirit that binds the profession together" and "clarifies how members view their responsibilities, apply their expertise and express their unique military identity."[43] The collective military identity is further reinforced through extended periods of interaction with experienced – i.e., socialized – in-group members and through peer-groups formed early on that build cohesion and morale through a shared history, further promulgating a shared identity.[44]

The CAF's socialization process and peer groups are physically instantiated through military standards of dress and deportment, which are meant to reflect military values and professionalism (e.g., self-discipline, duty, integrity). The military uniform is arguably the most basic example of a military cultural artefact, meant to both reinforce the member's professional self-concept and to transmit their professional affiliation and identity to others.[45] Uniforms provide a clear indication that the person wearing them belongs to the category of "military personnel," along with other individuating information (e.g., whether the wearer is a commissioned or non-commissioned officer and his or her branch of service and rank). Military dress therefore creates an immediately salient category that distinguishes military personnel from their civilian co-workers and reinforces a strong and salient identity for military personnel. In this sense, then, differences in dress between military and civilian personnel seem likely to promote differential levels of organizational and group identity.

The civilian side of the Defence Team has not undergone a similar socialization process – much less one aimed at creating a distinctive "civilian" identity. Nor is it common for civilians to have travelled through their careers with the same group of peers, which makes them less likely to have a shared history with their co-workers. Further, civilians do not share a common code of dress and deportment that marks them as members of specific jobs. As a result, civilians are likely to have less well-formed identities as DND civilians. Their identities as researchers, accountants and technicians, for example, are likely more salient in their senses of "who they are" than their social status as defence civilians.[46] Indeed, being a "civilian" may be no more meaningful for civilian personnel than being a "non-military" member of the Defence Team. [47] Sarah Hill's study of identity in National Defence Headquarters found that "No participants articulated the notion of a civilian identity (or identities) within the corporate culture."[48] The fact that civilian identities were not articulated, even though military participants singled out identity as a serious concern, is an important contrast. This observation is consistent with André Fillion's finding that there is an absence of discussion within the CAF surrounding the issue of defence civilian identity and that it may be advisable to "create an identity and sense of belonging for defence civilians."[49] By addressing this issue, he argues, cultural differences between the military and defence civilians can be reduced.

Hill's and Fillion's findings regarding the relative weakness of the civilian identity (compared to the CAF identity) found support most recently in the Defence Team Survey.[50] The survey contained a subscale on organizational identity that used James E. Cameron's model of social identity to measure three aspects of identity: cognitive centrality (i.e., the amount time spent thinking about being a member of a group), in-group ties (i.e., perceptions of belonging to a group), and in-group affect (i.e., positive feelings associated with being a member of a group). Civilian DND employees and CAF members were asked parallel questions meant to elicit the level of cognitive centrality, in-group affect, and in-group ties each group perceived in relation to their fellow members. Civilians were asked, for example, to rate their level of agreement with statements like "Being a DND employee is an important part of my self-image" and "I feel strong ties to other DND employees" on a 7-point scale ranging from *strongly disagree* to *strongly agree*. CAF members were asked similar questions on the same 7-point scale (e.g., "Being a CF member is..." and "I feel strong ties to other CF members."). Not surprisingly, CAF members indicated significantly stronger social identity than civilians across all three measures: in-group affect (military mean = 6.1; civilian mean = 5.9), centrality (military mean = 5.3; civilian mean = 4.4) and in-group ties (military mean = 5.7; civilian mean = 5.1).[51]

It is also worth mentioning that the especially strong and salient military sense of "who they are" and how they fit into the Defence Team may exacerbate the weakness of the civilian identity, because civilians may be unable to reciprocate with similarly strong self-defining statements.[52] As such, in addition to the importance of a super-ordinate Defence Team identity, civilian personnel may also need to have a clear and distinct sense of purpose and meaning that separates them from military personnel. Taken together, this research suggests that greater effort at encouraging a civilian defence identity may be beneficial for defence civilians and the Defence Team as a whole.

Of course, Hill's research also revealed some concerns about identity by military personnel from several perspectives.[53] Her interviews with senior military and civilian personnel from National Defence Headquarters showed, for example, that participants were concerned about the impact of lessening the strength of their environment identities (i.e., Army, Navy, Air Force) for the sake of emphasizing an all-service CAF identity. They worried that an all-service CAF identity might not sufficiently honour the important traditions and legacies of the past and that it may have a negative impact on how military personnel perceived themselves as individuals. In terms of military-civilian identity concerns, military personnel worried that without opportunities to train with civilians in a fully integrated way, true identity integration would be challenging. Nonetheless, they did see value in "a common 'front' presented by the CAF and DND in dealings with other government departments."[54] Notably, the senior civilian respondents indicated that the shift to a more integrated organization would result in their contributions as civilians being more valued.

Australian researchers Nick Jans and David Schmidtchen came to similar conclusions about military and civilian identity at Australian Defence Force (ADF) national headquarters, contrasting the "mainstream military and the Defence bureaucracy."[55] One of the core differences, they assert, is that the three military services each have "what scholars call a 'strong' culture because each has a strong sense of identity and clear and measurable functions." Inside ADF headquarters, by contrast, in which both military and civilian personnel serve, "the identity and functions of 'Defence' are less clearly defined. As an institution and as a 'culture,' it is an uneasy amalgam of the ethos of the Australian Public Service and the three Services."[56] Thus, it seems that the dynamics within the Australian Department of Defence mirror the military-civilian dynamics between DND and the CAF.

As noted earlier, social identity theorists argue that identity dynamics are heavily influenced by the status of one's own group relative to other groups.[57] Being a civilian employee who is not at the centre of the most prominent goal of the organization may make it more difficult to fully internalize an organizational identity that conduces to well-being and performance. In the next section, we examine some of the potential consequences of this identity disparity.

Potential Consequences of Social Identity Disparity on Defence Team Civilians

The strong and salient military identity and the comparatively weak civilian identity may affect interactions between military and civilian personnel within the Defence Team. Negative effects include the development of inter-group stereotypes and biases, the lack of a sense of belonging and identity threat. The literature suggests that civilians and military personnel do hold stereotypes of one another. For example, some CAF research shows that senior military officers perceive civilian and military personnel very differently. When provided with a list of 12 descriptors that could be used to describe military culture, senior military officers most frequently chose hardworking, disciplined and loyal, and they rated military personnel as having characteristics like strength, toughness, physical courage and the willingness to make sacrifices.[58] However, when the same military personnel were asked to choose descriptors for civilians, the most frequently chosen were materialistic, self-indulgent and hardworking.[59] Other research has indicated that the military community sees the civilian Defence Team "as risk-averse, process-oriented bureaucrats."[60] Meanwhile, some civilian personnel in the same study had negative stereotypes of military personnel, indicating, for example, that the military community is "rigid and difficult to penetrate."[61]

The weaker civilian identity may also affect civilian personnel's sense of belonging. They may come to believe that their military peers do not respect their contributions. By failing to distinguish key differences among civilian groups, military personnel may not treat civilian roles as having unique requirements or skills or may take a "one size fits all" approach when working collaboratively. At the same time, identity is particularly important because of the environment in which civilian DND personnel work. To fulfill their role inside National Defence, many civilian personnel are immersed in military culture and the military ethos,[62] and they must work to educate themselves about how to work with military personnel.

Because they are immersed in the strong military culture without a correspondingly strong identity, civilians may not perceive themselves as a distinct group or as one that makes unique contributions to National Defence. Social identity theory predicts that civilians may experience "identity threat," causing them to attempt to manage their identities. As we noted above, one of these management strategies is "individual mobility" (e.g., leaving the organization). Social identity research has shown that this occurs when low-status group members no longer wish to pursue group goals, and when they see themselves as being able to move outside of their groups (i.e., high permeability). As noted earlier, individual mobility can be either literal or figurative, and low-status group members may also choose to simply disengage psychologically from group goals. Losing experienced personnel because they are no longer motivated to serve DND's goals could pose a serious threat to its organizational effectiveness. Moreover, as discussed earlier in this chapter, the literature shows that identity-based tensions (e.g., the need to define one's group) have often given rise to intergroup conflict.[63]

A DEFENCE TEAM IDENTITY

The central question for this chapter is how research on social identity can be harnessed to enhance the work culture and collaboration between military and civilian personnel on the Defence Team. The first part of the chapter examined the central concepts in social identity theory, focusing on organizational identity and the personal and organization benefits of social identity maintenance. The second part examined the salient identities on the Defence Team and some of the issues that can arise when one member of a team has a strong and unique collective identity and the other has a weaker and more diffuse one. In this part, we look first at what social identity research suggests is the best way to optimize relations on the Defence Team to reap the benefits of social identity. In short, we argue that National Defence should promote both a super-ordinate Defence Team identity while concurrently fostering strong distinct military and defence civilian identities. In the next sections, we look at what has been done to foster a Defence Team identity and the nature of that super-ordinate identity.

A Super-Ordinate Defence Team Identity

Research suggests that National Defence should focus on simultaneously promoting a unified super-ordinate identity – i.e., the Defence Team – while also promoting distinct subgroup identities – i.e., military and civilian identities.[64] Dual identities allow members of two different groups the sense that they are "playing on the same team,"[65] and they have been shown to reduce stereotypes and intergroup biases between groups.[66] Research by S. L. Gaertner et al., for example, showed that people in multicultural situations who categorized themselves in terms of both a super-ordinate identity (i.e., American) and in relation to an ethnic subgroup identity (e.g., Asian) showed significantly less bias toward others than people who identified only with the super-ordinate category.[67] Establishing strong and salient sub-group identities (i.e., military and civilian) is also important, however, because a strong military identity is essential to military effectiveness and civilians need a sense of who they are within National Defence, beyond being the "non-military members of the Defence Team." Thus, the super-ordinate identity must complement the individual identities of both groups.

Leaders and managers can foster cohesion by establishing common opportunities between the two groups, by emphasizing their shared goals, and by addressing perceptions (or misperceptions) of unfairness between groups.[68] Of note, such initiatives are already underway. The CAF and DND have made various attempts at articulating and promoting a super-ordinate identity that can be shared by military and civilian personnel. An obvious example of promoting shared goals is the coining of the term "Defence Team," which is reported to have taken on greater significance in association with the CF Transformation effort arising out of Canada's 2005 International Policy Statement, and which seems to have been used more prominently in recent years.[69] A Defence Team website was also created with the motto "one vision, one mission, one team" to disseminate organizational information through a common platform.[70]

Moreover, there have been many examples of leaders at the highest levels explicitly emphasizing the value and role of both military and civilian personnel through a number of organizational messages. In a holiday e-mail to all personnel, for example, the Honourable Peter MacKay (former Minister of National Defence) and the Honourable Bernard Valcourt, Associate Minister of National Defence, wrote "We wish to extend our gratitude to everyone in the Canadian Army, the Royal Canadian Air Force, the Royal Canadian Navy and the Department of National Defence. Each and every member of the Defence family embraced this challenging year with the continued strength and passion that Canadians have come to expect from this outstanding team."[71] Similarly, General Tom Lawson, Chief of the Defence Staff, and CAF Chief Warrant Officer Bob Cléroux remarked to all DND and CAF personnel that "together, the members of the Defence Team have continued to uphold the finest traditions of service beyond self and delivering excellence in operations." Further, they explicitly reached out to say "To our civilian colleagues, we express our deepest admiration for your tremendous contributions to the successes of the Defence Team. The year 2012 has been marked by uncertainty and change, and, through it all, you have relentlessly continued the critical work needed for mission success."[72]

The orientation course for new DND employees also promotes a super-ordinate Defence Team identity while emphasizing the unique roles that civilians play in the organization. The expression "Defence Team" is used in the welcome letter signed by then Deputy Minister Robert Fonberg and then Chief of the Defence Staff General Walter Natynczyk, and DND civilian employees are referred to as "the Force Within." The manual for the course goes on to explain that the goals of the civilian workforce are aligned with those of the CAF – namely, to "defend Canada and Canadian interests and values while contributing to international security" – and that each DND employee "brings his or her unique set of skills and ideas to this task."[73] Following descriptions of each of the CAF's environmental commands, the manual explains how civilian personnel contribute to each of these commands, under headings like "Civilians Supporting Navy Operations," "Civilians Supporting Army Operations," and "Civilians Supporting Air Force Operations." All of this sets the stage for a super-ordinate Defence Team identity and for the unique identities of civilian personnel. And the analysis of social and organizational identity in this chapter indicates that these types of communications are valuable and ought to be continued.

While these efforts help build a shared sense of identity around the super-ordinate goals of National Defence, we suggest that a more robust sense of who DND civilians are as Public Service employees working to "defend Canada and Canadian interests and values" would be more conducive to reaping the personal and organizational benefits of having a meaningful organizational identity. We argue that the relatively recently proposed concept of a "defence professional" is a move in the right direction.

Defence Professionals and the Defence Team

In the wake of the terrorist attacks of September 11, 2001, defence leadership recognized that fundamental changes were required in National Defence to adapt it to the more complex and unpredictable security environment.[74] One of the proposed changes was closer civil-military cooperation at the political, strategic, operational and tactical levels.[75] General Rick Hillier (then CDS) responded to the new challenges in 2005 with the CF Transformation Project, which was designed to make the Canadian military more relevant, responsive and effective.[76] One of the major proposals in the project was an integrated Defence Team composed of Regular Force, Reserve Force and civilian personnel, often referred to as the "single solution."[77]

This civilian component of the single solution became the defence professional: "a Department of National Defence member of the Public Service Commission of Canada whose expertise, sense of identity and professional ideology distinguishes her/him from all other members of the public service and who works as a member of an integrated DND/CAF team whose primary focus is operational success."[78] Senior-level defence professionals would also possess a comprehensive understanding of war and conflict in the twenty-first century.[79] Defence professionals would work primarily in Canada, but could be expected to be employed at both the operational and tactical levels.[80]

The defence professional was modeled on the military professional concept articulated in *Duty with Honour*.[81] Like their military counterparts, defence professionals would have four defining attributes: expertise, responsibility, identity and professional ideology.[82] At the time of writing, each attribute still needed further articulation. Nonetheless, it has been suggested that the professional ideology of defence professionals be generalist in the sense that they should see themselves as employable in a wide range of roles across National Defence, especially as they become more senior members.[83] Their expertise is to be defence and security and their responsibilities – like their military counterparts – is to be the defence and security of Canada.[84] Clearly, the development and promulgation of this individualized concept would lead to a more salient and distinctive identity among civilian employees in DND, and it would also be conducive to a super-ordinate CAF-DND identity, with the identities of each side of the Defence Team having shared roots in *Duty with Honour*.

At the same time, developing defence professionals means creating an identity for public servants at DND that is qualitatively different from that of public servants elsewhere in the federal government. The extent of the ideological overlap between the defence professional and the military professional invites a number of questions, not the least of which is whether the defence professional identity is consistent with the Public Service identity and – more crucially – consistent with the mandate and the function of public servants within National Defence. Recall that there is a tension between maximizing organizational identity to reap the benefits predicted by identity theory – e.g., improved collaboration and increased personal well-being – and the function of civilian public servants within National Defence. As Gosselin,

Okros and English point out in their chapters in this volume, one of the functions that civilians in DND are meant to perform is a "challenge function" – i.e., to provide an outside perspective on complex problems and to bring civilian management practices into National Defence – among other roles. It stands to reason that the more civilians identify with their Defence Team counterparts, the less they will be able or inclined to perform what are oppositional functions. Any conception of the defence professional, therefore, must reconcile or at least strike a balance between strong social identification on the Defence Team and the oversight that civilians are meant to provide.

One solution is to root the super-ordinate identity of the Defence Team in the shared values of CAF military professionals and public servants. Values guide and shape behaviour, and they help individuals within a given organization foster a sense of common spirit. Military personnel are assumed to espouse the values in *Duty with Honour*, whereas civilian personnel are assumed to espouse the values in the *Values and Ethics Code for the Public Sector*.[85] No doubt, there are differences between the doctrines contained in these documents and the identities they foster. The CAF demands "unlimited liability,"[86] for example, and military service is often seen as a calling rather than a vocation.[87] Civilians are not obliged to accept unlimited liability and there is little clear evidence in the literature that working for the federal government is "a calling." Indeed, as Bentley argues, the Public Service continues to struggle with defining and embedding a concept of professionalism that all its members feel is accurate despite attempts at such reform.[88] Once again, therefore, it seems we are back to the fundamental differences between military and civilian members of the Defence Team: military personnel may see themselves in a distinct and unique category that can be breached only by those willing to make the sacrifices made by military personnel.

At the same time, *Duty with Honour* and the *Values and Ethics Code for the Public Sector* share many of the same core values – for example, loyalty, integrity, ethical behaviour and respect for democracy.[89] As Davis argues in this volume, moreover, there is also much overlap in the qualities and competencies expected of leaders in both organizations. Once this conception is filled out with the defence professional's unique knowledge base and focus on defence and security, we suggest that a strong and distinctive identity for defence civilians will emerge, one that is both conducive to the shared identity that fosters successful Defence Team relations and to personal well-being without sacrificing the special mandate of civilians inside National Defence. As Bentley proposed, though, defence civilians will develop an identity that is distinct from other public servants and more similar to that of their military colleagues.[90]

CONCLUSION

Department of National Defence civilians and Canadian Armed Forces military personnel work together in teams across National Defence under a common super-ordinate mandate. The success of these teams and the well-being of their members depend on their ability to forge trusting collaborative relationships. At the heart of trusting collaborative relationships is a sense of shared identity. Creating that sense of shared identity, however, is a challenge for National Defence. Military members of the Defence Team have a strong, salient, and visible collective identity that is both explicitly distinct from their civilian identities and closely aligned with the primary purpose of National Defence. Meanwhile, the civilians on the team have a weaker and more diffuse identity, and their function within National Defence is often characterized as supportive or secondary to the military function.

Social identity theory suggests that the weaker social identity of civilians – especially when it operates next to the strong and distinctive collective identity of military members – can lead to in- and out-group biases and to identity disparity for civilians, both of which can affect organizational performance and personal well-being. We argued that these problems could be overcome by promoting a super-ordinate Defence Team identity with which both military and civilian Defence Team members strongly identify, as well as a robust defence civilian identity that fosters a clearer sense of civilians' place within the organization and that matches the strong identity of military personnel. We argued that the introduction of the "Defence Team" concept and the messaging associated with it are important steps toward cultivating these elements of social identity within National Defence, and that these types of initiatives will help facilitate optimal integration and collaboration within the Defence Team.

ENDNOTES

1   National Defence and the Canadian Armed Forces, *Canada First Defence Strategy* [c. 2008], retrieved from http://www.forces.gc.ca/en/about/canada-first-defence-strategy.page

2   Canadian Armed Forces, Chief of the Defence Staff, *Duty with Honour: The Profession of Arms in Canada*, Government of Canada Catalogue Number: D2-150/2003-1 (Ottawa, ON: Canadian Defence Academy – Canadian Forces Leadership Institute, 2003), 13.

3   H. Tajfel, "Social Categorization, Social Identity and Social Comparison," in *Rediscovering Social Identity: Key Readings in Social Psychology*, eds. T. Postmes and N. R. Branscombe (New York, NY: Psychology Press, 2010), 120.

4   S. A. Haslam, N. Ellemers, S. D. Reicher, K. J. Reynolds, M. T. Schmitt, "The Social Identity Perspective Tomorrow: Opportunities and Avenues for Advance," in *Rediscovering Social Identity: Key Readings in Social Psychology*, eds. T. Postmes and N. R. Branscombe (New York, NY: Psychology Press, 2010), 342.

5   L. M. Roberts, I. H. Settles, and W. A. Jellison, "Predicting the Strategic Identity Management of Gender and Race," *Identity: An International Journal of Theory and Research* 8, no. 4 (2008): 269–306.

6   Subsequent refinements emphasized self-categorization theory in order to emphasize the intra-group processes as well as the intergroup processes relevant to identity (e.g., J. C. Turner, M. A. Hogg, P. J. Oakes, S. D. Reicher, and M. S. Wetherell, *Rediscovering the Social Group: A Self-Categorization Theory* (Oxford: Blackwell, 1987). These two theories, social identity theory [H. Tajfel and J. Turner, "The Social Identity of Intergroup Behavior," in *Psychology and Intergroup Relations*, eds. S. Worchel and W. Austin (Chicago: Nelson-Hall, 1986), 7-24] and self-categorization theory have since been integrated into the social identity approach [e.g., S. A. Haslam, *Psychology in Organizations: The Social Identity Approach* (London: Sage, 2001)].

7   J. C. Turner, "Social Categorization and the Self-Concept: A Social Cognitive Theory of Group Behavior," in *Rediscovering Social Identity: Key Readings in Social Psychology*, eds. T. Postmes and N. R. Branscombe (New York, NY: Psychology Press, 2010), 243-72.

8   Roberts, Settles, and Jellison, "Predicting the Strategic Identity," 269-306.

9   B. E. Ashforth and F. Mael, "Social Identity Theory and the Organization," *Academy of Management Review* 14 (1989): 20-39; S. A. Haslam, T. Postmes, and N. Ellemers, "More than a Metaphor: Organizational Identity Makes Organizational Life Possible," *British Journal of Management* 14 (2003): 357-69.

10   Tajfel, "Social Categorization, Social Identity," 119-28.

11   H. Tajfel and J. C. Turner, "The Social Identity Theory of Intergroup Behaviour," in *Psychology of Intergroup Relations*, eds. S. Worchel and W. G. Austin (Chicago, IL: Nelson-Hall, 1986), 7-24.

12 Tajfel and Turner, "The Social Identity Theory," 7-24.

13 M. Van Zomeren, T. Postmes, and R. Spears, "Toward an Integrative Social Identity Model of Collective Action: A Quantitative Research Synthesis of Three Socio-Psychological Perspectives," *Psychological Bulletin* 134 (2008): 504-35.

14 Tajfel and Turner, "The Social Identity Theory," 7-24.

15 Ashforth and Mael, "Social Identity Theory and the Organization," 20-39.

16 Z. Kunda, *Social Cognition: Making Sense of People* (Cambridge, MA: MIT Press, 1999).

17 Tajfel, "Social Categorization, Social Identity," 119-28.

18 Ibid.

19 T. F. Pettigrew, "Intergroup Contact Theory," *Annual Review of Psychology* 49 (1998): 65-85.

20 M. Sherif, O. J. Harvey, B. Jack White, W. R. Hood, and C. W. Sherif, *Intergroup Conflict and Cooperation: The Robbers Cave Experiment* (1954, 1961; Classics in the History of Psychology 1997), http://psychclassics.yorku.ca/Sherif/

21 See, Tajfel, "Social Categorization, Social Identity," 119-28.

22 Ibid.

23 H. Tajfel and J. C. Turner, "An Integrative Theory of Intergroup Conflict," in *Rediscovering Social Identity: Key Readings in Social Psychology*, eds. T. Postmes and N. R. Branscombe (New York, NY: Psychology Press 2010), 41.

24 J. C. Turner and S. A. Haslam, "Social Identity, Organizations and Leadership," in *Groups at Work: Advances in Theory and Research*, ed. M. E. Turner (Hillsdale, NJ: Erlbaum, 2001), 25-65.

25 Kunda, *Social Cognition*.

26 Ibid.

27 Turner and Haslam, "Social Identity," 25-65.

28 M. Hogg, "Managing Self-Uncertainty Through Group Identification," *Psychological Inquiry* 20 (2009): 221-24.

29 E.g., S. A. Haslam, S. D. Reicher, and M. Levine, "When Other People are Heaven, When Other People are Hell: How Social Identity Determines the Nature and Impact of Social Support," in *Social Cure: Identity, Health and Well-Being*, eds. J. Jetten, C. Haslam, and S. A. Haslam (New York, NY: Psychology Press, 2012), 157-74.

30 J. Jetten, C. Haslam, and S. A. Haslam (eds.), Social Cure: Identity Health and Well-Being (New York, NY: Psychology Press, 2012); G. Kreiner and M. Sheep, "Growing Pains and Gains: Framing Identity Dynamics as Opportunities for Identity Growth," in *Exploring*

Positive Identities and Organizations: Building a Theoretical and Research Foundation, eds. L. Roberts and J. Dutton (New York, NY: Psychology Press, 2009), 23-46.

31   Haslam et al., "The Social Identity Perspective Tomorrow," 357-80.

32   J. Ullrich and R. van Dick, "The Ingroup Psychology of Mergers and Acquisitions: Lessons from the Social Identity Approach," in *Advances in Mergers and Acquisitions*, vol. 6, eds. C. L. Cooper and S. Finkelstein (London: JAI Press, 2007), 1-15.

33   K. A. Jehn and K. Bezrukova, "The Faultline Activation Process and the Effects of Activated Faultlines on Coalition Formation, Conflict, and Group Outcomes," *Organizational Behavior and Human Decision Processes* 112 (2010): 24-42.

34   S. A. Haslam, J. Jetten, and C. Waghorn, "Social Identification, Stress and Citizenship in Teams: A Five-Phase Longitudinal Study," *Stress and Health: Journal of the International Society for the Investigation of Stress* 25 (2009): 21-30.

35   E.g., R. Van Dick, U. Wagner, J. Stellmacher, O. Christ, and P. A. Tissington, "To Be (Long) or Not To Be (Long): Social Identification in Organizational Contexts," *Genetic, Social, and General Psychology Monographs* 131, no. 3 (2005): 189-218.

36   Ashforth and Mael, "Social Identity Theory and the Organization," 20-39.

37   Haslam, Postmes, and Ellemers, "More than a Metaphor," 360.

38   M. Riketta, "Organizational Identification: A Meta-Analysis," *Journal of Vocational Behavior* 66 (2005): 358-84.

39   On organizational commitment, see Riketta, "Organizational Identification," 358-84; on organization performance, see F. O. Walumba, R. Cropanzano, and C. A. Hartnell, "Organizational Justice, Voluntary Learning Behavior, and Job Performance: A Test of the Mediating Effects of Identification and Leader-Member Exchange," *Journal of Organizational Behavior* 30, no. 8 (2009): 1103-26.

40   Department of National Defence, Report on Transformation 2011, available on request at http://www.forces.gc.ca/en/about-reports-pubs/transformation-report-2011.page.

41   The quotation comes from J. C. Wright, "'Service Before Self...Which Self?' Making Meaning of Military Identity at the Royal Military College of Canada" (paper presented at the Annual Meeting of the Canadian Sociological Association, Fredericton, New Brunswick, June 2011), 2.

42   *Duty with Honour*, 20.

43   Ibid., 21.

44   See also U. Ben-Shalom, Z. Lehrer, and E. Ben-Ari, "Cohesion during Military Operations: A Field Study on Combat Units in the Al-Aqsa Intifada," *Armed Forces and Society* 32, no. 1 (2005), 63-79.

45   Wright, "Service Before Self," 6.

46   Barbara D. Adams, Craig R. Flear, Andrea Brown, Michel H. Thomson, and Rachel M. Mcphail, *Civilian and Military Personnel Work Culture and Relations in CF/DND: Analysis Using a Social Identity Approach*, Director General Military Personnel Research and Analysis Contract Report 2012-003 (Ottawa, ON: Defence Research and Development Canada, 2012).

47   B. D. Adams, C. R. Flear, A. L. Brown, M. H. Thomson, and R. M. McPhail, *Civilian and Military Personnel Work Culture and Relations in CF/DND: Analysis Using a Social Identity Approach*, Director General Military Personnel Research and Analysis Contract Report 2012-003 (Ottawa, ON: Defence Research and Development Canada, 2012).

48   Sarah A. Hill, *Corporate Culture in the CF and DND: Descriptive Themes and Emergent Models*, Defence Research and Development Canada – Centre for Operational Research and Analysis Technical Report 2007-19 (Ottawa, ON: Defence Research and Development Canada, 2007), iv.

49   André Fillion, "The Integration of Defence Civilians within the Defence Team: How Far Can we Go?" (paper presented to Canadian Forces College, NSSP 9, June 2007), 26.

50   Irina Goldenberg, *Defence Team Survey: Descriptive Results*, Director General Military Personnel Research and Analysis Technical Memorandum 2013-026 (Ottawa, ON: Defence Research and Development Canada, 2013).

51   Ibid.

52   Adams et al., *Civilian and Military Personnel Work Culture.*

53   Hill, *Corporate Culture in the CF and DND.*

54   Ibid., 34.

55   Nick Jans and D. Schmidtchen, "Culture and Organisational Behaviour at Australian Defence Headquarters," *Australian Defence Force Journal* 158, (Jan/Feb 2003): 24.

56   Ibid.

57   Turner, "Social Categorization and the Self-Concept," 243-72.

58   Sarah Hill and F. Pinch, *Perceptions of Social and Cultural Gaps: Perspectives of Senior Canadian Forces Officers*, Directorate of Strategic Human Resources, Social Science Operational Research Team, Research Note 11/04 (Kingston, ON: Canadian Forces Leadership Institute, 2004).

59   Ibid.

60   Fillion, "The Integration of Defence," 2.

61   Ibid.

62   Ibid.

63   Van Zomeren, Postmes, and Spears, "Toward an Integrative Social Identity Model," 504-35.

64   Adams et al., *Civilian and Military Personnel Work Culture*; M. Hornsey and M. A. Hogg, "Subgroup Relations: A Comparison of Mutual Intergroup Differentiation and Common Ingroup Identity Models of Prejudice Reduction," *Personality and Social Psychology Bulletin* 26 (2000): 242-56.

65   S. L. Gaertner, M. C. Rust, J. F. Dovidio, B. A. Bachman, and P. A. Anastasio, "The Contact Hypothesis: The Role of a Common Ingroup Identity on Reducing Intergroup Bias," *Small Group Research* 25 (1994): 227.

66   Hornsey and Hogg, "Subgroup Relations," 242-56.

67   Gaertner et al., "The Contact Hypothesis," 224-49.

68   Adams et al., *Civilian and Military Personnel Work Culture*.

69   K. Banko, *The Defence Professional: Operationalizing the Concept*, Directorate Strategic Military Personnel Research and Analysis, Defence Research and Development Canada – Centre for Operational Research and Analysis Technical Memorandum 2008-17 (Ottawa, ON: Defence Research and Development Canada, 2008).

70   Defence Team website, last modified February 24, 2014, http://national.mil.ca/index-eng.asp

71   Peter MacKay (Minister of National Defence) and Bernard Valcourt (Associate Minister of National Defence), "Statement by the Minister of National Defence and the Associate Minister of National Defence on the Holiday Season" (corporate e-mail message, December 21, 2012).

72   Tom Lawson (Chief of the Defence Staff) and Bob Cléroux (Canadian Forces Chief Warrant Officer), "Holiday Message from the CDS and CFCWO," *The Maple Leaf* 15, no. 11 (2012): 2.

73   Department of National Defence, Assistant Deputy Minister (Human Resources – Civilian), Director General of Learning and Professional Development, *The Department of National Defence Civilian Employee's Orientation Guide*, National Defence ID Number: A-PD-007-000-AG-003 (published June 2003, revised June 2009), p. i.

74   L. W. Bentley, *Canadian Forces Transformation and the Civilian Public Service Defence Professional*, Canadian Forces Leadership Institute Technical Report 2007-01 (Kingston, ON: Canadian Defence Academy – Canadian Forces Leadership Institute, 2007).

75   Ibid.

76   Ibid.

77   Banko, *The Defence Professional*.

78   Bentley, *Canadian Forces Transformation*, 1.

79   Ibid.

80   Ibid.

81   Ibid.

82   Ibid.

83   Ibid.

84   Ibid.

85   Treasury Board of Canada Secretariat, 2011, retrieved from http://www.tbs-sct.gc.ca/pol/doc-eng.aspx?section=text&id=25049

86   Adams et al., *Civilian and Military Personnel Work Culture.*

87   Charles Cotton, "The Institutional Organization Model and the Military," in *The Military, More Than Just a Job?* eds. C. Moskos and F. Wood (Washington, DC: Pergamon-Brassey's, 1988), 39–56.

88   Bentley, *Canadian Forces Transformation.*

89   Treasury Board Secretariat, retrieved from https://www.tbs-sct.gc.ca/pol/doc-eng.aspx?id=25049&section=text

90   Bentley, *Canadian Forces Transformation.*

CHAPTER 9

CIVILIAN TRAINING AND MILITARY SOCIALIZATION

Justin Wright

The Canadian Armed Forces has been weighing the costs and benefits of in-service occupational training for junior non-commissioned members versus outsourcing their training to civilian institutions. One of the potential costs surrounds the "civilianizing" effect on military professionalism that outsourcing may have. The CAF's training system is considered the vehicle for socializing recruits[1] into the military ethos and the CAF identity. The formative experience of military training develops the new recruit into someone distinct – someone other than his or her civilian self. The CAF's socialization process has three basic aims that are not part of civilian education: the recruit must (1) come to place service before self, internalize the fighting spirit, accept unlimited liability and learn to maintain self-discipline; (2) become committed to the mission, to Canada and Canadian values, and to their fellow soldiers, sailors and air force members; and (3) adopt the professional identity and core values of the CAF.[2]

Civilianization of the CAF has long been a concern,[3] with new personnel seen as especially vulnerable to its influences.[4] For example, the 1978-79 *Combat Arms Survey* – which included the Military Ethos Scale (MES) – found that support personnel and junior NCMs tended to demonstrate comparatively less vocational and more occupational attitudes towards military service[5] (with the latter attitudes being indicative of civilianization).

But civilianization theory is not without its critics. S. B. Flemming noted the considerable impact of the *Combat Arms Survey* in his critique:

> The extent to which Cotton's MES has influenced the military at all levels is little appreciated. At the Combat Training Centre at CFB Gagetown, for example, a common topic among junior officers in

infantry phase training participating in discussions on leadership is the difficulty of leading troops more interested in being paid than doing their duty. More pointedly, during one session in the summer of 1987 several spoke ominously about a report (which they themselves had not seen) proving that 'more than half' of Canadian combat soldiers have said they would not go to war if called upon to do so. [These findings have] … reinforced strongly held military beliefs about the historical decline in the military commitment of Canadians.[6]

When the MES was administered again in 2004 through the Army Culture and Climate Survey,[7] the results demonstrated an almost identical distribution of attitudes towards military service, with junior NCMs again scoring the lowest in terms of vocational attitudes.[8] Civilianization, therefore, may not be a progressive problem in the CAF; the supposed indications of civilianization may be merely indicators of the incomplete socialization of junior ranks. Hence, the vulnerability of new personnel to civilianization cannot be assumed when examining traditional models of military training and socialization.

The focus of this chapter is thus the impacts and benefits of outsourcing military occupational training to civilian institutions, and, in particular, the initial training experiences of NCM trainees in these civilian educational settings. It begins with an examination of traditional military training and socialization theory, followed by a look at alternative training delivery and the reasons behind it. The third part examines a study of the effects of outsourced training on recruits, and the fourth reports qualitative research comparing in-service and out-sourced training.

MILITARY TRAINING AND SOCIALIZATION THEORY

Traditional models of military training are based on formal socialization, which includes tried and tested strategies, such as isolating new recruits, maintaining constant supervision over their training progress, and employing tactics meant to foster a common set of values and beliefs. One of the best treatments of formal socialization tactics is *Towards a Theory of Organizational Socialization*, in which J. Van Maanen and E. H. Schein outline a framework consisting of six tactical dimensions of socialization.[9] They propose that these dimensions consist of bipolar continuums and present categories of socialization techniques that are used by organizational leadership to ensure that newcomers adopt desired values and role orientations.[10]

Research building on Van Maanen and Schein's tactical dimensions of socialization regrouped their original dimensions to form a gestalt called "institutionalized socialization,"[11] which represents the set of socialization tactics commonly associated with formal socialization theory and practice. Institutionalized socialization tactics include the following:[12]

- Collective: putting newcomers together in groups and exposing them to common experiences and messages.

- Formal: isolating groups of newcomers from extra-organizational influences, as well as from established organizational members.

- Sequential: delivery of concise organizational knowledge through distinct and identifiable stages.

- Fixed: stages in the socialization sequence follow a predetermined timetable.

- Serial: socialization is facilitated through role modeling; experienced members teach the inexperienced and become active agents of socialization.

- Investiture: preserving the organization's status quo by bringing the newcomer to identify their role with the organization's core values and beliefs, so they see themselves as a "good fit" with the organization.

A useful metaphor for encapsulating this process is "socialization incubator,"[13] an artificial environment created to promote the rapid maturation of the socialized individual. Proceeding from the understanding that "clan-like" organizations, such as militaries and other highly structured organizations (e.g., civilian public service), hold newcomer socialization as a principal objective, the socialization incubator metaphor holds that the typical method adopted to achieve this objective is a specially constructed socialization climate in which newcomers are isolated from extra-organizational influences and factors.[14] Although this metaphor could be applied more broadly, it is especially apt when considering traditional military socialization, which includes physical relocation, isolation and supervision during initial training experiences.

There have been a few specific exceptions to this model (outlined below). But the socialization practices and tactics outlined above have generally formed the basis of the CAF's model of socialization and training delivery. These strategies and tactics have been the tried and tested way that the military "gets the job done" when it comes to training and socializing its new personnel.

At the same time, the CAF and its civilian partners – most notably the Department of National Defence – have continued to develop a more integrated and collaborative approach to operations, a change visible in the "Defence Team" concept. Given this heightened emphasis on an integrated Defence Team, it is perhaps appropriate that the CAF take advantage of new models of training and socialization that leverages alternative knowledge, perspectives and expertise. One way of achieving this is through outsourcing to civilian educational institutions the initial occupational training of new military personnel.

OUTSOURCING MILITARY TRAINING TO CIVILIAN INSTITUTIONS

Recent changes in operational- and strategic-level imperatives, most notably increased operational tempo and resource constraints, have led to the exploration of alternative approaches and strategies for enhancing training capability in the CAF. Under the aegis of the Individual Training and Education (IT&E) Modernization program, one such strategy, known as alternative training delivery (ATD), has explored a number of unconventional options to achieve CAF training requirements.[15]

ATD is not new in the CAF. The Royal Canadian Air Force has used contracted flight training and support (CFTS) for primary flight instruction since the early nineties,[16] for example, and the Royal Canadian Navy has been sending marine engineers to community colleges for portions of their training since 1981.[17] What is relatively new, however, is the acknowledgement that civilian training institutions can now accommodate a much larger portion of the military's training requirement, often at a much lower cost, which has led to an increased emphasis on leveraging ATD strategies wherever possible.

The term ATD[18] encapsulates a spectrum of training strategies, including contracting-in civilian instructors; "blended learning" approaches, such as on-the-job training (OJT), simulation technologies, and distance or e-learning; and outsourced training, such as tuition-based education or customized training provided through partnerships with civilian trade colleges. The focus of this chapter is the outsourcing of occupational training to civilian institutions and, in particular, on the initial training experiences of NCM trainees in civilian educational settings. The next section examines the results of a study of the effects of outsourced training on NCMs.

ATD and NCM Socialization Study

The CF IT&E Modernization initiative has explored several strategies for enhancing CAF training and education, including expanded initial occupational training programs for NCMs. Internal defence research has demonstrated that outsourcing initial training for selected occupations (such as vehicle technicians, avionic systems technicians, marine engineers) represents a significant cost savings when comparable training can be found in civilian institutions.[19] However, the same internal research noted that there is concern among some CAF leaders that removing new NCMs from the traditional military environment during the initial phases of training will have a detrimental impact on their socialization and the inculcation of the military ethos. This concern is most often expressed as "a failure to live the military chain of command," and it illustrates the strong influence of civilianization theory.[20]

The ATD and NCM Socialization Study was commissioned in response to these concerns. The aim of the study was to determine the impact of outsourced training on the early socialization of NCMs, including the identification of measures for evaluating the military ethos.[21] The project began with a thorough review and analysis of both military and academic research on organizational socialization and identity development,[22] which resulted in a conceptual model of the military ethos (Figure 9.1). The model contains four overlapping conceptual domains underlying the military ethos, including knowledge, motivation, behaviour and cognition.[23] Analysis of the socialization and identity development research within each of these conceptual domains yielded a number of suggested scales and measures, which were consolidated into a proposed NCM Ethos and Socialization Survey.[24]

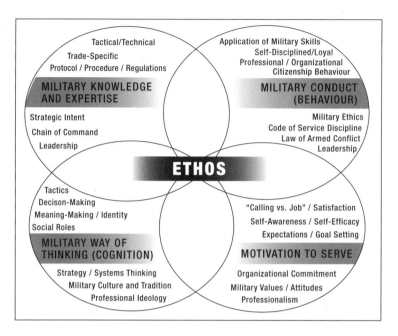

FIGURE 9.1: Military Ethos: A Model of the Underlying Concepts and Relationships[25]

Building on the conceptual development of the ethos model, some baseline qualitative data were captured to provide initial validation and to inform the final development of the NCM Ethos and Socialization Survey.[26] Qualitative data were collected through a series of focus groups with thirty-two NCMs who had received outsourced occupational training at civilian institutions, traditional occupational training at in-service schools, or both outsourced and in-service training. Participants were matched across occupation, service environment and unit of employment. A series of thirteen, one-on-one interviews with the immediate supervisors of the focus group participants was also conducted to capture the direct observations of immediate leaders regarding different training stream outcomes, including perceptions of the impact on the internalization of military values and the military ethos.

Ultimately, the focus groups and interviews were designed as a step in the development of the NCM Ethos and Socialization Survey, and thus were not intended to be generalized. However, much of the qualitative data that emerged speaks to the perceived effects on military personnel whose training and development has incorporated both military and civilian socialization experiences. The remainder of this chapter discusses a selection of these findings, situating them in the broader discussion of the benefits and drawbacks of civilian training alternatives for military socialization.

Outsourced Military Training: Perceptions of Outcomes

When discussing their perspectives on the merits and drawbacks of in-service versus outsourced occupational training, the focus group participants tended to favour their own individual experiences. Thus, outsource-trained participants typically saw their experience as positive, with no significant disadvantage, while in-service-trained participants typically viewed the cost of outsourced training – in terms of familiarity with the military environment – as a significant issue. Nonetheless, some of the focus group participants were more experienced personnel who had received outsourced training as part of an occupational transfer. The perspective of these participants proved invaluable, because they were able to offer richer insight into military socialization and identity development, having experienced both in-service and outsourced training and having significant military service. One experienced participant noted,

> Military ethos, and the values and the identity: that's all stuff that really builds up over time. It doesn't work to push that down on someone. Two years at a civilian school is not going to impact that process. You don't pick up so much of that in the first couple of years training in military schools that not doing that would make any difference. And the civilian college experience exposes you to a wider range of views and perspectives. It lets you see things from different angles....Basic training gives you a sense of being in the military, and what it takes. But it's only a few months. You don't lose anything from it because you've gone through a civilian college, and in reality there's not that much to lose.

This participant suggests that identity development and the inculcation of the military ethos are long-term processes, a view supported by the academic literature,[27] and one that calls into question the idea that a brief period of training in a civilian setting disrupts these processes. Perhaps most interesting, however, is the suggestion that civilian colleges expose military recruits to a "wider range of views and perspectives," the influence of which allows them to "see things from different angles." According to Robert Kegan's identity development framework, an individual's identity – defined as the act of "making meaning" of the world around them and their unique position within it – develops towards more complex stages as it is faced with different perspectives that challenge established mental schema and meaning-making narratives, incorporating those perspectives into a more complex meaning-making framework.[28] The participant's comments support this theory and suggest that military personnel who train at civilian institutions will have the opportunity, through exposure to a more diverse range of perspectives, to develop a more complex identity and meaning-making framework. For the Defence Team, a more complex meaning-making framework resulting from outsourced training experience may enhance a military member's capacity to communicate and collaborate with his or her civilian partners.

Indeed, some have argued that military and civilian personnel within the Defence Team have distinct cultures that reflect the different histories, roles, and socialization experiences of defence civilians and military members. The differences in attitudes, perceptions and behaviours can lead to misunderstandings and tensions, and can hinder integration between the two groups.[29] Exposure to a wider range of perspectives and more direct interactions with civilians through outsourced training may be conducive to a greater understanding of both cultures, and ultimately to the establishment of positive civilian-military working relations in the future.

Regardless of training experience, most focus group participants tended to view civilian college training to be as good as, or better than, in-service training in terms of the development of technical skill (with the caveat from in-service trained participants that it comes at the cost of familiarity with the military environment). In discussing the perceived benefits of their outsourced training experience, focus group participants cited a more in-depth study of the technical theory underlying the trade than is offered through in-service training; exposure to a wider range of applications of their trade skills, such as training on equipment or being introduced to specializations that are outside military applications; and receiving certification (i.e., a college diploma) at the completion of their training. These perceived benefits are important to consider because they point to some important differences in the nature of the training received at civilian institutions. For example, in explaining the benefit of a more in-depth treatment of trade theory to their military employment, one participant commented,

> The main difference is when you run into a problem in the shop. You draw on that broader civilian training and come up with workarounds or other options or approaches; you have more ability to troubleshoot problems that are bit unusual or outside the norm....The civilian program got a little deeper into the theory of the trade; it went beyond teaching the steps to fix something and explained why things worked the way they do. So that lets us approach a problem with a better understanding of what we're dealing with.

This participant suggests that outsourced training experience offers a more in-depth treatment of the trade theory, resulting in a perception of increased ability to problem solve, think critically and innovate within the context of applying trade knowledge on the job. Implicitly, this perception offers further support for the claim that outsourced training experience may lead to more complex ways of meaning-making than in-service training. Put another way, a training experience that results in increased capacity for critical and complex thinking may further prepare military members to communicate and collaborate effectively with their civilian partners.

Receiving certification for occupational training is another important point. Traditionally, military members who complete occupational training through in-service schools do not receive the civilian trade or technician certification – i.e., Red Seal Program certification – required to work as a licensed tradesperson in the civilian world. For military members exiting the CAF, their lack of certification generally means they are unable to leverage their military training and experience in seeking civilian employment in their occupation. However, the experience of CAF personnel who complete outsourced occupational training is quite different. Receiving journeyman certification opens up employment options should they choose to leave the CAF. Although it must be acknowledged that these civilian-trained members are contractually obligated to the CAF, the fact that they are trained and qualified in the civilian labour market – often in specialized technical trades with high demand – and still choose to serve in the military beyond their initial contract further challenges the assertion that outsourced training will disrupt the military ethos and socialization.

Certification also has implications for the identity development of these new CAF members, since their "professional/occupational" identity as a qualified tradesperson has also been validated and reinforced,[30] apart from their military identity. Recalling Kegan's framework, the integration of these multiple meaning-making narratives will result in the military member having a comparatively more complex mental schema and sense of self,[31] one that may have a greater degree of commonality with his or her civilian counterparts in the Defence Team.

Taking this a step further with respect to the identity development of CAF members and the integration of multiple meaning-making narratives, it has been suggested that the development of both unique (military or civilian) as well as common or "super-ordinate" (i.e., Defence Team) identities may facilitate collaboration between military and civilian personnel in DND and the CAF.[32] Through this dual identity, people can see themselves as members of two different groups that are nonetheless "playing on the same team."[33]

The literature provides both theoretical and empirical evidence that a super-ordinate and a unique military or civilian identity are beneficial to the work culture and relations within the Defence Team.[34] An unintended benefit of outsourced training may be to lay the groundwork for the development of a super-ordinate or Defence Team identity in the future.

Despite the perceived benefits of outsourced training, potentially negative consequences were also identified among focus group participants. In-service-trained participants tended to discuss outsourced training as coming at the cost of familiarity with the military environment. Some of their comments related to specific systems or procedures unique to the military, which outsourced trained personnel would not have encountered before arriving at their unit of employment. However, other comments spoke more broadly about military culture, social norms, established military convention, and nuances concerning how to navigate the chain of command (i.e., alluding again to the supposed effects of civilianization). For example, one supervisor remarked,

> Work ethic is a personal thing, so I wouldn't attribute that to a training environment. You can't make a lazy soldier more interested. But, knowledge of the military environment and military way of

doing things – the do's and don'ts and where those lines are – that's something you can't get at a civilian school.

Although outsourced training may have a number of benefits for the military member in terms of the application of their trade knowledge on the job and, potentially, in relation to their civilian Defence Team partners, the initial stages of their military training and socialization also require that they integrate into their military role and unit – to "live the chain of command." Outsourced-trained personnel may be approaching this process of integration from a more disadvantaged position than their in-service trained peers, which may have implications for adjustment to their organizational roles.[35] For example, one outsourced-trained participant reflected,

> The in-service guys have had a whole year to get to know each other and bond; it can be difficult to integrate into the group when you come in later. But that's where the military mindset comes in – once you're in the group, you're in. Everyone has that common experience because of basic training, and that experience becomes something you can share in common – helps you to relate.

The above remark acknowledges the difficulty that outsourced trained personnel can encounter when integrating into a military team. But it also suggests that social integration still occurs on account of the common experience of basic training that establishes the "military mindset." Arguably, the process of integration through a common frame of reference operates for both military teams and those consisting of military and civilian partners. It bears mentioning that collaboration and communication between military and civilian partners would likely be further enhanced if civilian members were able to develop a richer understanding of the nature and extent of military socialization, in order to see where their military partners are coming from.

CONCLUSION

The military ethos is at the heart of military professional identity and culture. The training system is the traditional vehicle through which socialization and military identity development operate. As the training experiences of CAF personnel become more complex, including through the incorporation of civilian training experiences and perspectives into their meaning-making activities, it becomes possible to imagine a military less isolated and more integrated with its civilian partners. However, it must be acknowledged that, as training experience becomes more complex, so too must the experience of socialization as multiple and integrated perspectives are brought to bear on the individual, the team, the unit, and the organization. Moreover, by embracing a more complex understanding of military training and socialization, the potential for increased capacity for communication, collaboration, and a common identity between military and civilian partners within the Defence Team will expand.

ENDNOTES

1   Of course, socialization and professional development and identity development are better viewed as career-long activities. See Justin Wright, *Towards the Development of a Measure of Military Ethos: Review and Analysis of Theory and Measures Related to Early Socialization and Training Delivery in the CF*, Canadian Forces Leadership Institute Technical Memorandum 2011-02 (Kingston, ON: Canadian Forces Leadership Institute), 45.

2   Canadian Armed Forces, Chief of the Defence Staff, *Duty with Honour: The Profession of Arms in Canada 2009* (Kingston, ON: Canadian Forces Leadership Institute – Canadian Defence Academy Press, 2009), 21.

3   S. B. Flemming, *Civilianization and Contemporary Social Theory: Alternative Approaches to Armed Forces and Society*, Project Report 439 (Ottawa: Operational Research and Analysis Establishment, 1988); Donna Winslow, "Canadian Society and its Army," *Canadian Military Journal* 4, no. 4 (Winter 2003-2004): 11-24.

4   Justin Wright, *Alternative Training Delivery and the Early Socialization of Non-Commissioned Members: Review and Analysis of Military Research and Related Concepts*, Canadian Forces Leadership Institute Technical Memorandum, 2010-02 (Kingston, ON: Canadian Forces Leadership Institute, 2010), 14.

5   On the Military Ethos Scale (MES) as part of the 1978-79 *Combat Arms Survey*, see Charles Cotton, "Institutional and Occupational Values in Canada's Army," *Armed Forces & Society* 8, no. 1 (1981): 99-110.

6   S. B. Flemming, *The Hearts and Minds of Soldiers in Canada: The Military Ethos Scale (MES) in Retrospect*, Staff Note 1 (Ottawa: Operational Research and Analysis Establishment, 1989), 10.

7   M. Capstick, K. Farley, B. Wild, and M. Parkes, *Canada's Soldiers: Military Ethos and Canadian Values in the 21st Century* (Ottawa: Director General Land Capability Development, 2005). It should be noted that, far from relying solely on the MES, the 2004 Army Culture and Climate Survey also examined a number of other dimensions that are considered to be interconnected with the military ethos, such as affective commitment; locus of commitment; professionalism; cohesion; job satisfaction; organizational citizenship behaviours; and career intentions.

8   Ibid., 29.

9   J. Van Maanen and E. H. Schein, "Towards a Theory of Organizational Socialization," in *Research in Organizational Behaviour*, ed. B. M. Staw (Greenwich, CT: JAI Press, 1979).

10   For a more comprehensive discussion of Van Maanen and Schein's socialization tactics framework, see A. M. Saks, K. L. Uggerslev, and N. E. Fassina, "Socialization Tactics and Newcomer Adjustment: A Meta-Analytic Review and Test of a Model," *Journal of Vocational Behaviour* 70, no. 3 (2007): 413-46. See also Justin Wright, *Towards the Development of a Measure of Military Ethos*, Canadian Forces Leadership Institute Technical Memorandum 2011-02 (Kingston, ON: Canadian Forces Leadership Institute, 2011).

11   G. R. Jones, "Socialization Tactics, Self-Efficacy, and Newcomer Adjustments to Organizations," *Academy of Management Journal* 29, no. 2 (1986): 262-79. See also Saks et al., "Socialization Tactics and Newcomer Adjustment," 413-46.

12   Ibid.

13   M. Ward, *An Analysis of Socialization Incubators in Selected Military Commissioning Institutions* (PhD diss., Southern Illinois University at Carbondale, 1999).

14   Ibid., iv-v.

15   L. G. Gillis and M. Russell, *A Study of Alternative Training Delivery in the Canadian Forces* (Kingston, ON: Canadian Defence Academy Press, 2009), 9.

16   Ibid., 18.

17   Ibid., 20.

18   Although the research on which much of this chapter is based makes use of the term "alternative training delivery" or ATD, it should be noted that this portion of the CF IT&E Modernization effort has since evolved and, at the time of this writing, is referred to as "Rationalized Training Delivery" (RTD). However, for the sake of continuity, this chapter uses the term ATD.

19   Gillis and Russell, *A Study of Alternative Training Delivery*, 34.

20   Ibid., 24.

21   Justin Wright, *Alternative Training Delivery and the Early Socialization of Non-Commissioned Members: Final Report on the Development of an NCM Ethos and Socialization Survey*, Canadian Forces Leadership Institute Technical Report 2012-03 (Kingston, ON: Canadian Forces Leadership Institute, 2012), iii. It is worth noting that these concerns

were aimed specifically at NCMs. As the CAF requires its officers to hold a university degree, the practice of officers studying at civilian institutions has been long established and is not deemed to be problematic for socialization or for instilling the military ethos. That these concerns have been raised specifically in relation to the training of NCMs in civilian institutions speaks to both the relative novelty of the idea (i.e., organizational/ cultural reticence towards change) as well as the underlying assumption that junior NCMs are more vulnerable to the perceived impact of civilianization.

22   Wright, *Alternative Training Delivery and the Early Socialization and Towards the Development of a Measure of Military Ethos.*

23   Wright, *Towards the Development of a Measure of Military Ethos*, 3.

24   Ibid.

25   Adapted from the CQ model in, Karen D. Davis and Justin C. Wright, "Culture and Cultural Intelligence," *Cultural Intelligence and Leadership: An Introduction for Canadian Forces Leaders*, ed. Karen D. Davis (Kingston, ON: Canadian Defence Academy Press, 2009), 9-25; see Wright, *Towards the Development of a Measure of Military Ethos*, for a detailed discussion of this model and its development.

26   Wright, *Alternative Training Delivery and the Early Socialization.*

27   Ibid. See also G. E. Harris and J. E. Cameron, "Multiple Dimensions of Organizational Identification and Commitment as Predictors of Turnover Intentions and Psychological Well-Being," *Canadian Journal of Behavioural Sciences* 37, no. 3 (2005): 159-69; T. S. Heffner and P. A. Gade, "Commitment to Nested Collectives in Special Operations Forces," *Military Psychology* 15, no. 3 (2003): 209-24; and J. P. Meyer, T. E. Becker, and R. Van Dick, "Social Identities and Commitments at Work: Towards an Integrative Model," *Journal of Organizational Behaviour* 27 (2006): 665-83.

28   Robert Kegan, *The Evolving Self: Problems and Processes in Human Development* (Cambridge, MA: Harvard U. P., 1982). For an applied example of Kegan's framework and methodology to a military population, see P. Lewis, G. B. Forsythe, P. Sweeney, P. Bartone, C. Bullis, and S. Snook, "Identity Development During the College Years: Findings from the West Point Longitudinal Study," *Journal of College Student Development* 46, no. 4 (2005): 357-73.

29   Irina Goldenberg and Filsan Hujaleh, *Partnership between Military and Civilian Personnel in Defence Organizations: An Annotated Bibliography*, Director General Military Personnel Research and Analysis Technical Memorandum 2012-020 (Ottawa, ON: Defence Research and Development Canada, 2012).

30   Meyer, Becker, and Van Dick, "Social Identities and Commitments at Work."

31   Lewis et al., "Identity Development During the College Years," 357-73. See also M. Jazvac-Martek, "Oscillating Role Identities: The Academic Experiences of Education Doctoral Students," *Innovations in Education and Teaching International* 46, no. 3 (2009): 253-64.

32   Barbara D. Adams, Craig R. Flear, Andrea I. Brown, Michael H. Thomson, Rachel M. McPhail, *Civilian and Military Personnel Work Culture and Relations in the Canadian Forces and Department of National Defence*, Director General Military Personnel Research and Analysis Contract Report 2012-003 (Ottawa: Defence Research and Development Canada, 2012).

33   S. L. Gaertner, M. C. Rust, J. F. Dovidio, B. A. Bachman, and P. Anastasio, "The Contact Hypothesis: The Role of a Common Ingroup Identity on Reducing Intergroup Bias," *Small Groups Research* 25 (1994): 227.

34   Adams et al., *Civilian and Military Personnel Work Culture.*

35   Saks, Uggerslev, and Fassina, "Socialization Tactics and Newcomer Adjustment," 413-46; see also K. Sang, S. Ison, A. Dainty, and A. Powell, "Anticipatory Socialisation Amongst Architects: A Qualitative Examination," *Training + Education* 51, no. 4 (2009): 209-321.

CHAPTER 10

THE DEFENCE TEAM: DOES GENDER MATTER?

Angela R. Febbraro

When visualizing the face of the two partners of the Defence Team in Canada, one is struck by the fact that the civilian partner is much more likely than the military partner to be female, even though both partners are predominantly male. In Canada, women constitute a relatively larger proportion of civilian personnel in the Department of National Defence (40.9%) than of military personnel in the Canadian Armed Forces (13.8% of the Regular Force).[1] A similar gendered demographic pattern is found in several other countries, such as the United States, the Netherlands, the United Kingdom, Sweden, Belgium, Germany, Estonia and Turkey.[2]

Yet little research has examined the Defence Team from a gendered perspective, and few analysts have asked whether gender matters in the Defence Team context. When gender has been considered in the military literature, the main questions have focused on the integration of women in the military, including the full integration of women into combat roles.[3] Within the civilian organizational literature, on the other hand, many studies have examined women in a variety of organizational contexts, but very few have examined civilian women working in a military or defence organizational context.[4] Moreover, although research on the Defence Team has recently begun to take off,[5] gender has rarely been a topic of inquiry when considering civilian and military personnel working together within the same defence organization.

An examination of gender within the civilian-military context – including associated team dynamics and intergroup perceptions of fairness – seems warranted, since military-civilian working relationships are likely to have important organizational implications (e.g., for employee engagement, performance and retention), and gender may define the experiences of personnel in unique ways within the organization.[6] Thus, the purpose of this chapter is to explore the question of whether gender matters in the context of the Defence Team. Indeed, a gender perspective may raise important new questions and reveal hidden complexities in the relationship between military and civilian members of the defence organization.

I first consider why gender might matter by examining theory and research on military culture from a gendered perspective. In particular, I examine the construction of masculinity in the military context – the notion of hyper- or hegemonic masculinity, the cult of masculinity and the masculine-warrior framework. I look at whether such constructions of masculinity present challenges, specifically for military-civilian working relationships in which military personnel are predominantly male and civilian personnel are more commonly female. I also draw on social and organizational identity theory in order to understand why gender might matter in the Defence Team context. Thereafter, I examine some of the empirical studies that have looked at gender in a civilian-military context. I suggest that an exploration of gender differences and similarities in organizational attitudes among civilian and military personnel may yield important insights for the Defence Team. Finally, I outline several directions for future research and for building the Defence Team, taking into account diversity considerations, including those regarding gender diversity.

WHY MIGHT GENDER MATTER? A LOOK AT CONSTRUCTIONS OF MASCULINITY IN MILITARY CULTURE

A number of analysts have looked at military culture from the perspective of how masculinity is constructed in militaries. Adopting a sociological approach, Karen Dunivin suggests that there are two models of American military culture: the traditional combat masculine-warrior model and the evolving model.[7] Under the traditional combat masculine-warrior model, combat is the military's core activity, from which its very existence and meaning is derived. Further, because the military is composed primarily of men, the culture of the military is also seen as largely shaped by men: soldiering is viewed as a masculine role, and the profession of war, defence and combat is defined by society as "men's work."

According to the traditional model, the military has recruited, trained and rewarded soldiers that embody its ideology, leading to a homogenous force comprised primarily of single, white, young men who view themselves as masculine warriors. Indeed, as Dunivin argues, a "masculine mystique" is evident as early as basic training when traditional images of independent, competitive, aggressive and virile males are promoted and rewarded. This has resulted, she argues, in a deeply entrenched cult of masculinity that pervades military culture, with accompanying masculine norms, values and lifestyles. Further, within the traditional model, military culture is exclusive, composed of masculine males holding conservative views. Women and gays/lesbians are viewed as outsiders or even deviants.

In contrast, as Dunivin explains, the evolving model of military culture promotes egalitarian and inclusive policies to support a diverse military force. It is certainly evident, as Dunivin and others have pointed out, that the contemporary American military has become more socially diverse, and that it increasingly includes women and minorities who perform non-traditional jobs previously performed primarily by white men.[8] However, even with such moves toward the evolving model, Dunivin argues that American military culture is still stuck in the traditional combat masculine-warrior model, and that this model persists even with the presence of "others" (e.g., women and gays/lesbians) who do not fit the stereotypical image of the masculine warrior. Further, a substantial body of literature shows that the bonding of men in predominantly male peer groups is often associated with hypermasculinity – i.e., expressions of extreme, exaggerated, or stereotypical masculine attributes and behaviours – even as the norms associated with hypermasculinity in the military are contradicted by other military norms that stress duty, honour, and discipline.[9] In any case, in addition to constructions of hypermasculinity, the traditional model of military culture is characterized by its monolithic view of women as outsiders – military women, by implication, but also, perhaps, civilian women.

Although Canada's military has made substantial strides in gender integration, American military cultural analyses, such as those by Dunivin and others, may also be applicable to the Canadian military context. Karen Davis and Brian McKee, for instance, suggest that the Canadian military still largely reflects a masculine warrior framework, in part because Canadian military policy and doctrine are increasingly dominated by the concepts *warrior ethos*, *warrior culture*, and *warrior spirit*.[10] Furthermore, Davis and McKee see this "warrior creep" as being unwarranted by current and future military requirements (e.g., changes in technology that reduce the need for brute strength, even within contemporary combat missions) and as inimical to the integration of women and many men. Research by Sarah Hill and Franklin Pinch provides some empirical corroboration for such a warrior framework in the Canadian military context.[11] Their survey found that senior CAF officers supported a traditionally structured military hierarchy and uniformity based on a conservative, masculine, and traditional cultural paradigm, and that they considered the Canadian military to be morally superior to the rest of society.[12] The authors pointed out that such attitudes could strain civil-military relations within the Defence Team, for instance, if such attitudes were to influence the military management of civilian personnel. Also worth noting is Hill's interview study of 26 military and 19 civilian senior decision makers in the Canadian military, which found that leadership, as practised by senior military personnel, had a highly directive quality that is considered well suited to the operational requirements of the military, whereas civilians' leadership style was reported to be more political, indirect and consensual.[13] Given that directive leadership has been traditionally associated with masculinity, and consensual/indirect leadership with femininity, one wonders whether there may also be a perceived gender dimension to these different leadership styles, based on masculine and feminine gender stereotypes and assumptions.[14] Hill's empirical work, however, did not include an examination of gender differences in attitudes or a discussion of findings in terms of gender constructs.

More recently, a study by Ramon Hinojosa examined hegemonic masculinities in the American military context.[15] Drawing on in-depth interviews with 43 men planning to enter active duty military service, Hinojosa explored how men construct a hegemonic masculinity by symbolically creating masculine hierarchies in which they situate themselves at the top. Through their discourse, the men positioned themselves as more morally oriented, self-disciplined, physically able, emotionally controlled, martially skilled, or intelligent than civilians, members of other military branches, different occupational specialties and different ranks. By casting other personnel – civilians and service members of different branches (i.e., Army, Navy, Marines, Air Force), different occupational specialties (i.e., infantry, artillery, supply, etc.), and different ranks (officer versus enlisted) – as less physically able, self-disciplined, willing to take risks, emotionally controlled, and intelligent, pre-active duty servicemen discursively dominated others, whether military or civilian, men or women.

The end result, according to Hinojosa, is that men construct hierarchies that subordinate others, while simultaneously placing their own perceived characteristics in positions of symbolic dominance. As Hinojosa further suggests, military service offers men unique resources for the construction of a masculine identity, defined by qualities tightly aligned with the military, such as emotional control, physical fitness, self-discipline, self-reliance, the willingness to use aggression and physical violence, and risk-taking. Thus, in addition to the external military rank system that ensures that some individuals, mostly men, maintain formal dominance over other men and women, Hinojosa claims that there exists an internal hegemony, one involving the symbolic hierarchal structuring of masculinities, such that some masculinity constructs are perceived as dominant and privileged over other masculinities and over femininities. In this view, Hinojosa suggests, hegemonic masculinities are extensions of everyday gendered social practice in which individuals construct gender identities in relation and opposition to other men and women.

As Hinojosa further explains, and of particular relevance to the present civil-military focus, one tactic for constructing an identity in line with hegemonic masculinity used by his participants was to compare the perceived qualities of military members to those of civilians. One way to achieve this was for participants to construct narratives in which they possessed greater self-discipline than civilians. Further, the emphasis on physical fitness was used by participants to imply that military personnel have the ability to handle the physical demands of the military, whereas civilians do not. Thus, the practice of rank-ordering civilians versus military personnel enabled the men in Hinojosa's study, symbolically at least, and as future military personnel, to dominate civilians by positioning them as less self-disciplined and less physically able. Indeed, by discursively comparing themselves to others, Hinojosa argues that the men symbolically waged "ideological warfare" on civilians and other military personnel,[16] setting themselves apart by suggesting that they were more self-disciplined, better physically capable, more emotionally controlled, more motivated by duty/honour/purpose, or more intelligent than others. As pre-active-duty service members, their ascendancy to the top of the hierarchies that they created occurred, Hinojosa suggests, as a verbal game of exclusion that relegated other men to "masculine ghettos" and symbolic subordination within the masculine hierarchy.[17]

What is particularly interesting about Hinojosa's study is that it involved pre-active duty men who were on their way to becoming full-fledged military personnel; thus, they were not quite civilians, but not yet full military personnel either. According to Hinojosa, these pre-active duty men saw themselves as superior to other military men, depending on their occupation, branch, or rank, and as superior to civilians, both men and women. One is left wondering, however, whether the men in Hinojosa's study would have discursively or symbolically positioned civilian men and women at the same level in their hierarchy or not. Given, for instance, the men's views of the importance of physical capability, and gendered assumptions about physical strength, it is possible that civilian women would have been ranked by Hinojosa's men at the very bottom of the hierarchy of hegemonic masculinity, positioned even lower than civilian men.

In light of these considerations, it is worth noting that some of the men in Hinojosa's study also discursively subordinated military or civilian personnel whose work involves sitting "behind a desk" to military personnel who work on the "front lines."[18] Similarly, some of the men felt that enlisted personnel had greater self-discipline and a stronger work ethic than officers. Accordingly, within the hierarchy of hegemonic masculinity, Hinojosa's men symbolically subordinated college-educated officers ("half-cocked micro-managers") to trained enlisted personnel, who they felt actually do the work ("sweating and working"), while the officers "get the medals."[19]

Given that some civilians who work in defence organizations sit behind desks and have university or college education, one wonders whether such civilians would hold a high position in the hierarchy of hegemonic masculinity in the view of Hinojosa's men. Such high status may be especially questionable for civilian women, who are likely to work in support, administrative or professional roles, as opposed to roles requiring physical strength or technical and mechanical expertise. And although military organizational culture may indeed be two-sided[20] – with one side represented by soldiers on the battlefield (the "teeth") and the other side reflected in military personnel working alongside civilians behind desks in corporate headquarters (the "tail") – the battlefield culture may still influence, and may even symbolically dominate the corporate culture.[21] In short, within the hierarchy of hegemonic masculinity – and drawing on Hinojosa's thesis – battlefield or warrior culture may be viewed as more valuable or superior to military corporate culture, and this differential valuation may subordinate civilian women in particular, who work in defence organizations beside male military personnel.

SOCIAL AND ORGANIZATIONAL IDENTITY

Social and organizational identity theory may also provide useful insights into the importance of gender in the Defence Team context.[22] According to social identity and self-categorization theory, the desire to categorize oneself as a member of a particular group is a natural human propensity. Categories may be based on age, gender, or any other characteristic that reflects membership in a social group, team, organization or other social entity – such as "military" and "civilian." As B. D. Adams et al. suggest, when military personnel see themselves as being prepared to make the ultimate sacrifice in the service of their country, it creates a significant divide between themselves and even respected civilian colleagues, opening the door for a strong in-group bias.[23] As civilians are not required to accept unlimited liability, they may be perceived as less committed than military personnel to their roles or as unable to understand the pressures that military personnel face. Adams et al. further suggest that even if military and civilian personnel are able to build strong working relationships, military personnel are likely to view themselves as members of a unique category that can be accessed only by those willing to make the same ultimate sacrifice.[24] In a sense, this perceived divide between military and civilian personnel on the basis of unlimited liability may be seen as analogous with the symbolic hierarchies constructed by the men in Hinojosa's study of hegemonic masculinity.

At an organizational level, the different goals and purposes of the Canadian military and the Public Service, for instance, are unique to each and thus have the potential to create divisions between military and civilian personnel. Although the two organizations are intended to work in partnership, the defence function is typically understood to reside with military personnel, with civilian personnel in DND typically viewed as playing a secondary, supportive role to defence. Given that supportive functions within civilian organizations have generally and traditionally been associated with females and femininity, the supportive roles of civilians within the CAF and DND may carry with them gendered connotations and messages about status and power.[25] For civilians, and particularly female workers in DND, not being in the organization's most prominent role – i.e., combat – may make it more difficult for them to fully internalize the organizational identity of the Defence Team and for the military to recognize the value and commitment of civilians – and perhaps especially the value and commitment of female civilians – to the defence organization.[26]

This conclusion would seem to be supported by Constance Anne Kostelac's analysis of civilianization in police forces, a pattern she argues reflects the gendered nature of police organizations in the United States.[27] As in the defence context, the majority of police officers are male, but the majority of civilian employees in police organizations are female. Further, civilian women tend to work in entry-level support roles (e.g., as secretaries, record clerks) – in jobs that fall outside the crime-fighting domain of "real police work." According to Kostelac, the support role held by civilian women is more in line with traditional domestic "women's work," while police work, reflecting hegemonic masculinity, carries with it the idea of "men's work." Kostelac further argues that these roles reinforce the distance between officers and civilian employees in the organization and set civilian support positions apart as more feminine, in contrast to the central, masculine role of the police officer. It follows that this central role versus supportive role positioning may also communicate messages about status and power within the defence organization, with those located at the centre possessing more status and power than those in more peripheral, supportive roles.[28]

Within the defence organization, several other factors differentiate military and civilian personnel and may thus contribute to social boundaries. Some of these differentiating factors may also carry with them gender connotations, as well as messages about status and power. For instance, as discussed earlier, research indicates that differences in leadership style may be one of the key areas of tension in the relationship between military and civilian personnel. Military commanders' leadership style tends to be agentic and highly directive, rather than consensual and participative, and this difference in leadership style may convey implicit messages about gender and power.[29] Interestingly, Hill's research also indicated that senior civilian leaders tended to accommodate a more directive leadership style when working with military personnel, but that military leaders did not typically reciprocate by shifting their leadership style in a more consensual direction when working with civilian personnel. The fact that military personnel did not reciprocate could be interpreted by civilians as a lack of inclusiveness, and it may have negative effects on their relationships with civilians. Moreover, the tendency of civilian personnel to accommodate the military style of leadership, without military personnel reciprocating, may also reflect the status of civilian vis-à-vis military personnel, with the latter having the higher status and power.

One might also ask whether differences in dress and deportment between military and civilian personnel carry similar implicit messages about gender, status, and power. As Adams et al. observe, military uniforms clearly indicate to both military and civilian personnel that the person wearing the uniform belongs to the category of "military personnel." Typically, military personnel with higher ranks are ascribed more status and competence by virtue of the barriers to advancement that they have had to overcome. The uniform may also convey messages about masculinity (e.g., the "man in uniform"), strength, and power. The attire of civilian personnel, in contrast, does not typically define them as having a unique function, nor is it linked with a long historical tradition or necessarily with competence, strength, or power – despite the wearing by some civilians, both male and female, of the "power suit."

Moreover, as explained in the next part of this chapter, perceived differences in organizational fairness may also contribute to civilian-military divisions, with implications for social and organizational identity and, ultimately, organizational commitment and performance. Research by Brian McKee and L. M. Williams, for instance, found that DND civilians perceived themselves as disadvantaged next to military personnel when it came to travel, training, assignments and hiring practices.[30] Similar perceptions were reflected in research by Sylvie C. Lalonde, in which civilians noted that their training budgets were highly limited compared to those of military personnel and that "civilians got the leftovers," rather than their fair share of resources.[31] From a social and organizational identity perspective, these perceptions may also contain a negative message to civilian personnel about their relative worth, their sense of belonging to the organization, and the long-term priorities of the organization in which they work. If military personnel do receive substantially more training opportunities and resources than civilian personnel, for instance, then this may imply that military personnel are viewed as more critical to the core functioning of the organization than civilians.

Indeed, this perceived military advantage in training and resources is consistent with the notion, previously discussed, that the ostensibly masculine work of military personnel may be viewed as more central to defence than the ostensibly feminine supportive work of civilian personnel. Once again, such views may undermine civilians' sense of organizational identity as part of the "Defence Team," which may in turn undermine civil-military working relationships, as well as civilians' organizational commitment and performance. Importantly, however, gender was not examined systematically in the research of either Lalonde or McKee and Williams.[32] McKee and Williams included an equal representation of male and female civilians (and no military personnel) in their study, but they did not report any specific gender comparisons.[33] The investigators did, however, find little or no differences between the opinions and perceptions of civilian employees who self-identified as members of an equity group and those who did not (3 of the 26 focus groups in the study were equity groups).[34] On the other hand, the vast majority (78%) of participants in Lalonde's study were civilian females; but again, no gender comparisons were reported, and no military personnel were included.[35] In any case, perceptions of organizational fairness among the civilian respondents in both studies seemed to reflect perceptions of organizational status. Whether they also signify a gender-related hierarchy within the defence organization, however, could be a fruitful area for future research.

The next part of the chapter reviews some of the few existing empirical studies that have looked at gender in a civilian-military context. Although not necessarily exhaustive,[36] the research review provides an indication of the range of issues that may be worthy of further study in the Defence Team context.

EMPIRICAL RESEARCH ON GENDER IN THE CIVILIAN-MILITARY CONTEXT

As noted earlier, previous empirical research on the Defence Team in Canada, particularly from the perspective of civilians,[37] has drawn attention to a number of issues that may affect civilian-military working relationships. For the most part, however, these studies have not incorporated gender into their analyses. Following is a summary of the findings of a few studies that have been conducted in the civilian-military context and that have included some analysis of gender. Given the paucity of research in this area, and the exploratory nature of this chapter, the studies are summarized in some detail in order to provide the reader with a sense of the range of issues that may be gender-relevant and worthy of further investigation, from the organizational to the individual level. Indeed, if it is the case that the Canadian military still reflects a masculine warrior framework, this may result in myriad effects, ranging from organizational effects (e.g., perceptions of organizational climate) to individual effects (physical and mental health issues). In any case, in most studies, gender was not the primary focus, but gender differences in perceptions or attitudes were discussed or revealed in findings.

One such study was the Defence Team Survey conducted in 2012 with CAF and DND personnel.[38] Participants in this survey included hundreds of civilian and military personnel of both genders. Thus, it was possible to examine gender differences in attitudes among civilian personnel and among military personnel, as well as to compare civilian personnel to military personnel on the basis of gender. Survey topics included perceptions of relationship quality, communication, respect in the workplace, inclusion, senior leadership messages regarding the Defence Team, the effects (for civilians) of working in a military context on career development and training opportunities, organizational fairness, supervision, job satisfaction, work engagement, organizational commitment and retention intentions. Results showed that, among civilian respondents, there were no discernible gender differences in work attitudes assessed by the survey. Likewise, among military respondents, most of the gender comparisons showed gender similarities. Thus, the main theme from this survey was one of gender similarity for both civilian and military personnel. However, a few notable gender differences were observed among military respondents. For instance, female military members reported higher levels of commitment (particularly affective commitment), higher levels of inclusion, higher levels of engagement, and higher retention intentions than male military members.

Considering separately the average ratings of both males and females on the Defence Team Survey, the ratings of civilian personnel and military personnel tended to be quite similar. For both genders, however, military ratings of senior leadership messages regarding the Defence Team were slightly higher than the corresponding civilian ratings. On a 5-point rating scale, the average ratings were 4.6 for both male and female military personnel and 4.1 for both male and female civilian personnel. Although the ratings were relatively high for all groups, the results suggest that – across both genders – military personnel seemed to have more favourable ratings than civilian personnel of the efforts of military leaders to promote the military-civilian Defence Team and to emphasize the importance of military-civilian employee cooperation. Thus, while senior leadership messages regarding the Defence Team may be perceived similarly by men and women, such messages seem to be perceived differently by military and civilian personnel.

In addition, survey findings indicated that the perceptions of overall organizational fairness of military personnel were slightly higher than those of civilians, perhaps especially those of civilian women. The mean rating of overall organizational fairness for civilian women was 4.8 out of 7, compared to 5.0 for civilian men and 5.2 for both military men and military women. Although the group differences were small, and would require future validation, these results suggest possible variations in the perceived fairness of work rewards, decision-making procedures, supervisor treatment, and DND/CAF treatment of its employees. Such findings seem consistent with previous research suggesting that DND civilians have concerns about organizational fairness.[39] The relatively low ratings also suggest that perceptions of organizational fairness could be improved for all groups – civilian or military, women or men. Indeed, the overall ratings of about 5 on a 7-point scale indicated only "slight agreement" with organizational fairness survey items.

Interestingly, the retention intentions of civilian women were found to be higher than those of military men in the survey (the average ratings were 4.7 vs. 4.3, respectively, out of 5). In comparison, the ratings of military women and civilian men were 4.9 and 4.8, respectively, and therefore also higher than those for military men. Once again, the group differences were fairly small. Still, along with other Defence Team Survey results mentioned earlier regarding organizational commitment and retention intentions (e.g., the lack of gender differences among civilians regarding commitment and retention intentions; the higher commitment and retention intentions of female compared to male military personnel), such findings seem to contradict gender stereotypes regarding the lower organizational commitment or lower retention of women compared to men.[40] In addition, the relatively low retention intentions of military men that were found in this survey may be worth further investigation.

Overall, the results of the Defence Team Survey, on their own, do not seem to provide clear or consistent evidence, for instance, of a masculine-warrior model within DND and the CAF; nor do they provide clear or consistent evidence that an evolved model has necessarily taken hold. Female civilians, for instance, seemed to perceive lower levels of overall organizational fairness than military personnel of both genders, but also reported higher retention intentions than military men. Moreover, the perceptions of female civilians were very similar to those of male civilians. Likewise, except for a few differences seeming to favour military women, the perceptions of military women were very similar to those of military men. Once again, the general pattern from the survey was one of gender similarity rather than gender difference. The small gender differences that seemed to occur do not reflect a consistent or easily interpretable pattern, and they would require further validation and potentially more in-depth investigation.

As mentioned earlier, few studies to date have focused specifically on gender within the civilian-military organizational context. One exception is a 1999 study by Stephen J. Brannen, Karen R. Brannen and Thomas W. Colligan, which investigated employee perceptions of the equal opportunity cultural climate at a large uniformed service medical centre in the mid-Atlantic United States.[41] This large-scale survey study, which included responses from 1,751 medical centre employees, compared male to female personnel, as well as military personnel (officers, warrant officers, and enlisted members) to civilian personnel (federal government employees).[42] Perceptions of climate were measured using the Military Equal Opportunity Climate Survey (MEOCS) developed by the Defense Equal Opportunity Management Institute to assist military organizations in improving organizational functioning and effectiveness and in assessing their equal opportunity climate. The MEOCS contained survey items on the following factors: sexual harassment and discrimination, different command behaviour toward racial minorities, positive equal opportunity behaviours, overt racist/sexist behaviours, reverse discrimination (at the medical centre, as well as in the military and American society), discrimination against women and minorities, attitudes towards racial and gender separatism, organizational commitment, perceived work-group effectiveness, job satisfaction, and overall equal opportunity climate. Thus, this study assessed gender differences in perceptions of organizational climate, but also focused on equal opportunity climate or diversity issues, including gender diversity issues, within a civilian-military organization.

In general, survey results showed that respondents viewed the equal opportunity cultural climate of their organization as above average. However, statistically significant gender differences in perceptions were found for most of the MEOCS factors. Compared to females, males generally held a more positive perception of the cultural climate in terms of perceiving less sexual harassment and discrimination against racial minorities and women. Males also perceived more reverse discrimination at the medical centre, in the military and in American society (with males viewed as the likely victims), held stronger beliefs that the races and genders should remain separate, and perceived a more positive overall equal opportunity climate than did females. Compared to males, females perceived less *overt* racist/sexist behaviour. The researchers speculated that males may be more aware of overt racist/sexist behaviour than females because males are more likely to engage in such behaviour in the presence of other males than other females.

Brannen, Brannen, and Colligan's study also revealed several differences between military and civilian personnel regarding equal opportunity or diversity climate, including gender diversity climate. Compared to civilians, military personnel reported more favourable perceptions of different command behaviours towards racial minorities, perceived more positive equal opportunity behaviours, reported greater job satisfaction, perceived less discrimination against racial minorities and women, and perceived a more positive overall equal opportunity climate. Civilian personnel, on the other hand, viewed reverse discrimination as less prevalent in the military and American society. On the whole, then, military personnel perceived the medical centre as reflecting an equal opportunity climate to a greater degree than did civilian personnel.

Brannen, Brannen, and Colligan make a substantive contribution to research on gender in the civilian-military context, as gender issues figured prominently in their analysis.[43] In addition, keeping in mind that the research was conducted over a decade ago, the findings could be interpreted as reflecting a traditional combat masculine-warrior model of military culture, one in which social homogeneity, rather than social diversity, is valued – and one in which masculine values define the organizational culture. Such a traditional model may help to explain, for instance, why females and civilians generally held a less positive view of the gender diversity climate (i.e., perceived more discrimination) than males or military personnel, at least at the time of study. However, it must also be noted that the analysis of the survey data was limited in that the military and civilian groups were not broken down by gender (or vice versa). Thus, although the perceptions of males and military personnel regarding diversity climate generally compared favourably to those of females and civilian personnel, civilian women were not compared to military men, civilian men were not compared to military women, and so on, for all possible group comparisons. However, the focus of Brannen, Brannen and Colligan's study on perceptions of organizational climate, specifically in terms of gender and other diversity issues, represents an important contribution to the civilian-military literature from a gender perspective.

In a similar vein, a 1997 study by Jacqueline Sharpe investigated the diversity climate at a large teaching military hospital in the United States, including aspects of the organizational climate related to ethnicity, gender, age, physical ability, sexual orientation, and job level.[44] The study included 1,252 participants (37% minority, 57% female, 25% officer, 30% enlisted, and 45% civilian). Like Brannen, Brannen and Colligan, Sharpe focused on perceptions of diversity climate (including gender diversity) in a defence organization, and presented results according to gender and civilian-military status. Results indicated that males, overall, had significantly more favourable perceptions of organizational climate, ethnicity climate, gender climate and job level climate than did females – a pattern which was consistent with Brannen, Brannen, and Colligan's findings. Further, the perceptions of officers, enlisted personnel, and civilian personnel differed significantly regarding gender climate: 21% of the civilian staff reported unfavourable perceptions of the gender climate, compared to 7% of the enlisted staff and 8% of the officer staff. Once again, as was found by Brannen, Brannen and Colligan, in Sharpe's study the perceptions of military personnel regarding diversity climate compared favourably to those of civilian personnel. Thus, it appears, based on these studies, that males and military personnel are generally more likely than females and civilian personnel to view the diversity climate (including gender diversity climate) of their defence organization in a positive way (i.e., to view the climate as functioning well in terms of diversity). Once again, although caution in interpretation is warranted, such patterns seem consistent with a traditional combat masculine-warrior model of military culture, in which masculine values define the organizational culture.

Interestingly, in Sharpe's study – which did break down military and civilian groups by gender – female officers had significantly more favourable perceptions of the gender climate than did enlisted women or especially civil service women, who were more likely to report unfavourable perceptions. Twenty-four percent of female civilians reported unfavourable perceptions of the gender climate, compared to 13% of the female enlisted staff and 15% of the female officer staff. Such findings, along with some of the Defence Team Survey results discussed earlier, indicate that organizational experiences and perceptions may differ to some extent for civilian women and military women. After all, military women, unlike civilian women, hold military status, and may embrace traditional military culture to a greater degree than civilian women, even if military women may also experience issues with gender discrimination. Further, nearly half of survey respondents (45%) rated the organizational climate as less than favourable concerning offensive remarks about women. In terms of recommendations, one participant called for military male officers to be trained to be more sensitive to both active duty and civilian females. In general, concerns about the advancement of women, and the lack of respect for civilian employees, were two of the major issues raised in the study.

In addition to research on organizational diversity climate, and the implications for gender, a few studies have examined individual health-related issues in civilian-military organizational contexts. For instance, Linda Duxbury and Chris Higgins' analysis of results from the 2001 Health Canada Work-Life Survey examined how Canadian military and DND civilian employees cope with work and family demands, work-family balance, changing work environments, and related stressors that affect their individual health.[45] Participants were 980 CAF members (12% female) and 555 DND civilian personnel (40% female). Results indicated that civilian and military personnel reported different work-life balance issues. In particular, CAF respondents reported heavy workloads, difficulties achieving a work-life balance, and having less control over their time and work situation than did civilians. Civilians, on the other hand, reported challenges such as lack of career development and recognition, and working in a non-supportive work environment. Indeed, almost one quarter of those in the DND civilian sample perceived their managers as non-supportive, compared to less than 10% of those in the CAF. Duxbury and Higgins also reported that the form of work-family conflict depended on the employee's gender and job type. For the most part, however, Duxbury and Higgins controlled for, rather than examined, gender differences, and thus shed relatively little light on gender in their study. Generally speaking, when gender was controlled for (i.e., men were compared to men, and women to women), managers, officers and CAF members reported more problems with balance than did other federal public service employees.

With respect to employee mental health, approximately half those in the DND sample reported high levels of perceived stress; one quarter were at high risk of burnout, and 30% reported high levels of depressed mood. When gender was controlled for, these levels of stress, burnout and depressed mood were the same as those of the total sample. Employees in the CAF sample (as well as managers and officers) were more likely to report high burnout, whereas non-managerial civilian members of DND were more likely to report high levels of stress (52% versus 47%) and depressed mood (33% versus 28%). Duxbury and Higgins suggested that these differences in stress and depressed mood were likely due to the higher number of women in the civilian sample (women are generally more likely than men to report that they are stressed and depressed). Recommendations (on the civilian end) included making the work environment more supportive, making career development a priority, and providing rewards and recognition. On the CAF end, recommendations focused on increasing members' sense of control, reducing workloads, and increasing work-life balance. Overall, such recommendations seem consistent with the goal of developing an evolving model of military culture, one that recognizes a diverse workforce with diverse needs – including the achievement of work-life balance. Yet the survey results may also indicate the possible persistence of the traditional masculine-warrior model within the CAF and DND, reflected in difficulties in achieving work-life balance, as well as in feelings of stress and lack of support.

While Duxbury and Higgins mentioned the potential impact of gender on their results, they did not seek to examine gender differences specifically, but rather sought to control for gender, as noted above. In contrast, John V. Civitello's 1997 study of stress levels among members of a United States Air Force medical facility did explore gender differences specifically.[46] Participants in Civitello's study included both military and civilian members in three squadrons: medical support, dental and medical operations. Of the 200 total staff, 173 were active-duty military (both officer and enlisted subgroups) and 27 were civilian employees. The military staff (40% female) included professional members, paraprofessionals and various technical support specialists, while the civilian staff (86% female) included mostly support persons assigned to various health clinics.

Among the most notable study results, and keeping in mind the large proportion of females in the civilian sample (i.e., the confounding of gender and military-civilian status), civilians were twice as likely as military respondents to report experiencing a severe level of stress (24% vs. 12%). For civilians, comparing job performance with others in the organization was the stressor most frequently identified (81%), while lack of reinforcement from leadership was also a major stressor for civilians (52.4%) – a finding that echoes the lack of support and recognition perceived by civilians in Duxbury and Higgins' study. Interestingly, civilians reported the highest level of burnout, but considerably less irritability toward others than reported by military respondents. Further, nervousness was reported by over half the civilian group (57.1%).

In terms of gender, the only stress symptom receiving a high response rate from both males and females in Civitello's study was fatigue (60.8% males, 53% females). Males were more likely than females to report burnout (54% vs. 36.4%) and irritability towards others (54% vs. 47%), and twice as likely as females to report nervousness (47.3% vs. 24.2%). Thus, for some symptoms, the male respondents appeared to experience higher stress levels than the female respondents. Such findings may serve as a reminder that it is not only or necessarily females that are disadvantaged within a defence environment. Indeed, considering Hinojosa's study of hegemonic masculinity, for instance, it may be that the hierarchical structuring of masculinities within the defence context plays a role in producing the stress symptoms experienced most acutely by some males, perhaps especially those males striving to achieve hypermasculine, stereotyped masculine attributes as military men. Although Civitello's study examined gender differences in stress levels in a civil-military context, the analysis did not break down the civilian and military results according to gender (or vice versa). Thus, such possibilities about the potential deleterious health effects of hegemonic masculinity on men or women, military or civilian – or other possible explanations for such findings – must await future research.

BUILDING A STRONG DEFENCE TEAM WITH GENDER IN MIND

Research on gender in the civilian-military context is still in its early stages and exhibits a range of methodological limitations. Yet the theoretical and empirical work that was presented here suggests that further research on the role of gender in the civilian-military context is worth pursuing – that gender may well matter for the Defence Team. Indeed, part of the challenge of building a strong civilian-military Defence Team may involve taking gender diversity into account.[47] By identifying shared values that transcend subgroups (e.g., quality of work, improvement of the organization), while at the same time embracing diversity, whether based on gender, military versus civilian status, or both, the potential advantages of diversity for the defence organization in terms of enhanced perspectives and broader approaches may be realized.[48]

Towards the goal of building a strong Defence Team, then, a better understanding of gender in the civilian-military context seems warranted. This chapter represents both a contribution to and a call for advancing this research program. We have seen in this chapter that hegemonic masculinity – or the traditional combat masculine-warrior model – may still define military culture to a degree; if so, it may have negative repercussions for members of the Defence Team, and the type and the extent of the repercussions may depend on whether the member is female or male, civilian or military. Indeed, the organizational experiences of both genders may differ by civilian and military status, among other identities, and thus are far from monolithic or immutable. Organizational experiences may also depend on the gender composition of a member's specific occupation (i.e., the experiences of women and men within female-dominated occupations may differ from experiences within male-dominated occupations within the defence organizational context). But this hypothesis requires validation. We have also seen that existing empirical research on the topic of gender in the civilian-military context is limited – studies are few, are often more than a decade old, and are often lacking in gender-based breakdowns of empirical results.

Nonetheless, the theoretical work and empirical studies highlighted here also suggest a number of potentially fruitful avenues for future investigation. For instance, future work could focus on the gendered implications of different military and civilian cultures within the Defence Team context: What are the gender implications of different leadership styles among civilian and military personnel or of different approaches to dress and deportment? Or, what are the gender implications, in terms of team dynamics and intergroup perceptions of fairness, of constructing civilians as playing a "support" role to the military, rather than as an equal partner within the Defence Team? And, further, is hegemonic masculinity still a feature of Canadian military culture, or is the culture moving towards a more evolved model? Given the paucity of existing research, qualitative interview research, in particular, could provide a useful starting point for the exploration of these questions. Such work could build on and complement some of the large-scale survey work that has been conducted on organizational climate, for example, including organizational fairness, cultural climate, and diversity climate – although such large-scale survey studies will also be required in order to provide a more up-to-date understanding of such issues. Still other work on the Defence Team could examine, from a specifically gendered perspective, issues of work-family balance and physical and mental health. Furthermore, future research should examine the issue of gender in the civilian-military context from an international perspective, in order to understand how the dynamics of gender and civilian-military status may play out in different national and cultural contexts. Whatever the future directions, it seems that gender may well matter in the civilian-military context – and that the Defence Team, like other organizational teams, could benefit from a consideration of gender.

CHAPTER 10

ENDNOTES

1   As reported by Arseneau and Cameron (this volume), the proportion of females in the Regular Force in fiscal year 2012-13 was 14%. The female representation for officers was 17%, and for non-commissioned members, 13%.

2   Such demographic trends are being documented through the work of the North Atlantic Treaty Organisation Science and Technology Organisation Human Factors and Medicine Panel Research Task Group 226 (NATO STO HFM RTG-226) on Civilian and Military Personnel Work Culture and Relations in Defence Organisations. This international research group consists of ten nations: Canada (lead nation), the United States, the United Kingdom, the Netherlands, Belgium, Germany, Switzerland, Sweden, Estonia, and Turkey.

3   See, e.g., A. R. Febbraro, "Gender and Leadership in the Canadian Forces Combat Arms: A Qualitative Study of Assimilation vs. Integration," *The Canadian Journal of Police & Security Services* 2, no. 4 (2004): 215–28; A. R. Febbraro and R. M. Gill, "Gender and Military Psychology," in *Handbook of Gender Research in Psychology: Vol. 1. Gender Research in Basic and Experimental Psychology*, eds. J. C. Chrisler and D. R. McCreary (New York: Springer, 2010), 671–96; D. Winslow, A. R. Febbraro, and P. Browne, "Diversity in the Canadian Forces," in *Cultural Diversity in the Armed Forces: An International Comparison*, eds. J. Soeters & J. S. van der Meulen (London: Routledge, 2007), 31-47.

4   A few studies have looked at the interaction between predominantly male military personnel and civilian women who work for non-government organizations and other non-defence government organizations. For instance, A. R. Febbraro explored challenges faced by such civilian women in terms of not being viewed by military men as equal collaborative partners or as credible leaders ("The Question of Gender in (Re)orienting to the Civil–Military Relationship," paper presented at the biennial meeting of the International Society for Theoretical Psychology, Santiago, Chile, May 2013). See also L. L. Miller, "From Adversaries to Allies: Relief Workers' Attitudes Toward the U.S. Military," *Qualitative Sociology* 22, no. 3 (1999): 181-97.

5   See B. D. Adams, C. R. Flear, A. L. Brown, M. H. Thomson, and R. M. McPhail, "Civilian and Military Personnel Work Culture and Relations in CF/DND: Analysis Using a Social Identity Approach," Contractor Report, Director General Military Personnel Research and Analysis [under review] (Ottawa, ON: Defence Research and Development Canada, in press); L. W. Bentley, *Canadian Forces Transformation and the Civilian Public Service Defence Professional*, Canadian Forces Leadership Institute Technical Report 2007-01 (Kingston, ON: Canadian Defence Academy Press, 2007); A. Fillion, "The Integration of Defence Civilians within the Defence Team: How Far Can We Go?" (research paper, Canadian Forces College, 2007); LCol. S. J. Gregory, "Change is the Mother of Invention: Changes in Canadian Forces Leadership Doctrine will Facilitate Leadership in Mixed Civilian/Military Settings" (research paper, Canadian Forces College, 2004); S. C. Lalonde, *Canadian Forces Health Services: Factors Affecting the Retention of Public Service Health Care Professionals in the Department of National Defence*, Director General Military Personnel Research and Analysis Technical Memorandum 2011-013 (Ottawa, ON: Defence Research and Development Canada, 2011); I. Lewis, "Public Service 2000 and Cultural Change in

the Department of National Defence," *Canadian Public Administration* 37, no. 2 (1994): 249-66; B. McKee and L. M. Williams, *Civilian Well-Being and Retention Project: Qualitative Findings*, Director Personnel Applied Research, Sponsor Research Report 2007-14 (Ottawa, ON: Defence Research and Development Canada, 2007); B. E. Van-Vianen, "Managing Civilians in the Canadian Forces" (master's thesis, Canadian Forces College, 2007).

6   M. Fine, F. Johnson, and M. Ryan, "Cultural Diversity in the Workplace," *Public Personnel Management* 19 (1990): 305-19.

7   Karen O. Dunivin, "Military Culture: Change and Continuity," *Armed Forces & Society* 29, no. 4 (1994): 531-47.

8   See, e.g., C. Moskos, "Diversity in the Armed Forces of the United States," in *Cultural Diversity in the Armed Forces: An International Comparison*, eds. J. Soeters and J. S. van der Meulen (London: Routledge, 2007), 15-30.

9   Leora N. Rosen, Kathryn H. Knudson, and P. Fancher, "Cohesion and the Culture of Hypermasculinity in U.S. Army Units," *Armed Forces & Society* 29, no. 3 (2003): 325-51.

10   K. D. Davis and B. McKee, "Women in the Military: Facing the Warrior Framework," in *Challenge and Change in the Military: Gender and Diversity Issues*, eds. F. C. Pinch, A. T. MacIntyre, P. Browne, and A. C. Okros (Kingston, ON: Canadian Defence Academy Press, 2004), 52-75. On the traditional notion of the warrior-masculine military culture, see A. D. English, *Understanding Military Culture: A Canadian Perspective* (Montreal: McGill–Queen's U. P., 2004) and Gosselin (this volume) regarding more recent movements toward a warrior framework in the Canadian military under the leadership of former Chief of the Defence Staff General Rick Hillier.

11   S. Hill and F. Pinch, *Perceptions of Social and Cultural Gaps: Perspectives of Senior Canadian Forces Officers*, Directorate of Strategic Human Resources Research Note 11/04 (Kinston, ON: Canadian Forces Leadership Institute, 2004).

12   Similarly, with regard to the civil-military gap in the United States, a survey showed that military respondents were younger, more likely to be male, and more conservative on social and moral issues than civilian respondents; see Thomas S. Szayna, Kevin F. McCarthy, Jerry M. Sollinger, Linda J. Demaine, Jefferson P. Marquis, and Brett Steele, *The Civil-Military Gap in the United States: Does it Exist, Why, and Does it Matter?* (Santa Monica, CA: Rand Corporation, 2007).

13   S. A. Hill, *Corporate Culture in the CF and DND: Descriptive Themes and Emergent Models*, Defence Research and Development Canada – Centre for Operational Research and Analysis Technical Report 2007-19 (Ottawa, ON: Defence Research and Development Canada, 2007).

14   See Febbraro, "Gender and Leadership in the Canadian Forces," 215–28. Despite these gender stereotypes, an extensive review of gender and leadership research indicates that women and men tend to be more similar than different in their leadership styles; see, e.g., A. H. Eagly and B. T. Johnson, "Gender and Leadership Style: A Meta-Analysis," *Psychological Bulletin* 108 (1990): 233-56.

15   Ramon Hinojosa, "Doing Hegemony: Military, Men, and Constructing a Hegemonic Masculinity," *The Journal of Men's Studies* 18, no. 2 (2010): 179–94.

16   Hinojosa, "Doing Hegemony," 191.

17   Ibid., 192.

18   Ibid., 189

19   Ibid., 191.

20   J. L. Soeters, D. J. Winslow, and A. Weibull, "Military Culture," in *Handbook of the Sociology of the Military*, eds. G. Caforio (New York: Springer, 2006), 237-54.

21   In a similar vein, research by Fillion indicated that the "military community sees the defence civilian team as risk-adverse, process-oriented bureaucrats" (*The Integration of Defence Civilians*, 2).

22   See, for example, H. Tajfel, "Social Identity and Intergroup Behaviour" and "Social Categorization, Social Identity and Social Comparison," in *Rediscovering Social Identity: Key Readings in Social Psychology*, eds. T. Postmes and N. R. Branscombe (New York, NY: Psychology Press, 2010), 77-96; 119-28; Tajfel and J. C. Turner, "An Integrative Theory of Intergroup Conflict" (ibid., 173-190); Tajfel and Turner, "The Social Identity Theory of Intergroup Behaviour," in *Psychology of Intergroup Relations*, eds. S. Worchel and W. G. Austin (Chicago, IL: Nelson–Hall, 1986), 7-24; T. F. Pettigrew, "Intergroup Contact Theory," *Annual Review of Psychology* 49 (1998): 65-85; Pettigrew and L. R. Tropp, "A Meta-Analytic Test of Intergroup Contact Theory," *Journal of Personality and Social Psychology* 90 (2006): 751–83.

23   Adams et al., "Civilian and Military Personnel Work Culture"; see also Goldenberg (this volume).

24   Adams et al. "Civilian and Military Personnel Work Culture."

25   See Febbraro and Gill, "Gender and Military Psychology," 671-96 and Winslow, Febbraro, and Browne, "Diversity in the Canadian Forces," 31-47.

26   For a more detailed discussion of the gendering of officer and civilian organizational status and positions, see Constance Anne Kostelac's "The Changing Face of Police Organizations: Trends in Civilianization" (unpublished dissertation, Arizona State University, 2008).

27   Ibid.

28   For a discussion of social identity based on gender, and how gender-based social categories are used to signify status and power, see Mary Crawford and Rhoda Unger, *Women and Gender: A Feminist Psychology*, 3rd ed. (Boston: McGraw–Hill, 2000). As they argue, the social construction of gender differences often reflects differences in social status and power.

29   Hill, *Corporate Culture in the CF and DND*.

30   McKee and Williams, *Civilian Well-Being and Retention Project*.

31   Lalonde, *Canadian Forces Health Services*, 11.

32   McKee and Williams, *Civilian Well-Being and Retention Project* and Lalonde, *Canadian Forces Health Services*.

33   McKee and Williams, *Civilian Well-Being and Retention Project*.

34   In Canada, the four designated equity groups are women, people with disabilities, Aboriginal people, and visible minorities.

35   Lalonde, *Canadian Forces Health Services*.

36   The research review focused on Canadian and American studies obtained through a search of PsycINFO, a database of more than three million records of peer-reviewed literature in the behavioural sciences and mental health, as well as studies identified in the annotated bibliography on partnership between military and civilian personnel in defence organizations compiled by Irina Goldenberg and Filsan Hujaleh, *Partnership Between Military and Civilian Personnel in Defence Organizations: An Annotated Bibliography*, Director General Military Personnel Research and Analysis Technical Memorandum 2012-020 (Ottawa, ON: Defence Research and Development Canada, 2012).

37   E.g., McKee and Williams, *Civilian Well-Being and Retention Project* and Lalonde, *Canadian Forces Health Services*.

38   For an in-depth analysis of the Defence Team Survey findings, see Goldenberg (this volume).

39   E.g., McKee and Williams, *Civilian Well-Being and Retention Project* and Lalonde, *Canadian Forces Health Services*.

40   Gender stereotypes suggesting that women are less committed to their jobs or show higher turnover compared to men are described in the psychology of women and gender literature. See, for example, Janet Shibley Hyde, *Half the Human Experience: The Psychology of Women*, 5th ed. (Toronto: D. C. Heath and Company, 1996) and Hyde and Nicole Else-Quest, *Half the Human Experience*, 8th ed. (Belmont, CA: Wadsworth Publishing, 2012), and Janice D. Joder, *Women and Gender: Transforming Psychology* (Upper Saddle River, NJ: Prentice Hall, 1999). Such stereotypes have persisted despite the lack of consistent evidence for gender differences in organizational commitment; see, e.g., Naomi Ellemers, Henriette van den Heuvel, Dick de Gilder, Anne Maass, and Alessandra Bonvini, "The Underrepresentation of Women in Science. Differential Commitment or the Queen Bee Syndrome?" *British Journal of Social Psychology* 43 (2004): 315-38.

41   Stephen J. Brannen, Karen R. Brannen, and Thomas W. Colligen, "Measuring Cultural Climate in a Uniformed Services Medical Center," *Armed Forces & Society* 164, no. 3 (1999): 202-8.

42   The study also examined differences between racial majorities and minorities. See Brannen, Brannen and Colligan, "Measuring Cultural Climate," 202-8.

43   Brannen, Brannen and Colligan, "Measuring Cultural Climate," 202-8.

44   Jacqueline Elaine Sharpe, *A Survey of Health Care Personnel's Perceptions Toward Diversity in the Workplace* (PhD diss., Old Dominion University, 1997).

45   L. Duxbury and C. Higgins, *The 2001 Work-Life Balance Study: Key Findings at the Department of Defence*, Director Human Resources Research and Evaluation Contractor Report 2002-02 (Ottawa, ON: Defence Research and Development Canada, 2002).

46   John V. Civitello Jr., *Perceived Stress Levels of Members of a U.S. Air Force Medical Facility* (PhD diss., Seattle University, 1997).

47   See Stephen B. Knouse and Mickey R. Dansby, "Percentage of Work-Group Diversity and Work-Group Effectiveness," *The Journal of Psychology* 133, no. 5 (1999): 486-94.

48   Knouse and Dansby, "Percentage of Work-Group Diversity," 486-94.

EDITORS' AFTERWORD

THE DEFENCE TEAM – A FUNDAMENTAL ALLIANCE

The importance of a building a strong and symbiotic partnership between military and civilian personnel within Canada's defence organization is not new. However, the explicit emphasis on this fundamental alliance, along with an increased interest in the factors that facilitate and challenge military-civilian collaboration has been increasing in recent years. Of note, much of the impetus behind the Defence Team concept comes from the post-Cold War, post-9-11 fiscal and security environments. Western governments are looking to downsize and streamline their militaries,[1] and efforts towards the optimal integration of the Defence Team in Canada have been undertaken in concert with the new NATO Strategic Concept called "smart defense," which prioritizes more efficient collective defence.[2] In the future, it seems, the effectiveness of both international and intra-national defence will depend on finding efficiencies through the optimal integration and utilization of the Defence Team. All of this makes the contributions in this volume especially timely.

The papers collected here show that building a Defence Team involves more than official endorsement of the concept. Turning two discrete institutions with two distinct cultures into a unified team brings with it a range of considerations, from the sociological and organizational level to the individual level. Our contributors have identified some of the main organization-level concerns: The historical reasons behind the expansion of DND and the promotion of civilians to senior positions was, in part, to effect greater oversight on behalf of the civil government (Gosselin); and the mandate and priorities of senior civilian managers can, at times, conflict with those of military leaders (Okros). Moreover, it is not always easy for military leaders to appreciate that civilian management principles are as important to military leadership as operational experience (English). At the same time, outsourcing some military training to civilian institutions might not have negative effects (i.e., civilianization) on the formation of junior members, and might even be conducive to stronger relations between military and civilian members of the

Defence Team (Wright). In addition, recent developments in HR modeling can provide insight into the optimal distribution of civilian and military occupations (Cameron and Arseneau). These analyses illustrate both the complexity and the interconnectedness of themes involved in understanding the Defence Team at the organizational or institutional level.

At the individual level, the core themes include culture, identity, roles, trust, power and control, integration, civilianization, differences and similarities, and attitudes and stereotypes. But the one overarching theme that connects this volume's chapters at the individual level is identity: CAF identity, civilian DND identity, and what it means to identify as a member of the defence team – that is, to adopt a super-ordinate identity (Goldenberg, Dean, and Adams). And the key to any super-ordinate conception of a Defence Team identity is, perhaps, complementarity without compromise. Military effectiveness depends on military cohesion, which depends on a strong, distinctive, and collective identity. Yet the Defence Team – as a team – also depends on a sense of shared identity to foster the level of trust necessary to a strong partnership (Thompson and Gill) and to dispel the stereotypes and ideological attitudes that impede such relationships (Febbraro). Nonetheless, our contributors have argued that highlighting the shared values and goals of military and civilian leaders in leadership training may go a long way toward building this sense of shared identity (Davis), and new research instruments like the Defence Team Survey can shed light on areas of concern at the individual level (Goldenberg).

Future analyses of the Defence Team could benefit from examining the various "mediate" identities – for instance, the identities of former military members who have become DND civilians, the identities of military reservists who might still retain a strong civilian identity, and the identities of DND civilians who have worked on operations directly alongside military personnel and who thus have shared common experiences to a degree that perhaps other DND civilians have not. Along with building common ground, do such common experiences play a role in shaping identities, particularly a super-ordinate identity? Further, might the themes explored in the present volume inform the next iteration of the Defence Team identity? Might the concept of the defence professional, for instance, represent the forerunner of such a future development, or even foreshadow what a future Defence Team identity might entail?

There is also no doubt that the issue of military and civilian personnel collaboration is becoming an increasingly topical issue internationally, as evidenced by terms like the "Whole Force Concept" in the UK, "One Defence Team" in Sweden, and the "Total Defence Workforce" in New Zealand. Indeed, the NATO Research Task Group on Civilian and Military Personnel Work Culture and Relations in Defence Organisations is in the process of examining a number of topics and themes that we have explored in the present volume, including demographic trends, issues around identity, culture, trust, and diversity, as well as policies and practices regarding the collaboration between military and civilian personnel within defence organizations.[3] Overall, the goal of this work is to better understand key aspects of civilian-military personnel integration from an international perspective. Understanding both the similarities and the differences between military-civilian personnel collaboration across defence organizations is aimed at identifying best practices and mechanisms for enhancing the effectiveness of these fundamental partnerships.

The Defence Team, comprising military personnel and civilian public servants, is the foundation of Canada's defence establishment. The men and women in uniform and their civilian counterparts work side by side to fulfil the mandate of the Minister of Defence. This volume offered multi-level analyses of the historical, political, strategic, organizational, sociological and individual level factors that have shaped and will continue to shape the Defence Team. Understanding the unique considerations, benefits, and challenges associated with this integrated workforce is critical to continuing to enable optimal military-civilian personnel collaboration. We hope that the analyses within this volume contributed to this effort.

ENDNOTES

1   See Department of National Defence, *Canada First Defence Strategy* [c. 2008], retrieved from http://www.forces.gc.ca/assets/FORCES_Internet/docs/en/about/CFDS-SDCD-eng.pdf

2   Peter Jones and Philippe Lagassé, "Rhetoric versus Reality: Canadian Defence Planning in a Time of Austerity," *Defence and Security Analysis* 28, no. 2 (June 2012): 140-51.

3   For more on this NATO Research Task Group, see http://www.cso.nato.int/activities.aspx?RestrictPanel=2.

CONTRIBUTORS

Barbara D. Adams has supported defence and security research as a consultant with Humansystems Incorporated for more than 10 years. She has a PhD in social psychology from the University of Waterloo. She has conducted research in a wide range of psychosocial areas, including social identity, team collaboration, psychological influence, individual readiness, trust, and ethical decision making.

Lise Arseneau holds a Bachelor of Science with Honours in Mathematics from Saint Mary's University and an MMath and PhD degrees from the University of Waterloo in combinatorics and optimization. She was employed as a defence scientist with the Department of National Defence in November 2000. She was posted to Director General Military Personnel Research and Analysis in November 2011 where she conducts research in the areas of attrition reporting and forecasting, as well as military occupational structure modeling and analysis. Her recent publications include "The Human Factors of Night Vision Goggles: Perceptual, Cognitive, and Physical Factors" published in the *Review of Human Factors and Ergonomics* in September 2011.

Amy Cameron is a defence scientist at Defence Research and Development Canada and holds a PhD in mathematics from the University of Ottawa. She is a member of the Workforce Modelling and Analysis team in Director General Military Personnel Research and Analysis (DGMPRA). Her research focuses on civilian and military occupational analysis and forecasting in support of human resources planning and management, and she is currently the lead researcher on DGMPRA's civilian human resources Forecaster tool.

Karen D. Davis is a defence scientist currently assigned to the Canadian Forces Leadership Institute. She has published numerous research papers, book chapters, and journal articles related to culture, diversity, gender, and leadership in the Canadian Armed Forces. Recent activities include contributing writer for *Leadership in the Canadian Forces: Leading the Institution* (2007); contributing writer/editor for *Women and Leadership in the Canadian Forces: Perspectives and Experience* (2007) and *Cultural Intelligence and Leadership: An Introduction for Canadian Forces Leaders* (2009); contributing writer/co-editor for *Transforming*

Traditions: Women, Leadership & the Canadian Navy, 1942-2010 (2010); and her PhD dissertation *Negotiating Gender in the Canadian Forces, 1970-1999* (2013).

Waylon H. Dean has been engaged as a science editor at Director General Military Personnel Research and Analysis since 2011. He is currently a doctoral candidate in philosophy at the University of Ottawa. His research interests include scientific method, logic, critical thinking, military ethics, political philosophy and ancient philosophy. He also specializes in science editing and technical writing.

Allan English served for 25 years in the Royal Canadian Air Force and the Canadian Armed Forces. He has taught undergraduate and graduate courses at the Royal Military College of Canada and at Queen's University, as well as courses in senior officer professional military education for officers in the ranks of major to brigadier-general at the Canadian Forces College, Toronto. He is currently an associate professor in the Department of History at Queen's University, where he teaches Canadian military history. He is a fellow of the Centre for International and Defence Policy located in the School of Policy Studies at Queen's.

Angela R. Febbraro received her PhD in applied social psychology and her MA in industrial/organizational psychology from the University of Guelph. She is currently a defence scientist at Defence Research and Development Canada – Toronto, where she is Leader of the Organizational Behaviour Group within the Socio-Cognitive Systems Section. A co-chair of the NATO STO HFM RTG-226 on Civilian and Military Personnel Work Culture and Relations in Defence Organisations, she has published and presented on military psychology, gender, cultural diversity, and reintegration issues for military personnel. Her current research focuses on the social and organizational aspects of effective civil-military interaction in the comprehensive environment. A former faculty member in community psychology at Wilfrid Laurier University, Dr. Febbraro currently holds an adjunct position in psychology at York University, and has taught several courses in the psychology of women, the psychology of gender, industrial/organizational psychology, and social psychology. Dr. Febbraro has served on the editorial board of the *Canadian Journal of Police and Security Services, Theory and Psychology*, and the *History and Philosophy of Psychology Bulletin*, and is a frequent reviewer for the *Psychology of Women Quarterly*.

CONTRIBUTORS

Ritu Gill received her PhD in social psychology from Carleton University, Canada. She started her career as a research manager in the Research Branch of the Correctional Service of Canada. Currently, she is a defence scientist at Defence Research and Development Canada – Toronto, where she conducts research examining trust restoration between military organizations and external clients or partners (e.g., indigenous populations, other government departments) as a means of enhancing mission success in international military operations. She has published several peer-reviewed publications in the areas of trust restoration, sexual harassment and gender discrimination. She served as a peer reviewer for the American Psychological Association's *Journal of Personality and Social Psychology Bulletin* and has taught psychology courses at Carleton University.

Irina Goldenberg received her PhD in social psychology from Carleton University in 2004, where her research focused on interpersonal trauma, posttraumatic stress, and emotional intelligence. She joined Defence Research and Development Canada in 2004, where she is currently leader of the Recruitment and Retention Team in Director General Military Personnel Research and Analysis, managing and delivering the program of research on recruitment and retention in the Canadian Armed Forces. As founder and co-chair of the NATO Science and Technology Research Task Group on Civilian and Military Personnel Work Culture and Relations in Defense Organisations, she also manages a comprehensive program of research on military-civilian personnel collaboration, both nationally and internationally. Prior to joining DRDC, Dr. Goldenberg taught in the Criminology Department at Carleton University and worked at Correctional Services of Canada. She is currently the Secretary General of the European Research Group on Military and Society, and she sits on the editorial board of *Res Militaris: European Journal of Military Studies*.

Daniel Gosselin has over 38 years of experience in the Canadian Armed Forces, having served in several command and staff assignments. He is completing a one-year assignment as the Senior Strategic Advisor to the Chief of the Defence Staff. He retired from the CAF as a major-general in 2011, and his last two tours of service included Commander of the Canadian Defence Academy and Director General International Security Policy at NDHQ. He holds three post-graduate degrees, in civil engineering, war studies, and public administration. He has also published articles and written book chapters on command, civil-military relations and defence management, and he teaches occasionally at the Canadian Forces College and the Royal Military College of Canada.

Alan Okros is a professor in the Department of Defence Studies, and he is the Deputy Director Academics at the Canadian Forces College, Toronto. From 2004 to 2008, he was an associate professor in the Department of Military Psychology and Leadership at the Royal Military College of Canada. He retired from the CAF in 2004 with 33 years service, having been responsible for four academically focused organizations, including the Canadian Forces Leadership Institute, where he led a multi-disciplinary team that produced CAF doctrine on leadership and professionalism, including *Duty with Honour: The Profession of Arms in Canada* and *Leadership in the Canadian Forces: Conceptual Foundations*. In addition to lecturing in a range of CAF professional development courses, he provides invited presentations internationally and is engaged in a number of research projects centred on leadership in the public domain.

Megan Thompson received a PhD in social psychology from the University of Waterloo. She joined the Department of National Defence as a National Sciences and Engineering Research Council Visiting Fellow, later becoming a defence scientist at Defence Research and Development Canada – Toronto. Dr. Thompson's research foci involve collaboration within diverse teams, with a focus on trust, optimizing moral and ethical decision making in military operations, and stress and resiliency in deployments. She has served on several international defence research panels (Panel Chair AG 26 The Comprehensive Approach to Operations; Canadian member NATO HFM 227 Collaboration in the Comprehensive Approach to Operations NATO HFM -179 – Moral Dilemmas and Military Mental Health Outcomes; National Lead, TTCP TP-10 Survival Psychology, National Lead TP-13 Psychological Health and Operational Effectiveness) and was a keynote speaker at the NATO HFM-142 Symposium on Adaptability in Coalition Teamwork. She has authored over 100 publications in the areas of team effectiveness, individual differences in judgment and decision making, deployment stress and resiliency, and moral and ethical decision making in operations and is on the editorial board of the American Psychological Association journal *Military Psychology*.

CONTRIBUTORS

Justin Wright holds an MA in sociology from the University of New Brunswick in Fredericton. His recent research has focused on identity development, military socialization, cross-cultural competency, and employment equity. He is currently employed as a defence scientist by Defence Research and Development Canada, Director General Military Personnel Research and Analysis. Mr. Wright has authored and edited several CDA Press publications, including *In Their Own Words: Canadian Stories of Valour and Bravery from Afghanistan, 2001-2007* (co-editor); *Professional Ideology and Development: International Perspectives* (co-editor); and *Cultural Intelligence and Leadership: An Introduction for Canadian Forces Leaders* (chapter author).

LIST OF ACRONYMS

ADF	Australian Defence Force
ADM	Assistant Deputy Minister
AFC	Armed Force Council
ASD	Alternative Service Delivery
ATD	Alternative Training Delivery
CA	Canadian Army
CAF	Canadian Armed Forces
CDS	Chief of the Defence Staff
CFHQ	Canadian Forces Headquarters
CFLI	Canadian Forces Leadership Institute
CFSI	Canadian Foreign Service Institute
CFSI CIL	Canadian Foreign Service Institute Centre for Intercultural Learning
CFTS	Contracted Flying Training and Support
CIL	Centre for Intercultural Learning
CMR	Civil-Military Relations
CQ	Cultural Intelligence
CSPS	Canada School of Public Service
DM	Deputy Minister
DND	Department of National Defence
DPS	Defence Policy Statement

LIST OF ACRONYMS

FOL   First Official Language

GLOBE   Global Leadership and Organizational Behaviour Effectiveness

IT&E   Individual Training and Education

KSA   Knowledge, Skills, Abilities

LDF   Leader Development Framework

MCCR   Management Command and Control Re-engineering

MEOCS   Military Equal Opportunity Climate Survey

MES   Military Ethos Scale

MRG   Management Review Group

NATO   North Atlantic Treaty Organization

NCM   Non-Commissioned Members

NDA   National Defence Act

NDHQ   National Defence Headquarters

NZDF   New Zealand Defence Force

OJT   On-the-Job Training

PME   Professional Military Education

LIST OF ACRONYMS

RCAF   Royal Canadian Air Force

RCN   Royal Canadian Navy

SJC   Special Joint Committee (of the senate and House of Commons)

SJS   Strategic Joint Staff

TISS   Triangle Institute for Security Studies

TTCP   The Technical Cooperation Program

WFA   Work Force Adjustment

WoG   Whole of Government

YOS   Years of Service

INDEX

INDEX